Industrious
Indian Anthropologists
(1920 – 2019)

Industrious Indian Anthropologists (1920 – 2019)

Editor
Samira Dasgupta
M.Sc, Ph.D

AGAM KALA PRAKASHAN
DELHI

First Published 2022

ISBN: 978-81-950098-6-2

Published by:
For **Agam Kala Prakashan**
34, Central Market, Ashok Vihar
Delhi - 110 052
Tel.: 91-11-27212195, 43513480
Fax: 91-11-27212195
Email: agamkala101@gmail.com, agambook@yahoo.com
www.agamkala.com

Composed by:
Sushil Kumar
Delhi - 110 052
Mobile: 9891395309

Printed in India

CONTENTS

PREFACE

There are number of industrious Indian Anthropologists (1920-2019) who are/were always placed behind the curtain/screen and not even in the field of discussion about their valuable contributions in the domain of anthropology. In this long span of 100 years of Indian Anthropology they are/were always marginalized and due to such the young generation are not aware of their noteworthy contribution in anthropology. I being the Editor of this volume know that there are many more among this list, but due to some technical constraints it is not possible to include all those scholars.

To my observation, it is found that the present day scholars are not interested for in-depth intensive field work, which is the lifeline of anthropology and also very much reluctant in writing their field impression with analytical frame. The major methodological tool of anthropological field work is participant observation. Some scholars are now-a-days are inclined and advocated for digital ethnography in various digital social platform; I am wonder how the data can be generated with modern electronic gadgets for this digital ethnography, and how those would be valid for any interpretation of intricate social matrix at the grass root level of our country?

Hence, in spite of all the available empirical resources, they are lagging behind. But they are very much active in digital social platform which appears to me as 'who will bell the cat'. Sorry to say, some among such scholars achieved high social position in anthropology discipline; discipline expects from such scholars, are expected to penetrate among many new horizons of anthropology for its future steps, through which the utility of the discipline can be established and felt by common people of our country.

The present treatise is a continuation of earlier three volumes viz. Doyens of Indian Anthropology (1920 -2019), published in 2019, 2020 and 2021 from this same publishing house that is, Agam Kala Prakashan, Delhi but this volume title is slightly different from earlier three volumes; the reasons are already mentioned earlier. The contributions of Industrious Indian Anthropologists (1920-2019) [along with some contemporary least known anthropologists] discussed in this treatise are chronologically arranged as per their year of birth.

The present treatise is a compilation of the selected contributions by the Industrious Indian Anthropologists (1920–2019) whose contributions were/are not only praiseworthy but their exposure to various field situation are also documented with their enrich data in published form. I hope the present volume will speak how and why the empirical field studies are helpful and important in anthropology discipline.

I also extremely grateful to Dr. Biman Kumar Das Gupta for submission of his write up on Dr. Amitabha Sarkar in the month of April, 2021; and perhaps this write up was his last academic involvement before his death due to Corona on 05.05.2021. Dr. Biman Kumar Das Gupta was a person with versatile knowledge, expert both in field work and interpretation of his data in analytical and theoretical frame work. It is our great loss that we lost a revered teacher.

I also express my sincere thanks to Dr.Amitabha Sarkar for his untiring support and help in making regular correspondence with the contributors of this volume and finally these are achieved.

In preparing this manuscript I personally thank to Sri, Debasish Biswas, EDP Section of Anthropological Survey of India for his labour in typing this volume and who also engaged in preparing the jacket of the volume. I also express thanks to the Publishing House for their co-operation in publishing this volume.

Kolkata
September, 2021

Samira Dasgupta
Editor

LIST OF CONTRIBUTORS

1. Professor Deepak Kumar Behera, Vice Chancellor ,KISS Deemed to be University KISS Campus-3 (KISS Higher Education Campus), P.O: KIIT, Patia, Bhubaneswar-751024.
2. Dr. Biman Kumar Das Gupta, Retd. Deputy Director, Anthropological Survey of India, Kolkata.
3. Prof. Jaydip Sen, Dept. of Anthropology, University of North Bengal, Darjeeling— 734013. West Bengal.
4. Dr. Dipak K Samanta, Retd. Assistant Anthropologist, Anthropological Survey of India, Udaipur. Residence:204. Divyajyoti Apartment, New Bhopalpura, Udaipur—313001. Rajasthan
5. Prof. Sumahan Bandhopadhyay, Department of Anthropology, Vidyasagar University, Midnapur. West Bengal.
6. Prof. P. Dash Sharma (Retd). Diganta Apartment, A-3, 3rd Floor, 11, New Santoshpur Main Road, Santoshpur, Kolkata 700075, West Bengal. E-mail: pdashsharma@rediffmail.com
7. Dr. Amitabha Sarkar. Retd. Superintending Anthropologist, Anthropological Survey of India, Kolkata. Residence : AG-44. Salt Lake, Sector-2. Kolkata—700091.

8. Dr. Bharati Devi, Retd. Assistant Anthropologist, Anthropological Survey of India, Kolkata.
9. Dr. Samira Dasgupta, Retd. Assistant Anthropologist, Anthropological Survey of India, Kolkata. Residence : AG-44. Salt Lake, Sector-2. Kolkata—700091.

CHAPTER 1

INTRODUCTION

Dr. Samira Dasgupta.

Learning habits of animals in their native habitats have demonstrated that they also learn from each other and pass on a considerable variety of skills. They have been observed to fashion simple tools from twigs, branches or blades of grass and then use them to fish, termites, which they eat, from their nests, they use rocks to break open fruits and nuts, while learning that take place in any human society is that human learning is cumulative and that of animals is not. Among humans each generation adds to the store of cultural knowledge, beliefs and techniques. The same is not true for animals as their learned traits are not cumulative.

To find out about Man, one must go among men. There is no other way. It is perhaps the most key contribution – anthropology has made to science.

The anthropologist attempts to bring to the surface the doctrine or set of principles elicited from act of speech. It should therefore come as no surprise that this analytical structure does not always correspond to the way the natives view their own society since they are rarely called on to analyze their actions in this way.

When I began my research at Western Regional Centre of Anthropological Survey of India, Udaipur in 1977 among the Bhil tribal women in Zawar Mines, Padla villages or in Rangey, Harup, and Holang villages of Birjia of Gumla district (now Jharkhand) for my Ph.D. dissertation work, I was interested in the way in which economic modernization had affected social life, I learned from the very outset of my work there that the contemporary villages were more egalitarian than it had been a generation earlier. In spite of that elements of hierarchy were still evident in naked eyes of everyday interaction as well as in the attitudes of villagers. Some among them had wealth and education which were treated as attributes to bring difference and respect, while others live in poverty, their children went half-clad or poorly dressed and they were treated disparagingly by others.

Despite this obvious difference, there are certain common things almost everywhere in the field experiences. All fieldworkers must made their presence acceptable to the people they study, select key as well as trustworthy informants find satisfactory means of recording, cross-checking of the data, classifying information etc. in other to interpretation of his/her hypothesis of the research work.

An anthropologist during his/her empirical study in field the chief research methodology is ***participant observation***. The degree to which an anthropologist is able to actually participate in community activities varies widely, depending on the rapport established, the permissiveness of the community, the temperament of the reaearcher and number of other local factors. In majority of the cases, fieldworkers not only do not become closely integrated into the community but remain conspicuous visitors at best. Their presence is constantly encumbered by pen, pencils, note book, camera, sunburn and nagging diarrhoea, all of which are reminders to everyone that they are outsiders. It is also reported that when an ethnographer studies his/her own society, and are therefore not set apart in appearance, they are still usually perceived as being different. This was brought home by William Whyte in his study of an Italian Street corner gang, the Nortons in Boston (1955 : 304).

II

According to some historians the origin of Social Anthropology is traced from David Hume and Immanuel Kant who were the first philosophers to define social anthropology. Hume was a British empiricist who argued that "experience was the only trustworthy source of valid knowledge". It was through that initiation of Hume that empiricism entered that social sciences including social anthropology.

Later anthropologist were interested in the study of primitives because it was held that they displaced institutions in their simplest forms and that it is sound method to proceed from examination of the more simple to examination of the more complex, in which what has been learnt from a study of the more simple would be an additional tool.

Anthropology distinguishes itself from the other social sciences through the great emphasis put on field work as the most important source of generating empirical data about society and culture. Field work aims at developing an intimate understanding as possible of the phenomena investigated.

III

Field work with Participant Observation in anthropology is essential and with such empirical experiences some scholars in anthropology who worked in Indian subcontinent produced valuable contribution in social sciences to understand the social fabric at grass root level of our country. Some of such contributions of eminent scholars in anthropology are illustrated here for justifying the importance of present volume where the contributions of some selected untiring anthropologists in India are illustrated.

L.K.Mahapatra

With the help of such field work in anthropology some scholars like L.K. Mahapatra who has studied social movement of Oraon, Gond, Khonds and others (1968, 1972) and defined tribal social movements as '*a social movement occurs when a fairly large number of people or an otherwise identifiable segment of their population deliberately band together for collective action in order to alter, reconstitute, re-interpret, restore, protect, supplant or create some portions of their culture or social order, or to better their life – chances by redistributing the power of control in a society*'.

Verrier Elwin

During 1943 Elwin came out with a small book (pamphlet) named, '*The Loss of Nerve*', wherein he has argued that the tribals are the original settlers of this land. *They lived with nature and their habits and way of life are conditioned by nature. When these tribals come in contact with the non-tribals, they are likely to shed their qualities of life; and there is their loss of nerve. They should be kept isolated from the mainline of civilization.* The proposition made by Elwin created a debate in India. Isolation in this case would keep them backward, ignorant, poor and illiterate and proposed a '*Public Park Theory*'. According to him the tribal area should be cordoned off from the main civilization. However, at the end of his life, Elwin changed his view and pressed for integration of tribals on the basis of their genius.

G.S. Ghurye

He contested the Elwin theory of 'Public Park', or isolation. His argument was that the tribals are a part of Hindu Society; they could be considered as backward caste Hindus and he came out with book entitled '*The Aboriginals, So-called and their Future*' in 1943. The said book was actually a rejoinder to Elwin. Ghurye's argument is that tribals all over the country are increasingly assimilating themselves into Hindu castes.

N.K. Bose

N.K. Bose another social anthropologist, a Gandhian himself, attempted to define Indian tribals are original inhabitants of the country and they are increasingly coming within the fold of Hinduism. While talking on Hindu method of tribal absorption (1941) he also advocates for a secular model for integrating the tribals.

Milton Singer and Bernards Cohn

Both of them discussed in their edited volume entitled "*Structure and Change in Indian society*" (1968), that the Indian social structure is not only in its change but also with in its continuity.

F.G. Bailey

Bailey has studied Khonds of Orissa. In his earlier work he studied the economic frontier of the castes (1957). In this study he argues that the castes have given a new dimension to the economy. He studies 'tribe', 'caste', and 'nation' (1960) and establishes their correlation. In this context he says that the Khonds are a tribal group in the sense that they share a common culture and speak a common language. From linguistic point of view, Bailey says that the tribe and caste have separate identities.In the same way, their structures differ in their political organization. Bailey further says that the tribal political system is segmentary. Its base is agnatic kinship.On the other hand, the caste political organization draws from social legislation. The Khonds have their political relations with the lower castes also. It is this the theme – that tribe, caste and nation – which constitutes the continuum of social change. In course of time the tribals assume the status of a caste and finally the caste lose their entity and integrate themselves in the nation. To him, tribal society is a segmentary society moving from its status of tribe to caste and finally nation.

A.C. Bhagabati

Prof. Bhagabati (1989) pointed out that the quality of change in the social organization itself of various tribal communities which is leading to change in material culture and habitational types. He has illustrated in support of his empirical observation that the Wanchos of Tirap disctict of Arunachal Pradesh; the Tribe practice Polygyny by hereditary class of **chief-tains** who belong to the *wangham* or royal lineage. In his study he observed during 1967 that some of the important chiefs in the Niausa Sub-division had as many as thirty wives each. The remainder were taken in as wives from a lower class and it was their burden to work in the field and attend to domestic chores in the chief's household. The traditional houses of these chief were with massive structures of wood, thatch and bamboo, built on platform. The internal arrangement of rooms was much like a vestibuled railway train, with compartments on either side of a central passage. Through this empirical study Dr. Bhagabati pointed out that this kind of house is going to disappear because none of the Wancho chiefs of to-day practices polygyny of such impressive proportion. Here, a change in social organization or social practice is going to alter the character of the habitation.

Uma Charan Mohanty

Dr. Mohanty (1989) is studying different groups of tribal communities (like Kota, Toda, Gadaba, Kandh and Saora) give much emphasis to the study of habitats of tribal people. According to Dr. Mohanty anthropologists are more interested in the cultural aspects of tribal habitats. The symbolic meanings of tribal habitats are more interesting and significant than that of the study of mere physical aspects. The tribal habitat not only shows ecological aspects and techniques of construction, but it also represents the symbolic aspects to tribal culture.

Mohanty in his studies also mentioned that the social structure of a community is best represented by its settlement pattern. A tribal settlement shows the distribution of clans in particular territories and so the lineages and families of each clan are also territorially represented. This territorial aspect is also represented beyond the clan level. Thus, there is interesting correlation between territorial aspect of the habitat and the structural aspect of the community.

Thus, all these observation has been made by Dr. U.C. Mohanty by virtue of his Participant Observation field work which is key tool for anthropological research.

IV

The present treatise is a collection of a few Indian untiring scholars during 1920 – 2019, whose contributions are not only praiseworthy by virtue of their painstaking field work in anthropology but their dedication to the discipline is well placed and remarkable till this date. This apart, it also deals with the concept of culture, Basics of Cultural Ecology and Study of Traditional Knowledge for Sustainable Development with special emphasis among Asur- a PVTG of Jharkhand which are very much relevant for a student of anthropology both in graduation and post-graduation courses in our country among various Universities.

References

Bailey, F.G. 1957. Caste and the Economic Frontier : A Village in Highland Orissa, Manchester : Manchester University Press.

Bailey, F.G. 1960. Tribe, Caste and Nation : A Study of Political Activity and Political Change in Highland Orissa, Manchester, UK; Manchester University Press.

Bhagabati, A.C. 1989, 'Lecture by A.C. Bhagabati, in Workshon on Tribal Habitat and Environment, Bhopal: Rashtriya Manav Sangrahalaya.

Bose, N.K. 1941. 'Hindu Method of Tribal Absorption' in Science and Culture, Vol. 7, pp. 188 – 194.

Director, 1989. Workshop on Tribal Habitat and Environment, Bhopal : Rashtriya Manav Sangrahalaya (Booklet).

Elwin, Verrier. 1943. 'The Loss of Nerve', The Statesman, Sunday, April 5.

Ghurye, G.S. 1943.The Aboriginals- So called and their future, Poona : Gokhale Institute of Politics and Economics.

Mahapatra, L.K. 1968. "Social Movements among Tribes of Eastern India with special reference to Orissa, Sociologist, Vol. XVIII, no. 1, Berlin..

Mahapatra, L.K. 1972. "Social Movements among Tribes in India", in Tribal Situation in India, (ed.), K.S. Singh, Simla : Indian Institute of Advance Study.

Mohanty, U.C. 1989. "Lecture by U.C. Mohanty, in Workshop on Tribal Habitat and Environment, Bhopal: Rashtriya Manav Sangrahalaya.

Singer, Milton and Bernards Coln, 1968. Structure and Change in India Society', Chicago: Aldine Publishing Company.

Whyte, William F. 1955. Street Corner Society : The Social Structure of a Italian Slum, Chicago : University of Chicago Press (2nd edition).

CHAPTER 2

CONCEPT OF CULTURE

Dr. Amitabha Sarkar.

Culture embodies the ideas and norms of a group. It is sum-total of the ideal patterns and norms of behavior of a group. Culture fulfills those ethical and social needs of a group that ends in itself. Culture possesses an order and system. Its various parts are integrated with each other and any new element that is introduced also gets assimilated. Culture evolves into more complex forms through division of labour that develops special skills and increases the interdependence among society's members.

One of the chief and remarkable characteristics of human behavior is the degree to which humans live in a world of symbols and conventional understandings. Anthropologists term it as culture. Here culture is conceived as the systems of commonly accepted meanings that serve as recipes or guidelines, for behaviour in any particular society. This symbolic capacity of the ability to bestow meanings on things or acts and then to live according to these meanings, is the distinguishing characteristic of all human societies. The activities of humans, in fact are deeply affected by these symbolic divisions. Man is the only animal, as one anthropologist has expressed it, perpetually "suspended in webs of significance he himself has spun" (Geertz, 1973).

II

Culture is the aggregate of human behaviour – verbal and non-verbal and its products are – material and non-material. It is very often referred to as the life of people which have their own culture. Culture is also used to convey various meanings in a general way. One uses culture to convey the social charm and intellectual's excellence. So Mathew Arnold (1960) has defined culture as sweetness and light. Some uses the term culture elite for the intellectual leader of a society. The sociologists MacIver and Sorokin have used the term culture for the moral, spiritual and intellectual attainments of man.

Sanskriti is a Sanskrit term for culture. The term Sanskriti is derived from *Sanskar,* means – learning of values and ritual performances. When one is born, he or she goes through various ritual performances as a result of which he or she is accepted into the various roles of society like that of an adult or an old. In other words we can describe, man who in the course of life performs and accepts various roles. The state of collective life through which he or she has to go by the performances of various rituals. *Sanskara* is *Sanskriti.* So *Sanskriti* is a process of refinement from one stage of life to another.

The anthropologists have used the term 'culture' in different ways. Tylor was the first anthropologist who defined "*culture is that complex whole, which includes knowledge, belief, art, morals, law, customs and any other capabilities acquired by man as a member of a society*". Here he has given emphasis on the social heritage as gift of a society to an individual. "I am inclined to say that heredity and learning from a group are the process by which the behaviour of organism is determined" (Tylor, 1871). In man, the heredity contributes such behaviour of sucking and swallowing – being a biological process of transmission. While the behaviour like speaking the language or wearing a cloth is learning from others – social process of transmission based on the capacity of man to learn. Transmission of behaviour by learning is found among the animal world, but the absence of speeches among them, however, limits the amounts of acquisition. Man alone has his acquisition.

Edward Tylor's was the first who specified that culture is learned and acquired, as opposed to being a biological trait. This was revolutionary against the backdrop of colonialism, racism, and social evolutionism -- the dominant ideologies of the 19th century. His definition is also one of the first anthropological definitions of culture.

Redfield defines culture "as an organized body of conventional understanding – manifest in art and artifact, which persisting through tradition characterizes a human group". Summing up both Tylor and Redfield's views on culture, it can be said that Tylor has emphasized on capabilities acquired by man as a member of society; while Redfield's points stand for persisting through tradition is the ability to learn from the group. But Lowie meant culture as the whole of social tradition.

Malinowski has pointed out that social heritage consists of both material and non-material parts. According to him, the culture is the total way of life and the instruments – mental, social and material out of which this way is made. On the one hand, one has social culture and on the other material culture. This view has been taken and modified by Bidney who has sociofacts, and mentifacts. This means that culture is the product of cultivation, industry, social organization and language, religion, art, etc. Radcliffe-Brown like Malinowski has taken the instrumental and humanistic view of culture but he regards culture as cultivation – the process of handing down and acquiring tradition as a result of which society exists.

Linton, Kluckhohn and Kroeber have said of culture on the plain of subjective nature of human understanding. According to Linton, culture is an abstraction from the reality which is the actual human behaviour. He used the term, social heredity for culture. Kluckhohn describes culture as a way of thinking, feeling and action and Gilling makes it clearer that culture is not activity but its patterning. He notes for a culture as each group, each society, has a set of behaviour patterns, which are more or less common to the members, which have passed down from generation to generation and taught to children and which are liable to change. These common patterns are called culture. Benedict stresses on the patterns of culture and not its content. Kroeber has said that culture includes speech, beliefs, customs, arts and technologies ideals and rules. That in short is what we learn from other men, from our elders or the past alongwith what we may add to it. According to Green, culture is the socially transmitted systems of idealized ways in knowledge, practice and belief. Along with the artifacts that knowledge and practice produce and maintain as the changed in time. Bose, N.K. speaks of culture as crystallized phase of man's life activities. It includes certain forms of acquisition, closely associated with particular objects and institution. Habitual attitudes of mind transferable from one person to another with the aid of mental images conveyed through speech symbols.

Man learns his behavior and behavior that is learnt denotes his culture. Thus culture is a system of learned behavior shared by and transmitted among the members of a group. Man begins to learn it since his birth. By picking up the culture and by tapping the heritage of his past, man becomes distinctively human. Man is therefore called the culture-bearing animal. Culture is not innate. Traits learnt through socialization, habits and thoughts are what is called culture. Culture is learned. Any behavior that is socially acquired is called learned behavior. Culture is inclusive of the expectations of the members of the group. It is a social product that is shared by most members of the group.

Language is the vehicle by which culture is transmitted. Man can inhabit present, past and future by language, i.e., he can built on what he has got from the past and transmit the present with additions to the future.

Records are made and preserved on stones, fire bed clay and metals from the very early days of mankind. Culture can accumulate little by way of knowledge and technology. It evolves into civilization only when written language comes into existence.

All cultures – primitive or modern, whether hunting, pastoral, or agricultural pattern contain the same type of economy, education, land, folklore, song and institution in a sequence of organization complexity. Cultural universality is also expressed in similarity in function. This is based on two factors:

i) Man being a biological species, his food, clothing, shelter, family life, etc., may all vary. But they represent the universal and basic need.

ii) Survival of man in all places and time; his economy, social control, education, political organization, religious beliefs and practices, etc., basic points are universal, but differences may be noted between a developed and an underdeveloped society.

From Tylor's definition of culture, it is evident that culture consists of commonly accepted and expected ideas, attitudes, values, and habits of individuals which they learn in connection with the social living. For an individual in his early years of life, culture is an aid of learning to get on more effectively in the world. Each new generation learns how to adjust to the physical and social world mainly from their progenitors. Gradually this new generation passes on to the next generation what he has learnt from the previous one, and what he has added to the cultural whole. Young and Mack, have used three words – *shared, learned* and *behaviour* for culture. Behaviour includes thinking, feeling and action. So any behaviour is a part of culture only when it is shared by members of a group. If only one person uses a neck-tie among the Santals, then this behaviour is not a part of Santal culture. Most of the Bengalis touch their elders feet when they go outside (at a distance place). This behaviour is shared, and is a part of Bengali culture. By learned behaviour one means more than attitudes and the ways of acting, which are formerly and consciously taught. Any behaviour which is socially acquired that comes through participation in a human group is learned. Of course, certain behaviour is determined by the inheritance. Such behaviour is not cultural. Hunger for food, is not culturally learned, but thought of fried rice or sweets as satisfying or bitter vegetables as repulsive is acquired and is a part of culture.

It is a difficult problem to note the importance of culture as a determinant of human behaviour. One is more likely to overemphasis the effects of heredity or the physical environment than to recognize how a large portion of his behaviour is composed of shared ways of doing things, to learn in a social environment. Every man likes to think of him as quite unusual kinds of food eaten, types of clothing worn, and forms of greeting used and many other components of culture with respect to uniqueness. The differences which one notes are small within the ways of behaviour expected and accepted in his society. The tests in clothing are in large, parts of culture. It is shared and learned behaviour. Man is the only creation of the God that possesses culture, the two most significant features of which are language and tools.

III

There are about 167 definition of culture which can be classified under following categories (Kroeber and Kluckhon, 1958).

	Category	No.
A.	Enumerative Descriptive	26
B.	Historical	22
C.	Normative	25
D.	Psychological	38
E.	Structural	9
F.	Genetic	40
G.	Incomplete Definition	7

IV

Anthropologists have identified many attributes **Ethos and Eidos:** This distinction as given by Kroeber highlights two different aspects of culture.Eidos is the formal appearance of a culture derived from its constituents. Ethos on the other hand is the disposition of a culture which determines its quality, its main themes and interests. According to Batson the first consisting of the total emotional emphasis of a culture is called ethos and the second consisting of the emphasis resulting from the cognitive processes operative within a culture is called eidos.

Explicit and Implicit Elements: The celebration of festivals when people are filled with joy, happiness, togetherness and a devotional fervour is an example of explicit element of our culture. However, behind every festival there are mythological stories or otherwise deep-routed meanings and implications and these could be termed as the implicit elements of our culture.

Broadly, culture can be conceived and expressed in tangible and intangible forms.

Tangible Cultural element: Cultural heritage in general consists of the products and processes of a culture that are preserved and passed on through the generations. Some of that heritage takes the form of cultural property, formed by tangible artifacts such as buildings or works of art.Tangible cultural elements can be physically observed, can be touched, that is, they are material objects. Many parts of culture, however are intangible, including song, music, dance, drama, skills, cuisine, and festivals. They are forms of culture that can be recorded but cannot be touched or stored in physical form, like in a museum, but only experienced through a vehicle giving expression to it. These cultural vehicles are called "Human Treasures" by the UN.

(http//www.unesco.org/culture/ich/doc/src/01851-EN). The intangible cultural forms may be explained –

Intangible cultural heritage includes oral tradition (including myth), performing arts, social practices, rituals, festive events, knowledge and practices concerning nature and the universe or the knowledge and skills to produce traditional crafts. For intangible to be kept alive, it must remain relevant to a culture and be regularly practiced and learned within communities and between generations. Hence, it is the cultural expressions that have been passed from one generation to another, have evolved in response to their environments and contribute to giving us a sense of identity and continuity (http//www.unesco.org/culture/ich/doc/src/01851-EN).

Reference

Arnold, Matthew. 1960 " *Culture and Anarchy"* in *The Complete Prose Works of Matthew Arnold,* Ed. R. H. Super, Vol. 5. Ann Arbor: University of Michigan Press.

Banerjee, Biswanath and Amitabha Sarkar. 1996 . Fundamentals of Social and Cultural Anthropology, Calcutta: Firma KLM Pvt. Ltd.

Barrett, Richard, A. 1991 Culture Conduct, California: Wadsworth Publidhing Company.

Geertz, Clifford . 1973 (Reprint). The Interpretation of Culture, U.S.A : Basic Books.

Kroeber, A.L. and Clyde Kluckhohn. 1958. Culture: A Critical Review of Concepts and Definations, Cambridge, Massachusetts: The Museum.

Tylor, E.B. 1871. Primitive Culture: Researches into the Development of Mythology, Philosophy,Religion, Language, Art and Custom, London: John Murray.

CHAPTER 3

INDUSTRIOUS INDIAN ANTHROPOLOGISTS

3.1. Durgadas Hazra (1925 --2016)

Dr. Dipak K Samanta

Shri Durgadas Hajra, a name amongst the stalwarts of the Anthropological Survey of India, was born on the first of February, 1925. His early days were spent in Dhanbad, now in Jharkhand. He also completed his primary education there. Later on, he completed his higher school education in Howrah, West Bengal, following which he graduated from Bangabashi College, Kolkata and later went on to complete his post-graduation in Anthropology from the University of Calcutta and specialised in Social Anthropology in the year 1949. His revered teachers were Prof. K.P. Chattopadhya, Prof. T.C. Das and the like.

He joined the Anthropological Survey of India, immediately after completing his P.G. programme and was posted in Kolkata. A classical ethnographer per excellence as he was had a remarkable contribution to this organisation and the discipline- anthropology too. He worked extensively in the central tribal corridor stretching from Assam in the north east to Gujarat on the west.

His contribution towards the Machida, the fishing community of Bherawal of coastal Gujarat, the Nagas of Assam, now a North-eastern tribe, the Dorlas of Bastar, Chhattisgarh and the Kolam of Yeotmal, Maharashtra are exemplary.

His commendable work with the various indigenous tribes will always be a topic of study for the present generation. Shri Durgadas Hajra along with Mr. Gohain worked with the Angami tribe, a sub-sect of the North- eastern Naga tribe. He was generous enough to share his experiences in encountering the study group and provide necessary titbits about impression management. His efficient team was always very supportive and he could handle his projects with expertise. Sometimes it was difficult to communicate with them, but he also started to share their meals, even if it was not palatable to him. This gave them confidence in sharing their life activities with him and his team members. He also learnt working knowledge of the Angami language to understand and simplify the issues.

Similar proficiency was also achieved by him when he worked with the Dorlas of Bastar. There are innumerable tribes in the Bastar region like the Marias (Dandami or Bison-Horn Maria), Murias, Dhuruwas, Halbas, Bhatras and the Dorlas. He worked with the Dorlas, where he used some methods of his own in addition to standard anthropological methods to befriend them. He would carry simple cotton fabrics, boiled sugar candies, attractive ribbons as gift items to take them into his confidence. In sixties when he conducted his long fieldwork (6 to 8 months at a stretch) was challenging specially in Bastar region. This hard working person never deterred even in the adverse days.

In Bheraval too Shri Durgadas Hajra while working with the Machiyar community, excelled in gaining their confidence. He would share meals, go for fishing trips and spend quality time with them to know more about them.

He applied the same methods to the indigenous tribe of Yeotmal, now Yavatmal who were the Kolams. He enjoyed every moment of his work, which actually brought contentment. His hunger for learning was incredible. These tours would sometimes extend up to six to eight months. This never deterred him from toiling hard to quench his thirst for learning and sharing more and more knowledge.

Most widely held works of Shri Durgadas Hajra are the books published by him. These are The Dorla of Bastar and Kolam of Yeotmal. Four editions of the first book was published in English and held by 63 libraries worldwide. It is a study of the Dorla tribe of Injiram Village, in Konta tahsil of Bastar District in Chhattisgarh, India. The second book was published in 1983 and held by 57 libraries worldwide. This book represented the field work with the Kolam tribe of Yeotmal, now Yavatmal in the year 1983.

He worked in close association with the stalwarts like Prof. S. C. Sinha, Prof. N. K. Bose, Prof A. K. Danda, and Dr. B. S. Guha. He retired in 1984 as Superintending Anthropologist, leaving an indelible mark on the human study. He lived a very fulfilling and a contended life. He left for his eternal abode on the 15th of October 2016.

Some of his Salient Publications are as:

Books:

1. 1970. The Dorla of Bastar, Calcutta: Anthropological Survey of India.(Memoir No.17).
2. 1983. The Kolam of Yeotmal, Calcutta: Anthropological Survey of India. (Memoir No. 49).

Articles:

1. 1959. The Dorla of Bastar, in Bulletin of Anthropological Survey of India, Vol. VIII (2), Pp: 75-84.
2. 1981. Ancestor Worship among the Kolam, in Bulletin of Anthropological Survey of India, Vol.XXX(1-2), Pp: 1-6.

3.2. Indera Paul Singh ((1928-2016)

Prof. P. Dash Sharma

On 28 September 2016 at about 11pm I received a message at Ranchi from Dr. Jatindera P. Singh and others, and the message conveyed was "Our beloved father Prof. Dr. Indera P. Singh left for his heavenly abode on 27th September 2016. Please join us for his "ANTIM ARDASS & KIRTAN" at Gurudwara Nanak Piao near Rana Pratap Bagh, GT Karnal Road, Delhi, on 2nd Oct. 12 noon to 1 pm." This message about the death of my research supervisor from his eldest son from Delhi had greatly saddened me that night.

On receiving the message I immediately sent a condolence message to Madam Balbir Kaur and Dr Jatindera. Thus ended my earthly link with my revered teacher who had immensely helped me to become what I am today in my academic field.

I was the second doctoral research student of late Professor Indera P. Singh in the year 1965. Inderjit Singh Bansal, his first Ph.D. student at that time was a research project fellow, and I was at the Office of the Registrar General of India, New Delhi, as a Junior Investigator.

My last meeting with Professor Indera P. Singh was in the year 2008, in the month of August, when I had an occasion to go to New Delhi on an assignment at Union Public Service Commission Office. In the evening of August 24 of that year my teacher had visited me at UPSC office, and took me to his home in north Delhi beyond Delhi University, at his Shakti Nagar residence covering a distance of about 12 kilometre by car. It was a wonderful evening that I had with my revered teacher Professor Singh and his family members, and that I cherished for many long years.

In the year 1993 I developed a special issue of *South Asian Anthropologist* as "Felicitation Volume on the Occasion of the 65th Year of Professor S. C. Tiwari and Professor I. P. Singh", as both of them had joined Delhi University as Lecturers in the same year 1953, and retired in 1993 within a gap of one month time. We are greatly happy that Professor Satish Chandra Tiwari is still with us, in May 2021 as I am drafting this article.

Professor Dr. Indera Paul Singh was born on 20 January 1928 at Amritsar, he died at the age of 88 years on 27 September 2016, after contributing a great lot in the field of anthropology. He completed his school studies in 1944 at Ramjas Higher Secondary School at Delhi, and then completed his Intermediate Science in medical stream from Hindu College, Delhi. He did his B.Sc. from Khalsa College, Amritsar, Panjab University in 1947, and then returned to Delhi and completed his Master's course in Anthropology from the University of Delhi in 1950 specializing in physical anthropology. Another stalwart of the Department of Anthropology at Delhi University, his class fellow Jai Dayal Mehra, specialized in social anthropology, under their mentor Dr. P. C. Biswas in the years 1948-50. Professor J. D. Mehra breathed his last on 30 July 2016. Their contemporary Dr. Manish Ranjan Chakravartii also completed his M.Sc. in Anthropology from the University of Delhi in 1951, but again shifted to Calcutta University for D.Phil. degree under the guidance of the great scholar Dr. S. S. Sarkar. From 1953 February to June 1953, Indera P. Singh worked as a research assistant for Professor Oscar Lewis who was doing a field study in Rampur village near Delhi with financial grant from the Ford Foundation's behavioural sciences division. [Lewis, Oscar (June 1956): "The Festival Cycle in a North Indian Jāṭ Village". Proceedings of the American Philosophical Society. *American Philosophical Society*, 100(3): 168-196.]

He had very often stated and considered Professor Oscar Lewis as his *guru* while conducting field studies in Sikh villages in Punjab. [Singh, Indera P., July-September 1958: A Sikh Village. *Journal of American Folklore*, American Folklore Society, 71(281): 503.]

From 1953 (September 1) to 1961 Dr. Indera P. Singh was a Lecturer in the Department of Anthropology of the University of Delhi. He became Reader in December 1961, and later became Professor in the same department in the year 1971 May, and remained in that position until his retirement from the University service in February 1993, after serving for forty long years.

He was the first recipient of a Ph.D. degree in anthropology from the University of Delhi, under the supervision of Dr. Prafulla Chandra Biswas (Ph.D., Berlin), Reader and the Head of the Department of Anthropology, who was the founder of the department at Delhi University. It was Sir Maurice Linford Gwyer (1878-1952), British lawyer and judge, the Vice-Chancellor of the University of Delhi from 1933 to 1950, who took much interest in creating anthropology department in his university and appointed Dr. P. C. Biswas as Reader and Head of the Department of Anthropology in 1947. Prafulla Chandra Biswas (1903-1984) got trained under Professor Panchanan Mitra (1892-1936) for his Master's degree in anthropology from Calcutta University.

Before becoming Lecturer in 1953, Indera Paul Singh obtained a 'specialized training in anthropology' during the years 1951-52 at Das Anthropologische Institute der Universität Frankfurt a. M. (Franz-Weidenreich-Institut) in Frankfurt. After returning from Frankfurt he completed his thesis research on the topic, "*Inheritance of Fingerball Patterns in a Human Population*", and was the first recipient of Ph. D. degree in anthropology in 1959 from the University of Delhi under the supervision of Dr. Prafulla Chandra Biswas, the titan in the field of dermatoglyphics research in India.

Dr. Indera P. Singh though specialized in physical anthropology with special interest in human genetics and growth studies, took much interest in village studies of north India, particularly in Punjab villages.

Professor Indera Paul Singh did extensive fieldwork in north India, particularly in villages of Punjab to understand the caste system among the Sikhs. According to Singer (Singer, 1958), Singh's analytical study of a Sikh village and of the changing traditions of Sikhs with regard to dominant traditions of Hindus illustrated "a process of differentiation that is fairly characteristic in Indian civilization. The analysis of Dr. Singh showed that there is heterogeneity between the lower and upper castes. [Singer, Milton, 1958 July-September: Traditional India: Structure and Change. *Journal of American Folklore*, American Folklore Society, 71(281): 191-204.]

Professor I. P. Singh and his research students had also conducted physical anthropological studies in north-western Himalayas, particularly among the tribal populations of north-western India, and among the people of Sikkim, during the years 1983 to 1987 extensively, and growth studies among the Bods of Ladakh, a high altitude population. In 1963 he had published a general anthropology book jointly in Hindi titled, *Manav Shastra Ki Roop Rekha* (Meerut: Kedar Nath, Ram Nath). In the volume *Anthropologists in India* (1970: 164-166) there are 31 titles of publications listed under Dr. Indera Paul Singh, authored singly and jointly. In 1968 Dr. Indera P. Singh and M. K. Bhasin published their most popular book titled, *Anthropometry* (Delhi: Bharti Bhawan), that helped the students a lot at that time. In 2004, they again jointly authored another book titled, *A Manual of Biological Anthropology* (Delhi: Kamla-Raj Enterprises).

The obituary by Professor Anup Kumar Kapoor of Delhi University (*J. Indian Anthrop. Soc.*, 2016, 51: 202-204) on Professor Indera Paul Singh indicate, “In total he has published five books; the most well-known is titled *Anthropometry*, and 218 articles.” Eight research projects were completed by him under the financial assistance of national and international bodies. Professor Indera P. Singh had successfully supervised 33 Ph.D. students for their doctoral thesis.

Professor Indera Paul Singh had mainly contributed in the field of dermatoglyphics, somatometric studies and growth studies, and had helped and took initiative in the establishment of new laboratories in the Department of Anthropology at Delhi University. He was the Head of the Department of Anthropology from 16 June 1968 to 6th June 1979, and from 4th April 1981 to 3rd April 1984. He was the longest serving Head of the Department after Professor Prafulla Chandra Biswas. During these periods he took initiative to develop laboratories particularly for the study of human cytogenetics, physiological studies, forensic studies and biochemical studies on human populations for researching in the department, and thus brought the anthropology department in the forefront with well-developed laboratories. His persistent efforts to expand the department in different specialized fields have been very successful.

For three terms Professor Indera P. Singh served the University of Delhi as the Dean of the Faculty of Science, in between the years 1971 and 1984. He was also the Proctor, possibly the longest serving Proctor of the University of Delhi, who served the University in that capacity from 1973 to 1992. For many years he was also the Chairman of Gwyer Hall Management Committee, and Delhi University Sports Council, and also served as a member of the Governing Body of many colleges affiliated to the University of Delhi. He was greatly involved in the administrative matters as a member the Executive Council, University Court and Academic Council of the University for more than twenty years. He was also a Member of University Grants Commission from May 1989 to 1992, and being closely associated with UGC was instrumental in founding many departments of anthropology in the country.

In his long academic life he was extensively involved with many professional bodies in India and abroad. Professor I. P. Singh was the President of Anthropology and Archaeology Section of the Indian Science Congress Association during the year 1968-69 Session. He was also the member of the Secretariat during the years 1973-78 of the International Union of Anthropological and Ethnological Sciences, and was the Vice-Chairman of the National Committee of Xth ICAES, and was the Secretary-General of International Congress of Anthropological and Ethnological Sciences that was held at New Delhi in 1978 from 10 to 16 December. Professor Lalita P. Vidyarthi of Ranchi University was the President of the Tenth ICAES that was held at New Delhi in 1978 December.

My association with Professor I. P. Singh always got strengthened that inspired me and gave me an invigorating feeling whenever he had visited the Anthropology Department of Ranchi University as an examiner in practical paper of postgraduate students on the invitation of his close colleague Professor Lalita Prasad Vidyarthi, the Head of the Department. His visit to Ranchi as an examiner or as a participant in national seminars, or as a member of UGC visiting team at Ranchi University, and on some other occasions during the years 1972 to 1980 had always had helped me in my endeavor to develop physical anthropology laboratory in the department. His attachment with Ranchi was also for visiting his relatives who were staying at Hatia in HEC complex, and I always had accompanied him during his visits to relatives.

I quote a few lines from the obituary note that Professor Vinay Kumar Srivastava of the Department of Anthropology of Delhi University [*he is no more with us, he died at New Delhi on 23rd December 2020, at that time he was Director of Anthropological Survey of India*], developed and circulated to his colleagues and students after the demise of Professor Indera Paul Singh on 27 September 2016. His obituary note reflects how much concern, affection and attachment Professor I. P. Singh had towards his students and the department even after his retirement from the University service. I quote the lines as follows: "Till quite recently, Professor Singh used to visit the Department to participate in seminars and make useful comments. He was exemplarily active after his retirement from the University and was a model for emulation. ..... I warm heartedly remember the day when in a seminar that day the Department had organized in August 2013, Professor Singh presented a kaleidoscopic account of the village of Daleka, based on his restudy that was funded by the Indian Council of Social Science Research. They (students) were enthralled and deeply touched by the fact that their great grand-teacher was presenting his paper along with them. .... Professor Singh's humility was the matter of talk later. Memories of association with him crystallizing in my mind and soul make me fuller than I am" (*South Asian Anthropologist*, 2016, 16(2): 221).

In difficult times and conflicting situations during the years of my doctoral research Professor Singh had always stood by my side extending a helping hand and encouraging me for the completion of my research work. What I admire in him is his great patience, cool and calm disposition whenever he had faced a difficult situation in administration and academic problems. He never ignored the problem but faced and solved it calmly. Professor Indera Paul Singh was an excellent person, a soft-spoken gentleman with humble attitude, who had great love and concern for his students and colleagues, and others whoever came close to him seeking help. A deeply religious person in life, and greatly secularist in administrative dealings, an ideal combination that he maintained throughout his life, a quality which is rare, seldom to be found in these days among teachers.

Some of the earlier research publications of Professor Indera Paul Singh as listed in *Anthropologists in India* [1970, Sachin Roy (ed.); and 1978, D. K. Bhattacharya (revised and edited)], published by Indian Anthropological Association, Delhi, have been presented here. It was found that in many cases pagination, volume number, publisher and place of publications, and the name(s) of the co-authors, etc are missing under the list of publications presented in the two volumes of *Anthropologist in India* (1970 and 1978). However, as far as possible, through cross-checking from other published sources, some have been rectified and have been presented here. During his long service of teaching and research for forty years at Delhi University, he was involved in many short and long-term research projects and thus had the opportunity and interest in involving himself by presenting papers singly and with co-authors in many national and international conferences and seminars. In many cases 'title of research publications are given but the references listed remained incomplete', those have been omitted here.

Some of his Salient Publications are as follows.

Books:

1. Biswas, P. C. and I. P. Singh 1960. *The Ex-Criminal Tribes of Delhi State*. Department of Anthropology, University of Delhi: Delhi.
2. Indera P. Singh 1963. *Manav Shasra Ki Roop Rekha* (with L. P. Vidyarthi and K. S. Mathur) (An Outline of Anthropology in Hindi,) . Kedar Nath, Ram Nath: Meerut.
3. Biswas, P. C. and I. P. Singh 1966. *Aspects of Indian Anthropology* (eds.). Proceedings of the Summer School in Anthropology, Dalhousie. Department of Anthropology, University of Delhi: Delhi.
4. Indera P. Singh and M. K. Bhasin 1968. *Anthropometry*. Bharti Bhawan: Delhi.
5. Indera P. Singh, S. C. Tiwari and Lalita Prasad Vidyarthi 1980. *Man and His Environment* (edited). Concept Publishers: New Delhi.
6. Indera P. Singh and M. K. Bhasin 2004. *A Manual of Biological Anthropology*. Kamla-Raj Enterprises: Delhi.

Research Publications:

I. Indera P. Singh 1950. Ex-inheritance of radial loop. *The Anthropologist*, 8: 47-50.
2. Indera P. Singh 1954. Inheritance of fingerball patterns. *The Anthropologist*, 1 (1).
3. I. P. Singh (in collaboration with Professor Oscar Lewis) 1956. Ceremonial and festival cycle in a north Indian Jat Village. *Proceedings of the American Philosophical Society*, 100(3): 168-196.
4. Singh, Indera Paul 1959. Inheritance of Fingerball Patterns in Human Populations. *Ph.D. Thesis, University of Delhi (unpublished).* [Results published through articles]
5. Singh, Indera P. 1960. Direction of whorls: Distribution and inheritance. *The Anthropologist*, 7(1-2):7-17.
6. I. P. Singh 1963. Caste and occupations in Simla Hills. In: Bala Ratnam (ed.), *Anthropology on the March*. Social Science Association: Madras.
7. I. P. Singh 1968. Inheritance studies in dermatoglyphics. In: P. C. Biswas and A. Sharma (eds.), *Proceedings Volume of the International Symposium on Dermatoglyphics,* pp. 133-136. Department of Anthropology, University of Delhi: Delhi.
8. Singh, Indera P. 1969. Physical Anthropology in India: Retrospect and Prospects. *Presidential Address to the Section of Anthropology and Archaeology of the 56th Indian Science Congress held at Bombay.*

9. I. P. Singh and S. L. Malik 1977. A study of human growth among high altitude female Bods of Ladak with remarks on morphological adaptation. *Anthropol. Kozl.*, 21: 63-70.
10. Malik, S. L. and I. P. Singh 1978. Growth trends among male Bods of Ladak – A high altitude population. *Am. J. Phys. Anthrop.*, 48(2): 171-176.
11. Malik, S. L. and I. P. Singh 1979a. Lung function in highlander Bods of Ladak. *Am. J. Phys. Anthrop.*, 51: 383-388.
12. Malik, S. L. and I. P. Singh 1979b. Ventilatory capacity among highland Bods: A possible adaptive mechanism at high altitude. *Ann. Hum. Biol.*, 6: 471-476.
13. Kapoor, Satwanti, Indera P. Singh and H. Bharadwaj 1980. Fat distribution in lean and obese young Indian women: A densitometric and anthropometric evaluation. *Am. J. Phys. Anthrop..*, 53:611-616.
14. Singh, Indera P., H. Walter, H. Strodtmann, M. Hilling, M. K. Bhasin and P. Veeraju 1981. Transferrin subtypes in six Indian population samples. *Human Heredity*, 31 (3): 152-155.
15. Singh, Indera P., Satwanti and R. Bhalla 1982. Influence of genetic and environmental factors on body temperature and patterns of subcutaneous fat distribution. *Presented at IIIrd International Congress of Auxology, in August 1982 at Brussels, Belgium.*
16. Singh, Indera P., H. Walter, Martina Stach and M. K. Bhasin 1983. Transferrin subtypes in four northwest Indian tribal populations and some remarks on anthropological value of this new polymorphism. *Am. J. Phys. Anthrop.*, 61(4): 423-428.
17. S. L. Malik and Indera P. Singh 1984. Ecology and human physiology in Ladak. In: John R. Lukacs (ed.), *The People of South Asia: The Biological Anthropology of India, Pakistan, and Nepal,* pp. 421-439. Plenum Press: New York.
18. Kapoor, S., A. K. Kapoor, R. Bhalla, and I. P. Singh 1985. Parent-offspring correlation for body measurements and subcutaneous fat distribution. *Human Biology*, 57(2): 141-150.
19. Singh, I. P. 1985. Medico-genetic problems of the tribal communities of India. *Keynote address*. In: Somnath Roy, Salil Basu and Anil Jindal (eds.), *Population Genetics and Health Care Issues and Future Strategies.* Proceedings of the Workshop on Population Genetics and Health Care, held during March 24-27, 1982, at Department of Population Genetics and Human Development, National Institute of Health and Family Welfare, Munirka, New Delhi 110067.
20. P. Mukhopadhyay and Indera P. Singh 1986. Intra-familial correlations among Mahalis. *Indian Anthropologist*, 16(2): 185-193.

21. Singh, Indera, P., M. K. Bhasin, H. Walter, V. Bhasin *et al.* 1986. Genetic studies of Pangwalas, transhumant and settled Gaddis. 4. Colour blindness, mid-phalangeal hair, ear lobe attachment and behavioural traits. *Anthropologischer Anzeiger*, 44 (1): 45-53.

22. Singh, Indera, P., M. K. Bhasin, Anu P. Shil, Madhu B. Sharma *et al.* 1987. Biology of the people of Sikkim, India. 2. Colour blindness, ear lobe attachment, mid-phalangeal hair and behavioural traits. *Anthropologischer Anzeiger*, 45 (4): 351-360.

23. Bhasin, Veena, M. K. Bhasin and Indera P. Singh 1991. Ecology, culture and development: Gaddis and Pangwalas of Himachal Pradesh. *Journal of Human Ecology*, 2: 253-302.

3.3.Pratap Chandra Dutta (1930-1994)

Dr. Bharati Debi.

Pratap Chandra Dutta was born on 1st August , 1930 in Kolkata. He was the eldest son of Dr.Prabodh Chandra Dutta and Smt. Pratima Dutta (Mother); his father was a renowned medical practitioner in Homeopathy.

His schooling was at Metropolitan Institution, Kolkata. After his graduation from Scottish Church College, he obtained his M.Sc. degree from the University of Calcutta. By deed of his devotion, sincerity, prudence and perseverance he achieved the PhD (1975) and D.Sc. (1976) degree from the University of Calcutta in two successive years. The title of his Ph.D. thesis was '*A cultural Historical Study of the Andaman Islanders'*.The of study was based on the findings of excavation of South Andaman Island. His D.Sc. thesis was entitled '*The Harappans: a Bio-anthropological study of the Skeletons discovered at Harappa.*' Both the thesis was published by the Anthropological Survey of India (An.S.I.) in 1978 and 1983 respectively. Usually he himself typed his manuscript on a portable type writer in order to avoid spelling mistakes or indentation.

After passing the M.Sc. examination in 1953, he was employed as a scholar trainee under the Archeological Survey of India (A.S.I..), New Delh. There he participated in excavations at different Harappan sites namely Ropar, Bara ,Kotla, Nihang khan and Kalibangnan.He obtained a certificate in Field Archaeology from Archaeological Survey of India in 1955.

He joined the AnSI in December, 1955 in the post of Senior Technical Assistant. Since then he worked in almost all the branches of Physical Anthropology like Bio-anthropological study of human population, demographics, middle phalangeal pilosity, inherited defective colour vision deficiency, taste sensitivity (P.T.C.) and human genetics. But his primary interest was the study of ancient human skeletal remains in India. His first major work was the publication of Human Remains from Harappa (1962) along with Sri Pabitra Gupta and Dr. Arabinda Basu, his colleagues in AnSI. This work was published as a Memoir of the Survey and received wide acclaim. It helped him to secure his place among the small community of Paleontologists in India.

He participated in almost all the archaeological excavations requiring the expertise of a Human Paleontologists and led many field parties in many parts of India. He participated in the excavation at Nagarjunakonda valley and Yellewswaram both are in Andhra Pradesh. He also excavated skeletons from Amirdhamangalam located in Chingliput district of Madras. All the above excavations produced human remains belonging to Palaeolithic, Mesolithic Neolithic and Megalithic cultures. Whereas the Syenaciti of the Purusamendha and other trenches at Kausambi in Uttar Pradesh yielded skeletons of Historical period. The site Sarai Nahar Rai in the Pratapgarh district of Uttar Pradesh produced first fossil record of 'modern man' in India. The site also yielded oldest earthen pot, so far South Asia is concerned, made by coiling technique and belonging to the Mesolithic culture. The pot was probably used as an item of grave and dated back c 8395 B.C. He excavated kitchen-middens in South Andaman bearing the relics of Great Andamanese.

He visited erstwhile Czechoslovakia in 1971 as a delegate of the Government of India to acquaint himself of the modern methods and techniques as applied in the field of Palaeo-anthropology and Paleontology.He also visited other European countries including United Kingdom and France, for his research purpose.

Dr. Dutta had been the Head of Physical Anthropology Division of the AnSI, Calcutta and thereby conducted and supervised the research projects of the institution. Simultaneously, he held the position of Head of Office- a position that was purely administrative in nature.

He was connected with many academic and professional bodies. He was an Associate Editor and then Assistant Editor of the Journal of the Indian Anthropological Society during 1965-70.He also held the position of Honorary Secretary and Treasurer of the society at different points of time. He was a member of the Indian Science Congress Association from was 1953 -68. He was associated with Calcutta University and Utkal University as a research guide and examiner. He was a member of the Editorial Board of the Journal Anthropology published from Brno, Czechoslovakia. He was also the Editor of the Journal Human Science and the Newsletter published by the AnSI. He was a member of the Science Advisory Committee of the G.B. Panth Institute of Himalayan Environment and Development, Almorah, Uttar Pradesh.

He participated in many national and intentional seminars and symposia, like 'Indian Anthropology Today' organized by Calcutta University in 1972; 'Three Decades of Development in Paleontology and Stratigraphy in India' organized by the Geological Survey of India at Hyderabad in 1980; International Symposium on 'Primates' organized by Jodhpur University, Jodhpur in 1982; International Symposium on 'Man and Environment' organized by the Indian Anthological Society at Calcutta in 1983; He was inspired to participate in the First International Congress in 'Human Paleontology' held at Nice, France in 1982.

He delivered courses during 1976-77 and 1977-78 sessions in Anthropology at the School of Archaeology, A.S.I., New Delhi. He chaired a major session on 'Skeletal Biology and Palaeo-anthropology' at the 10th International Congress of Anthropological and Ethnological Sciences in 1978, being nominated by the International Union of Anthropological and Ethnological Sciences. He also chaired the sessions on 'Physical Anthropology' in 1974 and 'Population Studies' in 1989, both organized by the Anthropological Society. On invitation he had addressed the annual seminar lecture of the Department of Ancient Indian History and Culture and Archaeology at Visva Bharati at Santiniketan in 1986.

In 1982 he launched a large scale exhibition on Human Evolution under the auspices of the AnSI to disseminate the knowledge evolution to people from all walks of life. The exhibition was first organised at the Ashutosh Birth Century Hall of the Indian Museum. It was inaugurated by Sri B.D. Pande, the then Governor of West Bengal. The Governor was so impressed that he spent 10 minutes more than his scheduled time limit. It was a grand success. It was held at many academic institutions in and around Calcutta. It was held at Pragati Maidan, New Delhi in 1983 and also at the Regional offices of the Survey at Dehradun in 1985, Mysore (1989), Jagdalpur of M.P. (now Chhattisgarh) in 1996 and in the session of the Indian Science Congress at Bangalore in 1986. It was held at different places of North 24 Parganas, Howrah, East Midnapur and also in different places of the country even after his retirement in 1988.

Bring inspired by the exhibition famous poet and writer Subhash Mukhopadaya wrote a serial in Bengali 'E*lem Ami Kotha Theke'* for the children's journal '*Anandamela*' published by the Anandabazar Group of Publication. He often used to meet Dr. Dutta and got his manuscript technically corrected. Even Dr. Dutta wrote an article on the topic in Bengali, being requested by the editor of *Kishore Bharati*, a popular Bengali journal for the youngsters in its prestigious 'Puja' issue. In later years he wrote a book entitled' Facts and Theories of Human Evolution'. The book was published posthumously in 1995.

In 1984 the Govt. of India constituted a committee of experts for examining and reporting to the Prime Minister whether the bone fragment kept in a steatite castket excavated at Pitrahwa, District. Basti in UP by the A.S.I. belonged to Lord Buddha or not. Dr. Dutta examined the collections and reported upon its status to the said committee.

Another feather was added to his cap when he was elected Fellow of the National Academy of Sciences, India in 1988 in recognition to his contributions in Biological Anthropology. He was the third living anthropologist to receive this honor.

Dr. Dutta did not raise much in the level of official hierarchy in the AnSI where he spent almost all his life. He superannuated in the post of Superintending Anthropologist. But the zeal and ardor with which he worked silently and steadily earned for him the appreciation of an anthropologist of eminence both at national and international level.

He was appointed as U.G.C. Visiting Professor at the post-graduate department of Anthropology and also History at the North Eastern Hill University. Shillong, in two successive spells during 1989-90 and 1990- 1991; he was in charge of the syllabus courses on Man and Culture, Palaeo-anthropology and Racial Biology. He also taught Indian Archaeology, Ethno-archaeology and Human Evolution at the History Department of the NEHU.

Dr. Dutt's list of publications in quite formidable. It consists of seven books (listed below). He has to his credit 69 research papers, published in national and international professional journals and also in edited collections. At least 26 of his papers were published in foreign journals, like *Nature* (Lond.); *Man* (Lond.); *British Medical Journal* (Lond.); *J. Royal Anthropological Institute* (Lond); *Current Anthropology* (Chicago); *Human Genetik* (Germany); *Anthropol Anzeiger* (Stuttgart); *Anthropologie* (Brno); *Acta Genet. Stat. Med (Basel); Acta Genet. Med Gemel (Rome); Ethnos (Stockholm); Wiener Volhe Milt.* (Viena); *Anthropos* and *Z. Morph. Anthrop.* Many of his papers were published in reputed Indian journals like *Man in India, Eastern Anthropologist, Human Science, Jr. Ind. Anthropological Society., Bull. Dept. Tribe, Culture, Folk ,Gauhati. University.*

Some of his List of Publications are :

A. Books:

1. 1962. *Human Remains from Harappa* (jointly with Pabitra Gupta and Arabinda Basu)
2. 1966. *Anthropometry in India* (jointly with Pabitra Gupta)

3. 1970. *Ancient Human Remains* (jointly with Pabitra Gupta and Arabinda Basu)
4. 1978. *The Great Andamanese: Past and Present*
5. 1983. *The Bronze Age Harappans*
6. 1987. *Ancient Human Remains from Ropar* (1987) (jointly with A. Pal, P. Gupta and Arabinda Basu)
7. 1995. *Facts and Theories of Human Evolution* (jointly with Bharati Debi),. Jaipur: Printece Well. Barring the last one all the books were published by the Anthropological Survey of India.

B. Articles:

1. 1967. "Physical Anthropology of the Gandhabanik and Population Variability in Southern West Bengal", in Bulletin of Anthropological Survey of India, Vol. XVI (3-4), Pp: 343-377.
2. 1986. "The Earliest evidence of Pottery in the World", in Human Science, Vol. 35 (2). Pp: 85-87.
3. 1975. "Physical anthropology in Czechoslovakia (A Report on the Czechoslovakia)", in Human Science, Vol. XXIV (1-2), Pp: 1-16.

Brief Communication:

1. 1985. "Prehistoric Research in India (1963-1984): a Review", in Human Science, Vol. 34 (2), Pp: 152-157. (Co-author Bharati Devi).

In his personal life he was a loving husband, affectionate father and a caring and dependable personality to other family members. His father died prematurely. He looked after his widow mother four young brothers and sisters. He helped them to settle in life; got them married and did not severe his tie till his death.

He was optimistic in nature with strong sense of positively. He was very systematic and methodical. He could draw people towards him by his amicable behavior and friendly attitude. He was a source of inspiration to his juniors.

On 7th Feb. 1994 he left for his heavenly abode leaving behind his wife, three daughters and innumerable friends and admirers.

Acknowledgement

I am indebted to Dr. Samira Dasgupta my colleague in the AnSI. for providing me the opportunity to jot down the few lines about Dr. P.C. Dutta - my mentor. I also owe to Smt. Mousumi Acharya and Sri Jayanta Acharya daughter and daughter-in-law of Dr. Dutta. Dr. Sikha chatterjee and Dr. Nabakumar Duary (my colleagues) for their co-operation in providing necessary information. Lastly but not the least, I thank my daughter Shaswati Bhattacharyya and grandson Aritra Bhattacharyya for their much needed and ungrudging help in the preparation of this script.

3.4. Binod Behari Goswami (1933--)

Dr Amitabha Sarkar

Dr Binod Behari Goswami, son of Late Sri Jatindra Chandra Goswami, is a renowned Cultural Anthropologist in India, born in Lucknow, U.P. in the year 1933. He has received his early education at Lucknow and got his post graduate degree in Anthropology from Lucknow University in 1956. He was Gold Medalist of his batch at Lucknow University. He retired as Joint Director of Anthropological Survey of India.During my personal interaction on 14th May, 2021 with Dr.Goswami, who is now located at Pune, narrated his anthropological journery at various eco-cultural set-up during his professional career through his memories.

He has his Ph.D dissertation on '*Mizo Unrest: A Study in Politicisation of Culture*', under the guidance of Prof. M.C.Goswami of Guwahati University and was awarded the degree in 1977. I personally heard from him during my posting period at Western Regional Center, Anthropological Survey of India,Udaipur, Rajasthan about his number of intensive field experiences among the Mizos on their food habits, data collection through group interviews and participative observations.

Dr.B.B.Goswami has been a "Visiting Fellow" at the Indian Institute of Advanced Study, Simla, from 1976-78. He is still considered as an authority on North eastern India as regards anthropological studies are concerned. His works on 'Toda' was well appreciated by wide range of scholars abroad. His chief thrust has been on Tribal State Formation (viz. "*The Mizos in the Context of State Formation in Tribal Politics*", 1987) and kinship alliance system. During discussions on the 'Purum' of Manipur, where structure and sentiment data were analyzed; and his works was referred in the Journal of 'American Anthropologist' by Rodney Needham around 1960-61. The original paper published in the 'Bulletin of Anthropological Survey of India' in 1960, entitled " *Kinship System of the Lushai*". Erstwhile Lushai are now jural Mizo .

His vast field experiences including study on Ethnography and Political Movement of Mizo, Mizo Hills, Manipur, Assam , Family & Kinship System of Lushai, Lushai Hills, Study of Sacred Complexes of Mysore , Study of Caste Panchayat at Bihar , Political Movement of North-east India and Toda of Nilgiri Hills (1965),deserves for worthy praise for their path breaking contribution in the field of Cultural Anthropology.

Dr. B B. Goswami during his tenure as Deputy Director of Anthropological Survey of India, Udaipur, has guided a Scholar of Cultural Anthropology in her research project entitled "Tribal Women Labourers in the Construction Industry". This project work (summary) was published in '*Human Science'* in 1986 and later in book form (name of the Book—'*In Search of Alternatives: Tribal Women in Desert Scenario'*) from Delhi in 1995.This also earned noteworthy comments from academicians on tribal laborer status in un-organised sectors, their role, deprivation even in their native villages inspite of making contribution to their respective families. He also has visited erstwhile Czechoslovakia as a part of Cultural Exchange Programme being an expert of Anthropology. He was a Founder Member of Journal entitled 'Ultimate Reality and Meaning', published from Canada.He taught in Nagpur University, M.Phil(Sociology) courses for a long time. He has also been involved in its Phd programme as a guide, examiner and expert member for 10 Universities in India.He has also been a prolific commentator and writer on Current Anthropology.

Some of his Salient Publications are as Follows:

Books:

1. 1974 (Reprinted in 1991). Chamundesvari Temple in Mysore, Calcutta : Anthropological Survey of India (Co-author S.G.Morab).
2. 1979. Cultural Profile of Shillong (ed). Calcutta : Anthropological Survey of India.
3. 1979. Mizo Unrest: A Study in Politicisation of Culture, Jaipur, Aalekh Publication, Rajasthan.
4. 1988. Marriage in India (Tribes, Muslims and Anglo Indian) (ed), Calcutta: Anthropological Survey of India .

5. 1997. Ethnicity, Politics and Political System in Tribal India, (ed). Calcutta : Anthropological Survey of India.

Articles (noteworthy out of more than 100 published):

1. 1960. Kinship System of the Lushai, Bulletin of Anthropological Survey of India, Vol. IX (2),Pp:81-88.
2. 1962. Mizo Laws of Inheritance, Bulletin of Department of Tribal Culture & Folklore Research, Guwahati.
3. 1963. Caste Panchyat among the Hindu Nai (Barber) of Patna City,Bulletin of Anthropological Surveyof India, Vol. XII(3-4), Pp: 155-163.
4. 1963. Working of a Caste Panchyat in Bihar, Bulletin of Anthropological Survey of India, Vol. XII(3-4) Pp: 129-141.
5. 1964. Tribal Panchyat in Rural and Urban Setting, Bulletin of Anthropological Survey of India, Vol.XIII(1-2), Pp: 1-8.
6. Bow and Arrow ceremony of the Toda-A new interpretation, Bulletin of Anthropological Survey of India, Kolkata (also filmed).
7. Outgroup and Ingroup-A study in typolisation of relationships. Man in India, Ranchi.
8. 1965. Bow and Arrow Ceremony of the Toda—an Interpretation, Bulletin of Anthropological Survey of India, Vol.XIV(1-2), Pp : 35-39.
9. 1970. Comparative Study of Sacred Complexes in India, in Journal of Social Research (Co-author).
10. 1974. Temple as a Civilizational Centre, in Journal of Social Research (Co-author).
11. 1974. Structural Phenomenon of Kinship with regard to the Lushai (Mizo), in Tribe, Caste and Peasantry (ed). K.S. Mathur and B.C. Agrawal, Lucknow: EFCS.
12. 1975. Out-group from the Point of view of In-group, Man in India, Ranchi.
13. 1975. Salvage Anthropology, Bulletin of Urgent Anthrop. Ethnog. Research, Vol. 17, Vienna.
14. Development and Centres of Anthropological Research in India in Ethnographia Polska, Vol.13,Warsaw, Poland.
15. 2002. The Tribes of Assam: A few Comments on their Societal and Cultural ties with the Non-tribes, in Tribal Situation in India (ed) K.S.Singh, Simla: Indian Institute of Advanced Study.13.16.1983. Cultural Adaptability of Violence, Human Science, Vol.32 (4), Pp: 237-247.
16. 1987. The Mizos in the Context of State Formation, in Tribal Politics and State System in Pre-Colonial Eastern and North-eastern India (ed). Surajit Sinha, Calcutta: K.P.Bagchi& Company (Pp: 307-327).
17. 1991. Ethnic-Cognition in North-east India, in Ethnonationalism: Indian Experience (ed). Arun Ghosh and R. Chakraborty, Calcutta: Chatterjee Publishers.

3.5. R.S. Mann (1936—2013)

Dr. Samira Dasgupta.
Dr.Amitabha Sarkar

Prof. Rann Singh Mann (R.S.Mann) was born on 15th November 1936 in a village in Delhi. All his elementary education was in Delhi. At the under graduate level he chose to study in the physical science stream. All through this and also for a while at post graduate level, he played volley ball for the University of Delhi. Finally he became the captain of the University team and represented Delhi University at several inter University competitions.

Being sensitized in village life, Rann Singh Mann found it easy to shift to social anthropology for M.Sc., which he completed in 1960. Almost within years of passing M.Sc., Prof. Mann was appointed as an Instructor in the Tribal Orientation and study centre in Udaipur. Here he came in regular contact with tribal group of Rajasthan and Gujarat. His romance with his roots, however, brought him back to his village in order to organize, plan and execute field work for his Ph.D. thesis. In 1973 he was awarded Ph.D on the topic *Social Structure and Social change in a Delhi Village*, by University of Delhi.

Very soon he was selected for the post of superintending anthropologist at the Anthropological Survey of India (AnSI). This again brought him back to Udaipur where AnSI had a regional station. Thus, having seen the Bhil, Bhilala, Mina, Garasia and Saharia tribes through time gave him the necessary insights into issues of social change leading to the publication of many meaningful papers on the subject. In the subsequent years, social change became one of his favourite perspective for studying tribes and multi caste villages. He got posted in various regional centers of AnSI and at almost each of these centers he brought out book volumes of great value.

Prof. Mann has published seven books. Most of his books till now are taken as the only reliable accounts of the contemporary status of tribes in remote areas. Of these *the Ladakhi, Nature-Man-*

Spirit-Complex and *The Bay Islanders* (where he has carried out two years field work in Andaman & Nicobar Islands during his official posting and discusses the ethno-cultural diversity of the islands as well as socio-economic problems with Jarwa and Onge ethnography) are worth mentioning. His research papers deal with such diverse topics as tribal polyandry, awareness and attitude of Minas and social barriers of nutrition among Indian tribes.

He has published extensively in the fields of ethnology, social and cultural change and anthropology, both theoretical and applied. In him one finds a rare combination of theoretician and empiricist as is reflected in his books entitled Anthropological and Sociological theory.

His publication entitled 'Aspects of Indian Anthropology', 1996 reveals that serious anthropological exploration in respect of unique customs, institutions and other ways of Indian tribes has been a long pending felt need in academic circle. Except some light surface reflexes the exercise on this front has, by and large, remained far short of analytical and structural analysis. This book meets the requirement of not only in-depth substantives but also of formal analysis in respect of polyandry, matriliny, chieftainship, serfdom, dormitory system, shifting cultivation etc. The two mounting emerging concerns of ethnicity and cultural ecology also find a detailed mapping with peoples cognition. In addition to dimensions of change and integration the fixity to and persistence of cultural traditions form yet another area in this presentation. This account of Indian social-cultural anthropology is rich at the level of interpretation and forms a valuable reading to all scholars interested in essence of tribal life and culture still forming a definite world.

His complete involvement in and passion for the subject soon saw him elevated to the position of Director at AnSI. This was at the time when the survey had undertaken a mammoth Project of bringing out a compendium of People of India in several volumes. Data were being collected by scholars from all corners of India and the head office had the almost impossible task of compiling them in a meaningful pattern.

It was shortly after this that he took a premature retirement from AnSI and came to Delhi and joined his Alma Mater the Department of Anthropology, Delhi University as a Professor. His vast empirical experiences in field and his continuous involvement in publishing in the past made him a very successful teacher. He took up to teaching many challenging paper for the specializing batches. He also successfully guided a number of Ph.D. thesis during this short period of service in the Department of Anthropology at Delhi University before he retired in 2002. He remained academically active and addressed research seminars and also helped AnSI in advisory capacity until the year of his death. On 1st September 2013, he expired after a brief illness.

Prof. Mann was a fun loving person who otherwise very serious in his work. I first met him in 1977 at Udaipur office. He was very cordial with juniors and encouraged and taught us in professional field work in anthropology. On those days office was opened on Saturday up to 2 P.M. It became a regular phenomenon after 2 P.M. on Saturday when Dr.Mann and other Seniors accompanied us to a nearby Bhil Tribal village and imparting training in field work and data collection; There was a Seminar Club at Udaipur office where juniors were supposed to present their field observations. This *guru-shishya* tradition is no more in existence now at AnSI.

Dr. Mann was a voracious reader and an excellent speaker.

Reference

Bhattacharya, D.K. 2013.'Prof. Rann Singh Mann (1936-2013)'. Indian Anthropologist 43(2): 101-102.

Some of His Salient Publications are as :

1. 1977. The Bay Islanders, Bidisa, Calcutta: Institute of Social Research & Applied Anthropology.
2. 1978. Problems of Indian Tribes : a Brief Review, Tribe, Vol.11, No.1. Pp:1-13.

3. 1978. On Structuralism, Social Structure and Beyond- an Analysis, Indian Anthropologist, Vol.8. No.2 (December).
4. 1979. Anthropo-Geography: an Important Methodological Issue, Man in India, Vol.59, No.3.
5. 1979. Social Structure, Social Change & Future Trends: Indian Village Perspectives.
6. 1980. Hakkipikki: Trapper and Seller, Calcutta: Anthropological Survey of India.
7. 1980. Indian Tribes in transition.
8. 1981. Nature-Man-Spirit Complex in Tribal India, (ed). New Delhi: Concept Publishing Company.
9. 1982. Economic Systems among the Western Indian Tribes, in Economics of the Tribes and their Transformation (ed). K.S.Singh, New Delhi: Concept Publishing Company.
10. 1986. The Ladakhi: A Study in Ethnography and Change, Calcutta: Anthropological Survey of India.
11. 1988. Tribal Women and Development.
12. 1989. Tribal Cultures and Change.
13. 1996. Aspects of Indian Anthropology, New Delhi: Concept Publishing Company.
14. 2000. Environment, Ecology and Culture Paradigms : Case of Ladakhi Tribe, in Studies on Man: Issues and Challenges (ed). M.K. Bhasin, Delhi: Kamla-Raj Enterprises.
15. 2002. Ladakh : Then and Now, New Delhi : Mittal Publications.

3.6 Satya Narayana Ratha (1936--)

Prof. Deepak Kumar Behera

Professor Satya Narayana Ratha joined Sambalpur University as the founder Professor and the Head of the newly created Post-graduate Department of Sociology and Social Anthropology on September 1976. By then, admission to the department was over. I was one among sixteen students including four girls. In the meantime three other teachers had joined. Classes started from September 15. We were sitting in a class room, temporarily allotted in the department of Life Sciences. A middle-aged tall, fair-skinned, handsome, well-dressed person entered the class room. We stood up. He waved his two hands to make us sit. He introduced himself and asked us, one by one, to introduce ourselves: name, institution and the subjects studied at the graduation level and reasons to change over to Sociology and Anthropology. To the last question, many of us had no answer.

When the formalities were over, he said, "now that you are going study a new subject, know what it is". He began defining the subject- Sociology, Anthropology, their development, their overlapping nature and their relationship with other disciplines that included almost all the subjects we had studied at the graduation level. We felt comfortable, as it dawned upon us that the subjects we had studied for two years are not to go waste.

As the days rolled over, we found him, punctual, clear in communication, cool and patient in responding to our queries and clearing our doubts. We came closer when he took us for field training. He is a very sensitive and meticulous fieldworker and is able to establish rapport with the informant within no time. Learning fieldwork under his guidance is a rewarding experience.

Later, when I undertook my doctoral research under his supervision, our relations became closer and homely. He used to pass on to me many doctoral dissertations coming to him for evaluation along with his evaluation report for me to understand the strength, weakness in the work and suggestions for improvements therein. Much later I realised that it was a part of his technique to make me familiar with research writings. As a teacher, I rate him the best among those I have been exposed to as a student.

II

Professor Ratha was born on 27th December 1935 in an orthodox Brahman family in a multi-community village in the Rayagada district of Odisha, where the Saora, a tribe is numerically dominant. A profile the village appeared in *Man in India* (1968: Vol.48, No.2).His father was a renowned Ayurvedic physician and a ritual specialist (*Purohita*). Professor Ratha's primary education was in the one-teacher school of his native village followed by High school (Then Board High School, now Boys' High School, Gunupur about ten kilo meters way). He passed Matriculation in 1954, Intermediate in science from Vikram Dev College, Jayapur in 1956; and Bachelor Arts from Sri Krushna Chandra Gajapati College, Paralakhemundi, in 1958, with History and Economics as optional. For about one year, he was a high school teacher, teaching History and English, before joining Utkal University to study Anthropology for the Master's degree, passing out in 1961 with specialization in Social and Applied Anthropology.

As a student he was good in studies and extra-curricular activities. He was the Secretary (1955-56) and the President (1957--58) of his College students' Union, won several prizes in debate and literary completions. He has a University Certificate in Spoken English, N.C.C. B Certificate. He was a good hockey player during his High School and College days.

III

Professor Ratha's tryst with professional Anthropology began immediately after the M.A. examinations, before results were out; as a Research Associate to Professor Cora Du Bois of Harvard University, U.S.A. After successfully completing the assignment, he joined The Tribal and Harijan Research and Training Institute (THRTI) , Government of Odisha, for a short period, before joining Gauhati University as a Lecturer (Now designated as Assistant Professor) on 2 January 1963; elevated to the rank of Reader (now designated as Associate Professor) in 1975.

During this period of about a decade and a half, Professor Ratha, had his Doctoral degree from Gauhati University, and conducted field studies among the Arleng (Mikir), Bodo Kachari, and in rural Assam, and published first-hand data based papers.

In 1976, he joined Sambalpur University as the founding Professor and Head of the Department Sociology and Social Anthropology, later renamed as the Department of Anthropology and Sociology; and still later, bifurcated into the departments of Anthropology and the department Sociology, which he, unsuccessfully tried to prevent. His teaching area covered all papers/ courses in the curriculum except Physical Anthropology

On his superannuation 1st July 1996, he was awarded the Emeritus Fellowship by the University Grants Commission. He completed the fulfilment of the conditions of the award and submitted the report, titled 'In Search of a Strategy for Sustainable Development' within the stipulated period.

His other superannuation assignments are: Honorary Director, Council of Analytical Tribal Studies, Koraput and "Director, Alluri Sitaram Raju Centre for Tribal Studies, Mahatma Gandhi National Institute of Research and Social Action "Hyderabad. Presently, he is back to his native village, working on a self-assigned project, like, Interaction between spoken Odia language and spoken Saora language, leading to death of a language (Saora) and emergence of new dialect (Odia) in South Odisha.

During this period of active assignments, Professor Ratha was associated with a number of National Academic and Administrative Institutions, Universities, as a Member, Life member, Consultant, Advisor, President, Vice –President, etc.

IV

Professor Ratha's research output includes three books, two edited volumes, two Project Reports and around seventy papers, of which ten are joint. They cover such areas as Caste, Community and Village Studies, Marriage and Kinship, Development issues, Palaeo-anthropology. Discovery of three Stone-age sites in Odisha goes to his credit.

In relation to caste in Bharat, Ratha's stand is that caste is an inclusive society, that castes are interdependent, and no caste can function in isolation. He has shown that even a tribal community, geographically juxtaposed with castes becomes a part of caste network, referred to as contribution to understand Social Organisation in India (Orans, Martin: 1969, Social Organization, Biennial Review of Anthropology, 1969, Vol. 6 1969, pp. 132-190, Published by Stanford University)

Dealing with tribal development issues he argues that inputs to improve the living conditions and lifestyles of any community must be culture friendly. In relation to the existential position of the tribes, his idea is that tribes are not ethnically different from the neighbouring so called non-tribal communities. The difference, if any, is due to their habitation isolation.

He has taken a stand that no population in India is non-indigenous. Communities resident in geo-politically defined and exclusive areas may be indigenous to that area, but they are also indigenous to India. Thus, in India there is indignity within indignity and that the entire Indian population is one source.

His Doctoral thesis (Caste as a Form Acculturation) was, adjudged the best among the award-winning thesis in Faculty of Arts of the University in the year 1972, and was published by the University (1977). The work is well received and has gone into a second print in 2017.

Professor Ratha often says that five persons in high esteem. They are his mother, his father, his primary school teacher, his professor A. Aiyappan, and Franz Boas. The first three do not need any explanation. He often recollects Professor Aiyappan saying, "Anthropology made me a better person." Brooding over the statement for he discovered its message while being exposed to Franz Boas' theory of Cultural relativism. This theory teaches one, Professor Ratha emphasizes, to respect dissent, respect other cultures and the only intellectual output in modern times as the key to world peace. In a lecture: Relevance of Anthropology, delivered in honour of Professor P. K. Bhowmick, he said that the 'Theory of Cultural Relativism' is the only intellectual input in the modern times to ensure global peace' and called upon 'Anthropologists unite the world'. I have been profoundly influenced by his fieldwork techniques and depth of knowledge. Professor Ratha's contribution to Indian Anthropology will be ever remembered by anthropologists across the globe. I really consider myself very fortunate to have him as my mentor.

Some of His Salient List of Publications:

Books Authored:

1. Caste as a form of Acculturation 1977, Gauhati University (2nd print 2017; GaudenTukel: A study of its Socio-economic implications (Project report financed by the Indian Council of Social Science Research)
2. Ethnographic profiles of (i) Dhulia, 2) Paika, 3) Gauda, 4) Kotia 5) Holva and Bentho-Oriya (Tribal Research and Training Institute, Government of Andhra Pradesh)

Edited:

1. Glimpses of Tribal Life in North-East India (Jointly with P. K. Bhowmick)
2. Sparks from *Bidisha*. Vol One, Tribal Development.

Articles:

A. Caste, Community and Village Studies

1966: Caste, and Occupation in an Assamese village (Jointly with M.C. Goswami and F. Nesha). *Man in India*, 46 (3)

1967: Gandhiji and Caste System, *Journal of the University of Gauhati*, VIII, (1)

1968: Caste in a South Orissa Village. *Man in India*, 48 (2)

1968: Caste and Occupation in two Peri-urban Assamese Villages.*The Eastern Anthropologist*, XXI (2)

1969: Madarbari: A Bodo Kachari Village in North Kamrup, Assam, *Journal of the University of Gauhati,* XX (2)

1969: Religion and occupational Differentiation, *Man in India*, 49

1970: A Village in South Orissa. *The North Eastern Research Bulletin*, Vo1-1, Department of Sociology, Dibrugarh University. 1971

1970: Hindu Jati Pratharar tha aru Adhunik Bharatatiar Bhumika.Nilachal. Vo1.9. No.2 (**Assamese)**

1975: Uttar-Purba Bharatara Adibasi Sanskruti (In Odia language and Assamese script to show the affinity of the two languages), Nilachal. Vo1:14. No.5

1976: Data on Caste: An Examination of Rigvedic Hymns in the Light of Watson's Hypothesis. *Man and Life*, Journal of the Institute of Social Research and Applied Anthropology, Vo1.2 No.1 & 2.

1982: Socio-economic stratification in a West Orissa Village, *Eastern Anthropologist*, 35 (4): 301-308

1985: Land Use and Human Relations: A case study of a Bada Kachari village, *Journal of Social Research*, XI (1-1)

1987: Towards an understanding of the Indian Caste System,*Journal of State Politics and Administration*, XI (1-2).

1992: Community Situation in Western Orissa: A Study in Ethos, Silver Jubilee Celebration Volume, Sambalpur University

1994: Western Orissa: An Ethnographic Profile, in S. B. Roy and A. K. Ghosh (ed) People of India: Bio-Cultural Dimensions (felicitation volume in honour of Dr K. S. Singh). Inter-India Publications, New Delhi

1995: The Problems of Identifying a Community: An emic view from a South Orissa Village (Proceeding of the Indian Science Congress Association).

B. Marriages and Kinship

1971: Menarikam: Matrilateral Cross Marriage Among the Komiti, Data from a South Orissa Village, Folklore, Vo1.XII, No.10

1971: External Influence on Danua Brahman Kinship Terminology: Data from a South Orissa Village, Proceedings of the 16th Annual Session of the Assam Science Society, Gauhati.

1977: A Comparative Note on Oriya and Assamese Kinship Terms. North Eastern Research Bulletin Vo1.VIIIsummer 1979. PP.36.41

1978: Brahmans of Assam: A Historical outline. Proceedings of the X International Congress of Anthropological and Ethnological Sciences, New Delhi

1980: Matrilateral Cross Cousin Marriage and Kinship Terminology: The Arleng Case, Tribes In N.E. India, (B.Dutta Ray edited), Shillong

1984: Mate Selection and Associated Factors: An opinion survey of Post Graduate Women Students (jointly with K. Vijayantimala) Man and Life.Vol.X

1988: Pattern of Marriage among the Converts to Christianity of Western Orissa in K. L. Bhowmick edited "Society and Culture". Inter-India publications, New Delhi

C. Applied and Development Anthropology

1978: Planning for Tribal Development (in *Tribal Problems Today and Tomorrow*, edited by P.C. Mohapatra and D.Panda pp,19-22, Sabari Cultural Society, Bhubaneswar.

1978: Anthropology and Community Development, Proceedings of the Post Plenary Session of the X International Congress on Applied and Action Anthropology, Calcutta

1981: Tribal Development Program: An appraisal (in L. P. Vidyarthi edited Tribal Development and its Administration), Concept Publishers, New Delhi.

1981: A Note on Tribal Education (in L. P Vidyarthi edited, *Tribal Development and its Administration*), Concept Publishers, New Delhi.

1982: Planning for Tribal Development: An Anthropological Approach (in Buddhadev Chaudhury edited Tribal Development in India), Inter India, New Delhi.

1983: A Note on the impact of Industrialization on the Tribal way of life: Observation from an Industrial fringe in Western Orissa, Journal of the Bihar Tribal Research Institute, Vo1XXV, No.1 & 2.

1988: Integrated Rural Development: Data from three West Orissa villages (Rural Development in eastern and North Eastern India. Ed. Madhu S. Mishra), Indian Institute of Management, Calcutta

1990: Displacement and Rehabilitation: Data from three resettled colonies around Rourkela Steel Plant, Orissa. Man in Asia, Vol.2 (Jointly with D. K. Behera)

1990: Rethinking Totemism: Man Nature Relationship in maintaining the ecological balance, Man in India, Vol. 70 (Jointly with D. K. Behera).

1990: Educating the Tribals,The Eastern Anthropologist, Vo1. 43 (Jointly with D. K. Behera)

1991: The Need for a sub-discipline of Action Anthropology and Sociology, Indian Anthropologist, V01.21.

1992: Tribal Development: A peep into the Problem, the Philosophy and the Program, Tribal Transformation in India, Vo1.II of Tribal Studies in India series T 148 Inter-India, New Delhi.

1992: Literacy in Tribal India: An evaluation, Tribal Transformation in India, Vo1.IV of Tribal Studies in India series T 150 Inter-India, New Delhi.

1992: Forest and Tribal Culture: An overview of the Man-Plant-Animal relationship, *Adivasi*, Vo1.XXXIII. No.1, Bhubaneswar

1994: Notes on Ecology, Economy and Religion: Data from a Bodo Kachari Village, Bulletin of the Department of Anthropology, Dibrugarh University.

2001: Welfare of the scheduled tribes and their development: The Orissa case, Journal of Rural Development, Special Issue on Welfare of Scheduled Castes and Scheduled Tribes in Independent India, National Institute of Rural Development, Hyderabad, Vol. 20, No. 1

2002: Relevant Education: Life-skill Approach in the context of Children of Disadvantaged and Marginalized communities- Micro data from Koraput district (National Consultative Meet on 'Education for Life' under Sarva Shiksha Abhiyan, N.C.E.R.T, New Delhi).

2002: A Suggestive micro-model of Community Education through Open Schooling in the context of Difficult to Reach Communities (in Enterprising Community Education, Ed. N.K.Ambasht, N.I.O.S).

2002: Migration into Assam- The Past History, the Present Realities and Future Implications, in *Ethnic Groups, Cultural Continuities and Social Change In North East India*, Ed By Indira Barua, Sarthak Sengupta, Deepanjana Dutta Das, Mittal Publications, New Delhi

2003: The Emerging Ethnographic Profiles of the Eastern Himalayas: Notes on SomeTribes of Arunachal Pradesh, *Tribes of North East India*, (Ed. Sarthak Sengupta), New Delhi, Gyan Books Pvt Ltd

2005: Tribal Welfare Administration And Development in Orissa Contemporary Society: *Tribal Studies, Vol. VI, Tribal Situation in India* pp 86-97 (Deepak Kumar Behera and Georg Pfeffer (ed.), Concept Publishing Company, New Delhi

2006: In Search of a Strategy for Sustainable Development (Research Report submitted to the University Grants Commission)

2009: Beyond the Tribal Society: To be or not to a Tribe in India (*Contemporary Society, Tribal Studies, Volume VIII: Structure and Exchange inTribal India and Beyond,* (ed.) Georg Pfeffer and Deepak Kumar Behera, New Delhi, Concept Publishing Company (pp.316-321)

2009: Outlining an Exercise to build a Field Model to Ensure Participation of the people for their Development (*Sustainable Development in Bonda Hills*, (eds.)Pyarimohan Mohapatra, K.K. Mohanty, P.K. Mohaptra,Council of Analytical Tribal Studies, Koraput).

2011: Resource Base and Livelihood Patterns of the LanjiaSaora: A Primitive Tribal Group of Orissa. In: V. Annamalai (ed.), "Resource Management and Village Panchayats: Experiences and Emerging Concern" pp.216-224, New Delhi, Kaniska Publishers).

2011: Women and Gender Relations in Tribal Society: The Case study of the Durua in Koraput district, South Orissa. In: D. Pulla Rao (ed.) 'Women of Disadvantaged Groups: Status and Employment: Essays in Honour of Professor K. S. Chalan pp.247-254), Serial Publications, New Delhi.

2012: Understanding tribes and their socio-cultural ethos for a sustainable policy for their development (in P. K. Misra, H.K. Bhat, K.K. Misra(eds.) 'Bio-Cultural Development of Scheduled Tribes: Policies and Issues pp.1-29, Rawat Publications, New Delhi)

2012: Forest, Food and Nutrition: Data from the Oraon, A Scheduled Community of Orissa (Jointly with Indira Naik in 'Women and Food: Studies from the Indian Sub-continent, LAP LAMBART Academic Publishing

2014: Food, Nutrition and Health: Data from the Kandha- A Tribal Group on the Andhra Pradesh Odisha border (Deepak Kumar Behera ed. Contemporary Society, Studies, Volume Nine)

2015: Durua: A Short Ethnography of a little known Tribal community in Koraput District, Yet to be scheduled (Jointly with Paresh Rath) in Vijay Prakash Sharma edited "Contemporary Indian Society in the beginning of 21 Century, Delhi Pp 9-16), Anmol Publications

2015: Rethinking Tribe and Tribal Cultures (*New Horizons in History and Culture,* Professor Manmath Padhy Felicitation Volume, (ed.),Benudhar Patra, Pratibha Prakasan, Delhi)

D. Palaeo-anthropology

1964: A Note on a PalaeolithicTool from Orissa, Journal of the Assam Science Society, VoI, VII,

1965: A Neolithic Celt from District Koraput, Orissa, Journal of the Assam science Society, Vol., VIII.

1969: Fluted Cores and Their occurrence in District Koraput, Orissa, The Eastern Anthropologist, VoI. XXII, No.3.

1970: A Note on the Occurrence of Palaeoliths in District Koraput, Orissa, Journal of the University of Gahuati, VoI, XXI, No.1

1988: Lower Palaeoliths from Kuchinda (Orissa): Man and Environment,VoI. XII (Jointly with D. K. Bhattacharya.)

E. Miscellaneous

1996: A Study on the post-Graduate students of Gauhati University: Their socio-economic Background and Educational Performance (Jointly with P. P. Gokulanathan), *Journal of the University of Gauhati*, VoI. VIII, No.1.

1968: Family of Orientation and Educational Achievement: Elite-in-Making (Jointly with the P.P.Gokulanathan), Journal of the University of Gauhati, VoI. XIX, No.1.

1968: A Bodo Kachari Folk Tale. *Journal of the University of Gauhati*, VoI, XX, No.1.

1972: Rabi SasyaraAchani: Iyar prastuti (**Assamese**) (Jointly with S. Dowerah). Nilachal No. 206-208. 15. 22. 29, Gauhati, 1972

1980: Eka Manab Gosthira Paribesiya Itihasa (**Odia**), *Saptarsi*, Special Number, June, 1980.

1985: Man and Nature Relationship: Life in a Kisan Hamlet of Western Orissa (Jointly with D. K. Behera). *Man and life*, VoI. II, No.3 & 4.

1988: Socio-economic responsibility of Tribal Women: A Case Study of Kisan of Western Orissa (Jointly with D. K. Behera) *Social Science and Social Concern* (Felicitation Volume in Honour of Dr. B. K. Roy Burman, Edited by S.B. Chakraborty, (pp108-116), Mittal Publication, Delhi.

1988: The Kisan Children at work: Data from a west Orissa Village (Jointly with N. K. Mahakud). Man in India, Vo1.I.

1998: Resettlement and Rehabilitation: A Case Study of the policy and the programs of the Mahanadi Coal Fields Ltd. Theme papers, Third Training Seminar on Resettlement and Rehabilitation (January 12-17, 1998) Gopabandhu Academy of Administration, Bhubaneswar.

2016: Understanding the Gender Issue: A Loud Thinking (in Gender Asymmetry in Contemporary India, (ed.)ItishreePadhy, pp.1-10, Mangalam Publication, Delhi)

Felicitation Publications:

My teachers, professional colleagues, and students from 16 countries have brought out 3 volumes of research papers in my honour. Professor Georg Pfeffer of Free University, Berlin (Germany) and Professor D. K. Behera of Sambalpur University are the Editors. Those volumes are:

1. Tribal Studies: Volume 1 Structure and Process, Concept, New Delhi, 1997.
2. Tribal Studies: Volume II Development Issues, Transition and Change, Concept 1997
3. Childhood and Complex Order, Manak, New Delhi, 1996.

3.7. Pashupati Prasad Mahato (1943—2019)

Prof. Sumahan Bandhopadhyay.

Activist Anthropologist

Pashupati Prasad Mahato was a rebel in anthropology. He had formal training in anthropology, and in fact was a bright student. He worked in Anthropological Survey of India, the largest government organization in the world. In spite of that, he pursued career more of an activist. He published very little in academic journals of anthropology compared to the magnitude of his huge writings. He was outspoken. He relentlessly fought for the rights of the backward classes of people being actively engaged in different organizations working with similar objectives. However, his central thesis of 'Nirbakization' or 'Cultural Memocide' seems to remain a seminal contribution to the understanding the Indian society in general and the plight of the marginal people in particular. His works can be cited as a valuable contribution to the study of socio-political dynamics in eastern India.

Pashupati Prasad was born to Anjali and Rabindranath Mahato in Dabar village in Purulia district on 29th October in 1943. His paternal grandfather Madanmohan Mahato was the first matriculate among the Kurmi Mahato of the region in 1919. And his maternal grandfather Rajkishore Mahato of Bagmundi was also among a few Mahato gentlemen who advanced in formal education during the early decades of twentieth century in Manbhum Chhotonagpur region. Both Rajkishore and Madanmohan were engaged in some respectable government service. It inculcated an environment for acquiring education and higher studies in the family. His father was also a government employee. Pashupati had his early education in his village. He passed matric (10 standard) from Purulia Zila School in 1959. He was an Intermediate Science Student in Jagannath Kishore College, Purulia from which he also earned his B.A. degree in 1963. Then, he went to Ranchi and took admission in Ranchi

University to study anthropology. He was introduced to Prof. L.P. Vidyarthi and Dr. Mrinal Roy with letter from his teacher Dr. Sudhir Karan to take admission in Anthropology in Ranchi University. His uncle (*meshomoshai* i.e. mother sister's husband) Professor Vishnu Charan Mahato inspired him to take anthropological interest in his own community of Kurmi Mahato. He stood first class first in M.A. Anthropology in the university in the year 1966. Long time after that he was awarded D.Litt in 1995 from the same university for his thesis titled '*Social Mobility Movement of the Kudmi-Mahatos of Purulia and Neighbouring Areas of Bihar and Orissa*'.

After passing masters, Pashupati started his career as a teacher in Gobindapur High School in 1966. He himself played a role in organizing this school when he himself was still a graduate student. But, the career in anthropology was beckoning him. Soon he left the job of school teacher to accept the tenured post of Research Scholar in CRI (Cultural Research Institute) where he worked for two years from 1967 to 1969. In 1970, he got a UGC research fellowship and joined under Professor L. P. Vidyarthi in Ranchi University. He was awarded a Senior Research Fellowship in Anthropological Survey of India in 1972 and he continued in that fellowship up to 1976, the year in which he was appointed in the permanent post of Research Associate in the same organization. He served the Anthropological Survey of India for long 27 years as a permanent employee and retired in 2003 as Assistant Anthropologist.

Dr. Pashupati Prasad Mahato was a prolific writer both in Bengali and English. He had liking for writing in Bengali in a popular style since he would like to communicate his ideological standing to the masses in vernacular language. His specialized area was performative traditions of Jharkhand and socio-political movements. His earliest writing published in 1969 was on the declining folkloristic culture of Jharkhandi region (Mahato,1969). He was among a few anthropologists who had written continuously in vernacular language. His articles were published in literary magazine like *Desh*. He wrote on a number of subjects mostly focused on the broad areas as mentioned above. These writings included topics like folk songs, folk dance, folk literature, ethnicity, social and political movement, economic relations based on land and agriculture, rights of the people, diverse marriage practices among the tribes, community-relations in Tripura. However, his most seminal contribution was the concept of *Nirbakization.*

Nirbakization

Pashupati Prasad Mahato's book "*Sanskritization vs Nirbakization – A Study of Cultural resistance of the People of Junglemahal*" which was published in 2012 is more and more relevant nowadays if we consider the metaphorical sense embedded in the title. It tells us about the narrative of the community, Kudmi-Mahatos which had to undergo "nirbakization" as a result of its confrontation with the over-arching Varna-Hindu civilization. However, a brand of emerging intellectuals educated in the colleges and universities countered the process and new scenario came out. Kshitimohan Sen in the introduction of his Bengali book *Jatibhed* (Sen,1353B) referred to Rabindranath Tagore who used the word 'Nirbak' (voiceless). Tagore was said to urge that it was necessary to write as much as possible on these voiceless peoples of India. This task must be taken up by the posterity as the poet laureate pledged. Pashupati was one among the posterity, who took up this task seriously. For him, the poet intended to mean a process of culturally silencing the toiling masses by the word 'Nirbak' which seemed to reflect a 'Culture of Silence'. Pashupati wrote:

> "*Ethnic groups under the spell of Nirbakization for more than two or three generations forget the creative excellence of their own language and idioms including aesthetics. This process we term as Smritiharan or memocide (killing of memories*)."(Mahato, 2012;Preface)

He felt so disturbed by this phenomenon that he began to collect the oral traditions, folk songs and other symbolic expressions of the people. Thus, it can be said that his studies on the socio-political dynamics and movements of the people was related to the study of performance. In this way, he contributed the concepts of 'Nirbakization', 'Memocide' to the sociological world in the one hand, on the other, he contributed significantly to the study of the politics of performance. This may be considered an exercise in Manchester school of anthropological study.

The process of "nirbakization", though discussed here with regard to a single indigenous community, is the reality for a vast number of small and large groups rest at the bottom of Brahminical hierarchy and remained outside this Varna system. These groups include in general understanding, the so called Dalits and Adivasis, however it has a broader implication at a cross-sectional level wherever there is a case of deliberate silencing of a just voice. In this context, it does not circumscribe only the above mentioned depressed or backward sections of the population; the process is well perceptible in so called higher classes and castes at different walks of life in social, political, economic, educational and cultural spheres. Though inherently a politically informed concept, "nirbakization" holds a much broader compass.

In defining "Nirbakization", Mahato writes (Mahato: 2000: 18)

"*The tribal/castes or Mulvasi-Dalit clusters of ethnic groups lost their cultural strength and forced to think and act accordingly to the idioms, symbols, signs and style of the dominant nationalities- accepting the rituals and religions through usurpation including food habits of the Brahmins or twice born communities. This process is to be known as Nirbakization or cultural silence.*"

He adds that-

"*By the term Nirbakization I intend to mean the processes of cultural silence.*"

(Mahato, 2012:36)

He studied the process of Nirbakization ethnographically in three villages in West Bengal, Jharkhand and Odisha. In the village of Talpat in the Bandowan block of Purulia, he saw how the Nirbakization was at work to silence the people in articulating their own traditional song to the common masses of the area and general people. The educated school going boys and girls were feeling shy at singing the jhumur and other songs in public, however, they were fluent in their performance at their traditional *akhra.* By way of Sanskritization the dominating culture actually effaced the traditional lore and practices of the so called low caste or tribal people by sheltering them in a berth of the hierarchic system and inculcating their own practices on these assimilated communities. Therefore, we come across an anti-thesis of Sanskritization by a subaltern scholar. This also informs his theoretical formulation in the following way:

"*...from cultural silence generated a tremendous voice of protest which led to the formation of nationality in Jharkhand region with sustained political and cultural movement.*" (Mahato,2012:43)

Study of performances

Dr. Pashupati Prasad Mahato was himself a gifted jhumur performer. Besides this, he is rated as one of the established scholars in the the study of performative traditions of Jharkhand, Manbhum and Jangalmahal regions. He wrote about Jhumur, Nachni, Natua dance, Chho dance and masks. He gave an exposition of the theory of 'Tribal-Folk Continuum' with reference to the literary works of a native Jharkhandi poet Binandiya Sing. Apart from this, he used the 'continuum' model in many of his other studies. For example, Nachni dance appeared to him as a reflection of folk-classical continuum since some of the classical markers of Indian dance tradition could be noticed in this dance formed practiced and performed mostly by a section of outcaste women. According to Mahato (2013), the Jhumur songs can be classified into two main types – i.Bhaduria and ii.Darbari or Nachnisalia or Zamindari. He considered this folk song to be the elan vital of the culture of this vast stretch of Jharkhand region. His detailed work on the three regional *Chho* (also pronounced as *Chau*) traditions of eastern

India connected with Purulia, Mayurbhanj and Seraikela. He has described the characteristic features that distinguish three 'schools' of Chho dance which he extensively studied in different locations for years. One of his own arguments was related to the actual name of the dance – whether it was 'Chho', 'Chhau' or 'Chha'. He was in favour of using the word *Chho,* and was vehemently against using the word 'Chhow' for the dance form. He had his own argument for this. Besides, he also provided empirical data that showed the use of the word by the performers themselves. He was not only a docile researcher, but a crusader to fight against any kind of misinformation or misinterpretation on the researched topic. He used to refer to a misinterpretation as done by a noted university professor and celebrated folklorist on the use of mask to cover the face of chho dancer which he vehemently opposed and engaged himself in a long intellectual battle against it (Mahato,1978; Chatterji,2009).

Chatterji (2009) wrote that Dr. Mahato presented Jharkhand as an 'autonomous cultural region' that had only a superficial connection with the folk culture of West Bengal. However, it is apparent from the writings of Dr. Mahato that he thought of a more deeper affiliation with the culture of the country as once he wrote: '…to know the people of Jangalmahal and Jharkhand means to have a key to know the people of India.'(Mahato,2012:43) In fact, his idea of folk – classical continuum with regard to some of the performative genre of this region seems to indicate an intimate connection of this region with the rest of India.

Subjectivity of Kurmi-Mahato identity

Pashupati Prasad Mahato used to take pride as a student of Anthropology. His assertion in support of the cultural relativistic stand of the subject lends him a foundation to fight against any ethnocentric bias. At the same time, he exposed the unethical and cunning use of the subject in dividing and subjugating the people of our country. He even used the words 'Nritattwer chalaki' (Cunningness of Anthropology) to describe this act.

As an anthropologist, he studied his own society and people, the Kudmi-Mahato. The Kudmi-Mahatos were categorised as tribe before 1931. Later they were classified as OBC (Other Backward Classes) by the state government. However, he was in support of the claim for tribal status for the Kudmi-Mahato. He never hide his identity as an insider. To quote from Mahato(2012:68):

"The investigator is himself a Kudmi-Mahato and he is also well-known in different parts of the region in Kudmi-country, so he has got some advantage in gaining entry into the social life of the Kudmi-Mahatos of different villages in the entire region."

To quote from him again (ibid):

"In the field I made a conscious effort to combine my professional training as an anthropologist with my value involved role as cultural revivalist and a performer of the folk songs of Jharkhand. This combination gave me some advantage to proceed deeply into the stability of social situation."

Therefore, his case reflects the subjective location of the fieldworker as well as an auto-ethnographic exercise, at least in part. His identity as a Jharkhandi was very much prominent in a number of his deliberations (Mahato,1970, 1982,2012). He wanted to portray a larger cluster of tribal solidarity through his idea of 'Hor Mitan' that included Scheduled Tribes like Santal, Munda, Oraon along with the Kurmi – Mahatos on the other. According to him the divisive mechanism perpetrated by the colonial power resulted into the ruptures among the communities who had a close connection with the land. Therefore, he took up the study of the land ownership among the tribal and other neighbouring communities (Mahato, 1983).

Mahato as an Activist

Dr. Pashupati Prasad Mahato was known beyond his immediate academic circle as an activist and subaltern or Dalit intellectual. Though I am not in favour of using the words like Dalit or subaltern to qualify his academic credentials, yet his fight for the rights of the backward and deprived sections of the populations cannot be undermined. He, as I felt through my association with him, did not judge the person by his or her caste or community, but by the social location and deprivation he or she is experiencing. So, the target of his scathing attack was the attitude or mentality the Brahminic cult propagates not the individual Brahmin (here, Brahmins also denote the upper caste or class). He was the Secretary of the West Bengal Backward Classes Federation. He met the members of the Backward Classes Commission under the leadership of B.P. Mandal at Darjeeling in 1980 to submit the demands of the backward classes of people. He again gave deposition before State OBC Commission later to stake the claims of the Kudmi-Mahato people.

Dr. Mahato retired from AnSI in 2003. After retirement, he visited Australian National University, Cambridge University, Sussex University and Peking University. He became a member of the Executive Council of the Sidho-Kanho-Birsha University of Purulia. He was associated with the Asiatic Society of Bengal as a member of its Anthropology Sub-Committee. He was also a member of the '*Adivasi O Loksanskriti Kendra*' (Tribal and Folk Culture Centre), Government of West Bengal.

He left for his heavenly abode on 28th February,2019.

References

Bandyopadhyay,S. 2019. Chole gelen Adivasider Kacher Lok Pashupati Prasad. *Dainik Statesman*, 4 March

Chatterji, R. 2009. *Writing Identities – Folklore and Performative Arts of Purulia, Bengal.* IGNCA and Aryan Books International. New Delhi.

Sen, Kshitimohan, 1353B. *Jatibhed.* Visva-Bharati Granthalaya. Kolkata

Some of His Salient Publications are:

1. 1969. *Jharkhandi Khsiyaman Lok Sanskriti.* Pub. By Bishnupada Soren. Jhargram
2. 1970. Ami Jharkhandi (I am Jharkhandi). *Srijan*
3. 1978. Chho Nach (A rejoinder to Dr. Ashutosh Bhattacharya). *Desh*: 29 April.
4. 1982. *Jharkhander Vidroho o Jiban.* Sujan Publication. Calcutta
5. 1985. *Adivasi Arthaniti o Bhumi Byabastha.* B.B. Prakashan. Calcutta

6. 1994. The Status of the Kudmi-Mahatos. *Social Change* 24(1&2).
7. 2012. *Bharater Adivasi o Dalit Samaj*. Purbalok Prakashan. Kolkata
8. 2012.*Sanskritization vs Nirbakization – A Study of Cultural resistance of the People of Junglemahal*. Purbalok Prakashan. Kolkata.
9. 2013. *Performing Arts of Jangalmahal and Jharkhand*. Purbalok Prakashan. Kolkata.

3.8. Asit Baran Das Chaudhuri (1943--)

Prof. Jaydip Sen.

I happened to be associated with Asit Baran Das Chaudhuri since my days in the Master's course in Calcutta University. It was way back possible in the year 1989 when the M.Sc, first year classes were held in the lecture theatre of the Department that a bearded Professor whom we knew subsequently as ABDC walked in to teach us Evolution. In his classes he used to talk about Darwin, the voyage of the HMS beagle, the life of Dobzhansky and so on. Slowly we began to be awed by his knowledge. His room was the last one in the corridor and he was totally involved with his work.

It was only when I joined as UGC-NET JRF under Prof. Das Chaudhuri that I became close to him. I found him to be a very encouraging teacher and supervisor. He was very punctual and was in the department by 9.30 am and used to leave around 8.00 pm. I learnt a lot from this great man, a man whose works I believe cannot be surpassed by us even today. I still remember that he also used to encourage the students, regardless of their specialisation in the subject. When I wrote my first paper, I had given his name as the first author. Immediately he called me and told me that since I wrote the paper, it is I who should be the first author and he gave his justifications. This is one principle that I follow even today with my students. He used to say write papers in good journals as one day we all shall retire from our profession and then meet our destiny with the Almighty. The papers shall survive not the number of seminars one attended or number of selection committee one went to.

Prof. Das Chaudhuri was born on 31st of December, 1943 in Assam. He completed his graduation in Anthropology (Hons) from the University of Calcutta. Later in the year 1973, he was awarded the Ph.D. degree in Anthropology from the University of Calcutta. The title of his Ph.D. thesis was "*Genetics of Quantitative Variation of Human Head Hair*". He was the recipient of the prestigious Humboldt fellowship offered by the Alexander von Humboldt

Stiftung of erstwhile West Germany in 1979-1980. He joined the Anthropologisches Institute (now named as Institute for Human Biologiae Universitat Hamburg) and continued research in the area of human quantitative genetics. Later he worked in the field of Cytogenetics with Prof. Dr. G. Flatz, Director, Human Cytogenetik Labor, Medizinische Hochschule, Hannover. Prof. Das Chaudhuri then furthered his research into population and family areas and concentrated on human hair micro-morphological variables. He was subsequently awarded the D.Sc. degree on the basis of these studies by the University of Calcutta. He joined the Department of Anthropology, University of Calcutta as Reader and became Professor in Anthropology in the year 1998. He retired as Professor and was later UGC-Emeritus Fellow in the same department. He is also a fellow of the West Bengal Academy of Science and Technology. He was also President, Section of Anthropological and Behavioural Sciences (Including Archaeology and Psychology & Educational Sciences), Indian Science Congress 2009 at Shillong.

The major research contributions of the great person may be summed up as follows:

a) The utilization of twin, family and population models for the first time in the sub-discipline of biological anthropology for a comprehensive understanding of the genetic basis of qualitative and quantitative human hair micro-morphological variables such as diameter and cross-section.
b) A modification of Martin's micro technique for hair analysis
c) Fundamental research in twin studies relating to inheritance of twinning, biology of twinning and twin zygosity.
d) Development of efficient sequential search procedure for twin diagnosis using gene frequency of genetic markers.
e) Extraction of four factors of dermatoglyphic variables using a multivariate method of factor analysis which showed that each finger was a discrete part of the digital

complex comprising of ten fingers and not a separate entity acted upon by independently by genes involved.

f) Understanding of the determinants of anthropometric and metabolic risk factors for coronary heart disease.

g) For the first time from the domain of biological anthropology in India, use of human hair as a biomarker to toxic elements such as lead using flame atomic absorption Spectrophotometry.

h) Effect of consumption of ground-water contaminated with arsenic on age at menarche and reproductive wastage.

i) Initiating the Six-month certificate course in Forensic Anthropology under CUIIPP in the Department of Anthropology, University of Calcutta.

Prof Das Chaudhuri has authored more than fifty research publications in various international and national journals. To many of us, this may seem to be miniscule, but one has to look into the quality of his publications. His publications appeared in such famous journals such as Human Heredity, American Journal of Physical Anthropology, Zeitschrift für Morphologie und Anthropologie, Bulletin of Environmental Contamination and Toxicology and Acta Geneticae Medicae et Gemellologiae: Twin Research. He has also completed a number of UGC Major Research Projects.

Some of his important research publications are given below:

1. Das-Chaudhuri A.B. Genetic basis of hair medulla by twin study. Am. J. Phys Anthropol.. 1976 Jan; 44(1):51-3. doi: 10.1002/ajpa.1330440107.
2. Das-Chaudhuri A.B. A twin study of the structure of human hair medulla. Hum Hered. 1976; 26(3):167-70. doi: 10.1159/000152800.
3. Das-Chaudhuri A.B. An enquiry into the genetic basis of human scalp hair cross section (area) by twin study. Z Morphol Anthropol. 1977 Jul;68(2):226-32.
4. Das-Chaudhuri A.B, Chopra V. Genetic basis of hair histomorphological variables. Am J Phys Anthropol. 1983 Jan;60(1):1-6. doi: 10.1002/ajpa.1330600102.

5. Das-Chaudhuri A.B, Chopra VP. Variation in hair histological variables: medulla and diameter. Hum Hered. 1984;34(4):217-21. doi: 10.1159/000153466
6. Das-Chaudhuri A.B. Human scalp hair genetics by twin study. Prog Clin Biol Res. 1978;24 Pt C:261-7.
7. Das-Chaudhuri A.B. A Supplementary note on Human Hair Medullation. Hum Hered. 1978;28(2):86-8. doi: 10.1159/000152947.
8. Das-Chaudhuri A.B. Genetic basis of human scalp hair weight: a twin study. Ann Hum Biol. 1980 Jan-Feb;7(1):77-81. doi: 10.1080/03014468000004061.
9. .Das-Chaudhuri A.B. Genetics of quantitative variation of human scalp hair diameter. Prog. Clin. Biol. Res. 1981;69 Pt C:231-8.
10. Das-Chaudhuri A.B. A note on Martin's method of hair microtechnique for preparing cross- section. Anthropol Anz. 1981 Jun; 39(2):135-7.
11. Chaudhuri, A.B.. Efficient Sequential Search of Genetic Systems for Diagnosis of Twin Zygosity. Acta geneticae medicae et gemellologiae. 1991,.40 :159-64. 10.1017/S0001566000002592.
12. Das Chaudhuri A.B, S. Basu, S. Chakraborty. Twinning rate in the Muslim population of West Bengal. Acta Genet Med Gemellol (Roma). 1993;42(1):35-9. doi: 10.1017/s0515283600042268.
13. Chaudhuri, A.B. Cytogenetical and Anthropometric Studies on Clinically Diagnosed Patients with Down Syndrome. Journal of Human Ecology. 1996, 7 : 35-39. 10.1080/09709274.1996.11907189.
14. Nandi, Arpita and A.B. Chaudhuri, Trace Element Copper and Chromium Concentration Levels in Blood of Non-Insulim Dependent Diabetes Mellitus (NIDDM) Patients. Journal of Human Ecology. 1998, 9: 397-398. 10.1080/09709274.1998.11907394.
15. Ghosh A, K.Bose, A.B.Das Chaudhuri. Comparison of anthropometric characteristics between normotensive and hypertensive individuals among a population of Bengalee Hindu elderly men in Calcutta, India. J R Soc Promot Health. 2000, Jun;120(2):100-6. doi: 10.1177/146642400012000207.
16.. Sen J, A.B. Das Chaudhuri. Brief communication: Choice of washing method of hair samples for trace element analysis in environmental studies. Am J Phys. Anthropol. 2001, Jul;115(3):289-91. doi: 10.1002/ajpa.1083
17. Bose K and A.B.Das Chaudhuri. A comparative study of adiposity and central body fat distribution of normotensive and hypertensive older Bengalee Hindu women of Calcutta, India. Coll Antropol. 2001 Dec;25(2):521-7.
18. Chakraborty, Shila and A.B.Das Chaudhuri, Heritability of Some Important Parameters of the Antioxidant Defense System Like Glucose-6-Phosphate Dehydrogenase, Catalase, Glutathione Peroxidase and Lipid Peroxidation in

Red Blood Cells by Twin Study. International Journal of Human Genetics. 2001, : 1-4. 10.1080/09723757.2001.11885764.

19. Ghosh A, K Bose and A.B.Das Chaudhuri. Age and sex variations in adiposity and central fat distribution among elderly Bengalee Hindus of Calcutta, India. Ann Hum Biol. 2001 Nov-Dec;28(6):616-23. doi: 10.1080/03014460010025167.
20. Ghosh A, K. Bose and A.B. Das Chaudhuri. Association of food patterns, central obesity measures and metabolic risk factors for coronary heart disease (CHD) in middle aged Bengalee Hindu men, Calcutta, India. Asia Pac J Clin Nutr. 2003;12(2):166-71.
21. Bose K and A.B. Chaudhuri. Age variations in adiposity and body fat composition among older Bengalee Hindu women of Calcutta, India. Anthropol Anz. 2003, Sep;61(3):311-21.
22. Ghosh A and A.B.Das Chaudhuri, A. Explaining body composition by some covariate factors among the elderly Bengalee Hindu women of Calcutta, India. The Journal of Nutrition, Health & Aging., 2005, 9:403-6.
23. Ghosh A, D. Chatterjee, A.R. Bandyopadhyay and A.B. Das Chaudhuri. Age and sex variation of body mass index and waist circumference among the Santal children of Jharkhand, India. Anthropol Anz. 2006, Mar; 64(1):83-9.
24. Sen J and A.B. Das Chaudhuri. Effect of arsenic on the onset of menarcheal age. Bull Environ Contam Toxicol. 2007 Sep;79(3):293-6. doi: 10.1007/s00128-007-9206-7.
25. Sen J and A.B.Das Chaudhuri. Arsenic exposure through drinking water and its effect on pregnancy outcome in Bengali women. Arh Hig Rada Toksikol. 2008 Dec; 59(4):271-5. doi: 10.2478/10004-1254-59-2008-1871.
26. Nissimov J.N and A.B. Das Chaudhuri. Hair curvature: a natural dialectic and review. Biol Rev Camb Philos Soc. 2014, Aug; 89(3):723-66. doi: 10.1111/brv.12081.

3.9. Amitabha Sarkar (1952 –)

Dr. Biman Kumar Das Gupta
Dr. Samira Dasgupta.

Amitabha Sarkar was born on 5th Devember 1952 in Calcutta to a businessman's family. His father Late, Naresh Chandra Sarkar was an engineer and contractor and mother Smt. Alaka Sarkar – a housewife. He has one brother- Samitava Sarkar. Amitabha Sarkar's early childhood education was at Darbhanga, Bihar. He completed his B.Sc (Honours) in Anthropology in 1972 from the University of Calcutta and then his Masters in Anthropology in 1974 from Calcutta University. He has joined Anthropological Survey of India in March, 1977 initially as Senior Technical Assistant. Prior to that he was a bank employee where he worked for about six months and then left for the job of Anthropological Survey of India Udaipur, Rajasthan. He was retired from Anthropological Survey of India as Superintending Anthropologist in December, 2012.

Empirical Studies and Research Output

Dr. Sarkar during his tenure at Anthropological Survey of India, Udaipur, carried out his Ph.D. dissertation work among the Dhodia for a period of six month at a stretch, when it is informed that he stayed with the Dhodia in the villages for collection of empirical data on Dhodia community. In 1986 Dr. Sarkar received his Ph.D. degree from Calcutta University. His Ph.D. work was guided by Prof. Biswanath Banerjee, one of the *Sishya* of Prof. Nirmal Kumar Bose. The title of his Ph.D. dissertation was 'Impact of Industrialization among the Dhodia of South Gujarat'. The chief findings of his thesis was – " *it is evident that the changes which have taken place in the way of life of Dhodias of the impact village as well as in the industrial township for the last two generations are more around the periphery than the core of their traditional cultural life" (*Sarkar, 1994*)* .

During his association with AnSI he carried out several field works in a number of research projects since 1977-2012 in Rajasthan, Gujarat, West Bengal, Chhattisgarh especially in undivided Bastar district, South Bihar (now Jharkhand), Malkangiri and Koraput districts of Odisha etc.

Some salient features of his field impressions are illustrated here. The study of Ethno-science among the Abujh Maria - a half clad tribal group as well as a PVTG of Chhattisgarh as a co worker with Samira Dasgupta. The work deserves a noteworthy contribution in the domain of anthropological research. The same study was also published in 2005 from Mittal Publication, New Delhi.

Studies were done among the Toto - a PVTG of West Bengal and the Asur -a PVTG of Jharkhand. Both the tribal communities were studied holistically, jointly with Dr.Samira Dasgupta, and especial emphasis was given on their belief system, world view and ethno- medical practices, where use of local herbs / plants / tubers were used for ailment which were documented.

The study centering on Dusehra festival of Bastar shows how centripetal social force is active which brings harmony of various tribal and non-tribal communities in one platform and ultimately existence of harmonious environment occurs. Further, it is also informed that he has initiated a research work along with Samira Dasgupta on state formation of Bastar with special emphasis on role of Danteshwari Mata – the tutelary deity of Bastar Maharaja; one section of such work is already published from New Delhi, 2010 entitled "Religious belief and practices. Portrayal of the integrative Process" in 2010 from New Delhi.

Further, Dr. Sarkar has also studied Banbibi cult at Sundarban- who is appeased by all section of Sundarban being survival strategy in such dreaded terrain where the existence of Royal Bengal Tiger is very much in evident. Here, cultural syncretism has been observed (2010, 2018).

At the end of his official carrier he has carried out a study on social audit assessment along with six other members of

Anthropological Survey of India. The team was multi-disciplinary, where there were two cultural Anthropologists- Samira Dasgupta and Dr. Sarkar.He took the maximum pain in designing the project, including methodology and data collection. Finally this work was published under the caption 'Fuming Forest' from New Delhi, 2014 and earned a notable review observation where with empirical data the social situation of Jungle Mahal (Study area) was analyzed and presented.

In spite of his official superannuation from Anthropological Survey of India Dr. Sarkar has serving the discipline – Anthropology by virtue of his vast exposure to various field situation in different eco-cultural zones of our country and a study has been made among the Kandh - Pano community of Odisha jointly with Samira Dasgupta for establishing identity through empirical data and the same is also published from New Delhi in the year 2016.

It is also found that following the principle of Prof. N.K.Bose in his study 'Peasant life in India: A Study in Indian Unity and Diversity (1961), Dr. Amitabha Sarkar has also attempted to identify some Cultural attributes of Indian Communities in various eco-cultural zones in the form of Little Tradition. He presented those in published form to establish that in spite of variation, there is a strong pulse of harmony among all ethnic groups and which is identified as Indian diversity are signature by great heritage (2018).

Lastly, it is to be mentioned that with his active initiation and with the help of Samira Dasgupta he was able to document the contribution of Indian Anthropologists during 1920 – 2019 and published three volumes of Doyens of Indian Anthropology (1920-2019) wherein contribution 69 Indian scholars were documented (2019, 2020, 2021). There is also a publication where he is one of the co-editors of the volume, entitled "Retrospect of 100 years of Indian Anthropology (1920 – 2019)" where development of the branches of the discipline are dealt till date with expected new dimensions of anthropology (2020).

Reference

Bose, N.K. 1961.Peasant Life in India : A Study in Indian Unity and Diversity, Calcutta : Anthropological Survey of India (Memoir :8; Reprinted in 2009).

Sarkar, Amitabha, 1994. Dhodia : Industrialisation and Change in a Primitive Community, New Delhi : Gyan Publishing House.

Dasgupta, Samira and Amitabha Sarkar. 2005. **Reflection of Ethno-Science:Study on the Abujh Maria**, Delhi: Mittal Publications.

Sarkar, Amitabha and Samira Dasgupta, *2010. Religions Belief and Practices* (A Portrayal of the Integrative Process), New Delhi : Agam Kala Prakashan,

Sarkar, Amitabha, Samira Dasgupta and et al. 2014. *The Fuming Forest : An Analytical Critique*, New Delhi, Mittal Publications,

Sarkar, Amitabha, Samira Dasgupta and Dhananjay Senapati. 2016. *Indigenous People : In Search of Identity* (A Quest for Social Identity of Pano or Kui Domanga), New Delhi : Mittal Publications.

Sarkar, Amitabha, Samira Dasgupta. 2018. *Little Tradition in a Culturally Pluralistic Nation* (ed.), New Delhi : Aayu Publications, **2018.**

Some of his Salient Publications are –

List of Published Books :

1. *TOTO: Society and Change (A Sub-Himalayan Tribe of West Bengal)* Calcutta: Firma KLM Pvt. Ltd., 1993.
2. *DHODIA:Industrialisation and Change in a Primitive Community,* New Delhi:Gyan Publishing House, 1993.
3. *Spectrum of Tribal Bastar,* Delhi: Agam Kala Prakashan, 1996. (Jt. Author-Amitabha Sarkar and Samira Dasgupta)
4. Fundamentals of Social-Cultural Anthropology, Calcutta: Firma KLM Pvt. Ltd, 1996. (Jt. Author-B. N. Banerjee and Amitabha Sarkar.)
5. *Frontiers of Social Anthropology,* New Delhi: Gyan Publishing House, 1996. (Jt. Author- Samira Dasgupta and Amitabha Sarkar.)
6. *Ethno-Ecology of Indian Tribes: Diversity in Cultural Adaptation, Jaipur:* Rawat Publications, 2000. (Jt. Author-Amitabha Sarkar and Samira Dasgupta.)
7. *Reflection of Ethno-Science: Study on the Abujh Maria,* Delhi: Mittal Publications, 2005. (Jt. Author- Samira Dasgupta and Amitabha Sarkar.)
8. *Religions Belief and Practices* (A Portrayal of the Integrative Process), New Delhi : Agam Kala Prakashan, 2010 (Jt. Author – Amitabha Sarkar and Samira Dasgupta).
9. *Mal Paharia Culture at the Crossroad*, New Delhi : Agam Kala Prakashan, 2011 (Amitabha Sarkar, Samira Dasgupta).

10. *Traditional Knowledge in Indian Society*, (ed.), Amitabha Sarkar, A.V. Arakeri, Suresh Patil, Kolkata : Anthropological Survey of India, 2012.
11. *Rhythm of Tribal Culture – an Unveil Saga*, Germany, Lambert Academic Publishing 2012 (e-book released on 19.10.12) – Joint by Samira Dasgupta, Amitabha Sarkar (ISBN : 978-3-659-24217-5).
12. *Traditional Wisdom and Sustainable Living : A Study on the Indian Tribal Societies*. (ed.), H.R. Mandal and Amitabha Sarkar, New Delhi and Kolkata , Anthropological Survey of India. and Gyan Publishing House, 2013.
13. *The Fuming Forest : An Analytical Critique*, New Delhi, Mittal Publications, 2014.
14. *Indigenous People : In Search of Identity* (A Quest for Social Identity of Pano or Kui Domanga), New Delhi : Mittal Publications, , Amitabha Sarkar, Samira Dasgupta, Dhananjay Senapati, 2016.
15. *Dimensions of Anthropology* (A Prismatic Panorama), New Delhi : Kalpaz Publications, Amitabha Sarkar, Samira Dasgupta, 2016..
16. *Attributes of Culture* (Reflection of Cultural Itinearies from a Multi-Cultural Nation), (ed.), Amitabha Sarkar, Samira Dasgupta, Naba Kumar Duary, New Delhi : Aayu Publications, 2016.
17. *Little Tradition in a Culturally Pluralistic Nation*, (ed.), Dr. Amitabha Sarkar, Dr. (Mrs.) Samira Dasgupta, New Delhi : Aayu Publications, 2018.
18. *Doyens of Indian Anthropology (1920-2019*), (ed.), Amitabha Sarkar and Samira Dasgupta, Delhi : Agam Kala Prakashan, 2019.
19. *Doyens of Indian Anthropology (1920 – 2019), Part - 2*, (ed.), Amitabha Sarkar and Samira Dasgupta, Delhi : Agam Kala Prakashan, **2020.**
20. *Retrospect of 100 years of Indian Anthropology, (1920 – 2019*), (ed.), Biman Kumar Dasgupta, Samira Dasgupta & Amitabha Sarkar, New Delhi : Aayu Publication, 2020.
21. *Doyens of Indian Anthropology (1920 – 2019), Part-3*, (ed) Amitabha Sarkar, Delhi : Agam Kala Prakashan, 2021.

List of Published Papers:

1. "Some Aspects of Cultural Behaviour of Dhodia of South Gujrat", Vanvaiati. Vol. XXV, No.4, 1977.
2. "Some observation on Cultural of Poverty in a Bengal village", *Journal of the Guiarat Research Society*. Vol.40, 1978.
3. "A Brief Review of Land Tenure System and its Effect on Agricultural Labourer", *Indian Anthropologist*. Vol.9, No.2, 1979.
4. "Ritual Value of Paddy in Bengal", (Jt. Author), *Folklore*. Vol.20, No.3-4,1979.

5. "A Position of Agricultural Labourers in Two villages of West Bengal", *Bulletin of the Cultural Research Institute*. Vol.XIII, No. 3 & 4, 1979.
6. "Marriage Rites among the Kharias : A Case Study", (Jt. Author), *Vanvaiati*. Vol.XXVIII, No.l, 1980.
7. "Cultural Anthropology : Historical Background and Recent Development", (Jt. Author), *Bulletin of the Cultural Research Institute*. Vol. 14, No. 3 & 4,1980.
8. "Behind the Tribal Movement", (Jt. Author), *Tribe*. Vol.XIII, No.l, 1981.
9. "Agrarian Social Structure, in a Bengal Village", *Bulletin of the Cultural Research Institute*. Vol.XV, No.l & 2, 1982.
10. "Education of Tribal Women : An Appraisal", (Jt. Author), *Bulletin of the Cultural Research Institute*. Vol.XVI, No 1-4, 1984.
11. "Bhagat Cult and its Role in Tribal Society: A Study of the Dhodia in South Gujarat", *Folklore*. Vol.26, No. 10, 1985.
12. "Continuity of Traditional Craft (Weaving) in a religious Urban Spot", *Bulletin of Cultural Research Institute*. Vol.XVII No. 1-2, 1987.
13. "Problem of Subsistence of a Small (Migrant) Population", (Jt. Author), *Journal of the Gujarat Research Society*. Vol.46-47, No.3, 1984/85.
14. "Changing Pattern of Marriage Practices among the Dhodia", in *Marriage in India*,(ed.), B.B. Goswami et al., Anthropological Survey of India, Calcutta, 1988
15. "Impact of Industrialization among the Dhodias of Gujarat", Human Science. Vol.37, No.3, 1988.
16. "Dhodia : A Tribe in an Industrial Setting", in *Accultration and Social Change in India : An Inter-disciplinary Appraisal*, (ed.), S.C. Panchbhai and M.K.A. Siddiqui, Anthropological Survey of India, Calcutta, 1989.
17. "Tribal Women in Industrial Arena", in *Profiles of Tribal Women in West Bengal*,(ed.), Ratna Gupta, sp. Series 34, Scheduled Castes and Tribes Welfare Department, Govt, of West Bengal, 1990.
18. "A New Light on Munda Social Organisation", (Jt. Author), *Man in India*. Vol.70, No.2, 1990.
19. "Need and Requirement of Documentation in Ethnographic/Anthropological Museum", *The Journal of the Anthropological Survey of India*. Vol.39, No.2 & 3, 1990(Jt. Author).
20. "Parhaiya : Culture and Environment", *Bulletin of Cultural Research Institute*. Vol. XVIII, No. 1 & 2, 1992 (Jt. Author).
21. "Life and Culture of Bastar Tribe", *Manorama Year Book*. 1992.
22. "Bi-cultural Role of Tribal Labourer in Industrial Milieu", *Man and Life*. Vol. 18, No. 3&4, 1992.

23. "A Tribal Economy in Transformation", *Journal of Social Research*. Vol. XXXI, No. 1 & 2, 1988.
24. "Study on Abujh Maria - A Primitive Tribe of Bastar", *Giriian Sanskriti*. Vol.l, No. 1, January, 1993 (Jt. Author).
25. "The Birhor - A Semi-Nomadic Tribe of Bihar : Problems and Suggestion", *Man and Life*. Vol.20, No.3 - 4, 1994.
26. "A Note on the Rise of Cultural Pluralism in Chotanagpur", (Jt. Author), *Man in India*. Vol.75, No.2.
27. "BHATRA", in *Encyclopedic Profile of Indian Tribes*, (ed.), By Sachidananda and R.R. Prasad, Vol.l, New Delhi : Discovery Publishing House, 1996 (Jt. Author).
28. "DOKRA - A Dwindling Art of Bastar", *Journal of Human and Environmental Sciences*. Special Inaugural Volume, January, 1996.
29. "Ethnic Conflict : Unrest Among Autochthons of Jharkhand", *Social Change*. Vol.25, No.4, December, 1995.
30. "Ethnic Tension" who are Local?" *Bulletin of the Tribal Research Institute*. Bhopal, Vol. XXIII, No.l, June, 1995.
31 "Community and Ethnicity : The Determination of Identity of Tribal Bastar", (Jt. Author) in *Tribal Identity in India : Extinction or Adaptation*, (ed.), By Kalyan K. Chakraborty, Indira Gandhi Rashtriya Manav Sangrahalaya, Bhopal, 1996.
32. "Ethnic-Situation in Tribal Bastar", *Sp. Issue Souvenir. Dandakaranava Samachar*. 17th January, 1998.
33. "Prakeetir Koley Bastar", *Pratikhan*. January, 1998.(in Bengali).
34. Bastarer Adibasi Sangeet O Ghotul", *Prasangva Loksangeet*(ed.), Premendra Majumdar, Calcutta : UBI, Staff Welfare & Cultural Society, 1998, pp.609-615. (in Bengali).
35. "Aranyer Spandan", (Jt. Author) Souvenir. Sarbojanin Durgotsav, Lake Town Adibasibrinda,, 36th Year, 1998 (Bengali, 1405),(in Bengali).
36. "Cultural Mosaic and Folk Dances of Tribal Bastar", in *Tribal Dances of India*, (ed.), R.D. Tribhuwan and et.al., New Delhi, Discovery Pub.House, 1999.
37. "Urskal - The Megalithic Monuments at Bastar", *Bulletin of the Tribal Research Institute*. Bhopal. Vol.XXVI, No.l, 1998.
38. "Dorla - Under the Shadow of Supernatural Beliefs", *Journal of Indian Anthropological Society*. Vol. 34, 1999.
39. "Use of Herbal Medicine in Tribal Bastar" (Jt. Author), *Man and Life*. Vol.25, No. 3 & 4, July - Dec, 1999.

40. "Religious Beliefs and Practices of Tribal Bastar", (Jt. Author), in *Tribal Religion : Change and Continuity*, (ed.), M.C. Behra, New Delhi, Commonwealth, 2000 (pp. 157-167).
41. "Cultural Mechanism of Ethnic Boundary Maintenance among Dhodia", *South Asian Anthropologist*. Vol.21, No.2, 2000.
42. "*Adibasi Sanskritetey Shilper Prabhav*", *Palikrit*. Vol.2, No. 1, 2001,(in Bengali).
43. "Trend of Industrialization among the Dhodia - Some Observations", *Man in India*. Vol.81,No. 1 & 2, 2001, pp.219 - 225.
44. "Challenges Towards Indian Primitive Tribal Cultures in the Context of Traditional Environment". In *Rethinking of Indian Culture Challenges and Responses*, (Edited) Sitakant Mahapatra, Cuttack : Institute of Oriental and Orissa Studies, 2001
45. "Ethnicity and Regional Unrest", *Man And Life*. Vo.27, No.3 and 4, July - Dec, 2001.
46. "Bison Horn Maria in the Light of New Ethnography", in *Indian Tribal Life*, (Edited) Chaturbhuj Sahu, New Delhi : Sarup & Sons, 2001 (Ch.10, pp. 106-113). (Jt. Author)
47. "Configuration of Tribal Culture of Bastar", Bulletin of the Tribal Research Institute, Bhopal, Vol.XXVIII, No. 1 & 2 (June-December), 2001 (Jt. Author).
48. "Impact of Urbanization and Changes in Social Milieu - Analysis with reference to Mangrove Tribes", in *Population Stablisation and Development*, (Editor-in-chief), Dr. Baidyanath Misra, Cuttack, The Universe, 2002 (Jt. Author, pp.463-466).
49. "A New Dimension on Social Organisation of Abujh Maria of Tribal Bastar : Communion between Celestial and Terrestrial Life", *Journal of the Indian Anthropological Society*. Vol.38, No.l, 2003 (Jt. Author).
50. "Synthesis of Tribal Religion and Hindu Cults in Bastar", *in Culture. Religion and Philosophy : Critical Studies in Syncretism and Inter-Faith Harmony*. (ed.), by N.K. Das, Jaipur : Rawat Publications (pp.280-294) (Jt. Author), 2003
51. "Sustainable Development in Relation to Traditional Wisdom of Bison Horn Maria". *Man And Life* , Vol.30, No. 1 & 2, 2004 (pp.91-96).
52. "Bison-Horn Maria in the Midst of Forest Environment", *Folklore Research Journal*. No. 14, 2004 (Forest and Folklore : Special Number).
53. "Problem and Prospects of Sundarban Tourism", *Journal of Social Anthropology,* Vol.2, No.l, 2005 (Jt. Author,).
54. "Communion Between Celestial and Terrestrial World – Nature – Man, Celestial World Complex among the Abujh Maria; in *Primitive Tribes in Contemporary India*, Vol. I, New Delhi : Mittal Publication, 2005, (ed.),

Sarit Chaudhuri and Sucheta Sen Chaudhuri, pp. 247-251, (Jt. Author). [First author Samira Dasgupta].

55. "Sustainable Growth of Population in relation to Customary Laws among the Abujh Maria; *Jr. of the Indian Anthropological Society,* Vol. 40, No. 223, 2005 (Jt. Author with Samira Dasgupta).
56. "Formation of Ethnic Identity, Cultural Symbol and Social Unrest – A Prelude," in *Social Unrest,* (Proceedings of the First Inter–Congress), (ed.), Ajit K. Danda and et al, Kolkata : Indian National Confederation and Academy of Anthropologists (INCAA). 2006.
57. "Syncretism at Sundarbans : Anthropological and Linguistic Dimensions, *"The Oriental Anthropologists*, Vol. 6, No. 1, 2006 (Gautam K. Bera, Asok K. Mukhopadhyay, Amitabha Sarkar).
58. "Socio-Cultural Changes in the Tribal Milien of Bastar,"in *Societies and Culture in India,* Vol. I. (Tribal Issues), (ed.), A.K. Haldar and Pradip K. Bhowmick, Kolkata : R.N. Bhattacharya, 2008 (pp. 215-22), [Section – IV, Continuity and Change], [Joint paper with Samira Dasgupta].
59. "Perception of Indigenous Knowledge for Health Care among Bastar Tribes,", *The Eastern Anthropologist*, Vol.59, No. 3-4, 2006 (Jt. Author, Samira Dasgupta 2nd author), pp. 453-455.
60. "Land Ownership Pattern among Bastar Tribes," in *Land and Forest Rights of the Tribals Today*, (ed.), By R.M. Sarkar, New Delhi, Serials Publicaztions, 2006, pp. 109-117.
61. "Social Stratification of Bastar Tribes,"*Man in India,* Vol. 85, No. 3 &4, July – Dec., 2005 (Jt. Author – Amitabha Sarkar is first author).
62. "Socio-Cultural Adaptation as a Means of Survival Strategy at Sundarban,"*Journal of Social Anthropology*, Vol. 4, No. 1, 2007, (pp. 45-52) (Jt. Author).
63. "Stratification of Bastar Tribes", *Studies of Tribes and Tribals* (Journal), Vol. 5, No. 2, December, 2007.
64. "Sustainable Development in relation to Traditional Wisdom of Bison.-Horn Maria", in Indigenous Science and Technology for Sustainable Development", (edited0, V. Subramanyam, Jaipur. Rawat Pubvlication, 2007 (pp. 133-139).
65. "Perception of Indigenous knowledge for Health Care among Bastar Tribes, in *Tribal Ethno medicine-Problem and Prospect*, (ed.), A.K.Haldar, P.K. Singh and P.C. Coomar, ISRAA, Bidisha, 2008.
66. "Tribal Architecture and Concept of culture of Space", *Man in India",* Vol. 87, No. 3 & 4, July-December, 2007.
67. "Sparks of Globalisation and its Impact among the Toto – a Primitive Tribal Group", in *Primitive Tribal Groups in India : Tradition, Development and*

Transformation,(ed.), By R.M. Sarkar, New Delhi; Serial Publication, 2008 (pp. 146-161).

68. "Role of Tribal Women Towards Community Development", in *Portrait of Anthropological Research,*(ed.), Debabrata Mondal & et. al, New Delhi : Sarup Book Publishers Pvt. Ltd., 2008. (Jt. Author), pp. 265-278.
69. "Combs as Expression of Creativity and Cognitive Symbol of Love," in *The Eastern Anthropologist",* Vol. 61, No. 2, 2008.
70. "Identity vis-à-vis Survival Strategy: Two Case Studies," in *Identity, Cultural Pluralism and State: South Asia in Perspective*, (ed.), N.K. Das and V.R. Rao, Delhi; Anthropological Survey of India and Macmillan, 2009.
71. "Aspects of Tribal Culture in the Forest Environment of Bastar," in Studies of Tribes and Tribals (Journal), Vol.7 No.2, 2009 (pp.81-89) (Jt. Author – Amitabha Sarkar &Samira Dasgupta).
72. "Role of Indigenous Knowledge for Sustenance," in *Environmental Issues and other Essays*, (ed.), Ajit K.Danda & Indu Talwar, INCCA Occasional Papers No. 12, Jhargram : INCAA and New Delhi : IGNCA, 2010 (pp. 87-103) (Jt. Author).
73. "Mal Paharia Belief System", in *Environmental Issues and Other Essays*, (ed.), Ajit K. Danda & Indu Talwar, INCAA and New Delhi : IGNCA,2010 (pp. 151-186). (Jt.Author).
74. "Autonomy of Culture :Socio-Cultural Adaptation among the Tribe," in *the Eastern Anthropologist*, Vol. 63 No. 1, ppo. 127-133, 2010 (Jt.Author).
75. "Fusion of Identity being Survival Strategy," in *Man in India,* Vol. 90, No. 3-4, 2010 (pp. 521-558).
76. Ban Bibi –The Mother Cult of Sundarban : an Observation of Fission and Fusion in Belief System," in *Journal of Social Anthropology*, Vol. 7, No. 1-2, 2010 (pp. 55-66) [Jt. Author]
77. "Indigenous Knowledge for Sustenance: An Introspection of Tribal India," in *Indigenous Knowledge in Traditional Folk Programme : Genesis, Development &Applications*, (ed.), R.M.Sarkar, New Delhi; Serials Publicatins, 2011 (pp. 266-257) (Jt. Author).
78. "Economic Status of the Tribal Communities and Government Response", in *Jr.of Anthropological Survey of India*, Vol. 60, No. 1, 2011 (pp. 19-23)
79. "Methodology of Studying Indigenous Knowledge," in Jr.of *Anthropological Survey of India* Vol. 60, No. 1, 2011 [Jt.Author] (pp. 76-82).
80. "Cultural Diaspora : Tribal Migration as a Survival Strategy", in *Cultural Pluralism : The Indian Scenario*, (ed.), S.A. Azeez Saheb, B.F. Kulirani, K.K. Misra, Bhopal and New Delhi: IGRMS and Gyan Publishing House, 2012.
81. "Ghotul and Muria: an Institutional Cultural Heritage," Man in India, Vol. 91, No. 3-4, 2011 (pp. 441-460) (Jt. Author).

82. "Dooarser Hathchani" in *Smaranika*, Calcutta AG Block Durga Puja Committee, 2011.(in Bengali).
83. "Is Modernisation a Curse? Capitalist Trend in a Tribal Area", *Many Faces of Development* (ed.), Rajat K.Das and D.K. Midya, Jhargram, INCAA, 2012.
84. "Dharamraj Ritual : As a Process of Transformation into Hindu Fold" ,in *Eastern Anthropologist,* Vol. 64, No. 2-3, 2011, (pp. 271-278) [Joint Author].
85. "Cultural Diversity and Repository of Indigenous Knowledge among the Indian Tribal Groups for Sustenance," in *Multidisciplinary Approaches in Angiosperm Systematics*, (ed.), G. Maiti and S.K. Mookherjee, Kalyani : Kalyani University.
86. Introduction", in Traditional Knowledge in Indian Society (ed.), Amitabha Sarkar, A.V. Arakeri, Suresh Patil, Kolkata. Anthropological Survey of India, 2012. (pp. 1-16).
87. "Toto Society and Culture with special emphasis on Ethno-medical Practices," in *Traditional Knowledge in India Society*, (ed.), Amitabha Sarkar et al, Kolkata:. Anthropological Survey of India,. 2012 (pp. 17-84) (Jt. Author).
88. "Traditional Knowledge for Sustenance : An Introspection among the Asur," in *Traditional Knowledge in Indian Society*, (ed.), By Amitabha Sarkar, et.al. Kolkata: An.S.I. 2012 (pp. 233-264). (Jt. Author.
89. Ïndigenous Knowledge in the Ecological Context of the Sundarbans, West Bengal : A Note, in *Mastermasai – the teacher*, (ed.), Dipak Piplai, Adhyapak Biswanath Bandhopadhyay Smritiraksha Samiti, 2012 (in Bengali)..
90. "Ïntroduction", in *Traditional Wisdom and Sustainable Living Sustainable Living : A Study on the Indian Tribal Societies*, (ed.), Hrishikesh Mandal and Amitabha Sarkar, New Delhi, Anthropological Survey India. and Gyan Publishing House, 2013, (pp. 17-27).
91. "Ä study on Traditional Wisdom among Bison-Horn Maria of Bastar," in *Traditional Wisdom and Sustainable Living : A Study on the Indian Tribal Societies*, by Hrishikesh Mandal and Amitabha Sarkar, New Delhi, Anthropological Survey India and Gyan Publishing House, 2013, (pp. 183-248).
92. "Ä Study on Traditional Wisdom among the Munda and Oraon of Sundarban," in Traditional Wisdom Societies, by Hrishikesh Mandal and Amitabha Sarkar, New Delhi, Anthropological Survey India and Gyan Publishing House, 2013, (pp. 301-347).(Jt.Author).
93. 'Andaman Dwippunjer ek Adibasi', (in Bengali), in *Argya,* Darbhanga : Darbhanga Durga Puja Samiti, 2013.(Subarna Jayanti Barsha, Bengali Year, 1420).
94. " Banbibi of Sundarban", in *Mandrasaptak*, Kolkata: Allahabad Bank Recreation Club, Subarna Jayanti Barsha, 2013. (Pp: 190-196).

95. "Sherni Sangram O Purushtantra", in *Naiya* (Utsav Sankha), (ed) Ramanuj Chattopadhyay, Kolkata : Mastul, 2013 (Bengali Year, 1420).
96. "Indigenous Knowledge and Intellectual Property Rights for Sustainable Development among the Toto" , in *Tribal Development : Issues and Challenges* (ed.), Dr. Robin D. Tribhuwan, Pune : Tribal Research and Training Centre, 2013 (pp. 189-219) (Jt A. Sarkar and Samira Dasgupta).
97. "Cultural Definition of Illness Etiology and Herbal Therapy among Tribal India," *Man in India,* Vol. 94, No. 1-2, Jan-June, 2014.
98. "Nirmam Nishturata", in *Naiya* (Utsav Sankha),(ed). Pinaki Mukhopadhyay, Kolkata: Mastul, 2014 (Bengali Year, 1421), Pp: 83-84.
99. "Tribal Concept of Diseases and Treatment among the Toto," in *Health and Tribes in India* : *Challenges and Opportunities*, (ed.), by K.N. Dash, Sarup Book Publishers Pvt. Ltd., New Delhi, 2015 (pp. 331-356) [Jt. Author].
100. "Developmental Paradigm : Up in the Arms against the State : an anthropological analysis of insurgent in the Junglemahal of West Bengal, in *Proceedings: International Seminar* : *Development, Resources and Livelihood*, organized by Dept of Anthropology (UGC – SAP), University of Hyderabad, Feb. 12-13, 2015, pp. 443-467. [Jt. Author].
101. "Cultural Practices of Bakung – A Sacred Drum among the Toto," in *Indian Culture and Art* : *Continuity and Change* Vol. II ((ed.),Dr. Agam Prasad, Delhi : Swati Publications, 2015, [pp. 441-449], (Jt. Author).
102. "Culture of Communication : Ritual Symbol, Cultural Ethnos among the Mal Paharia" in A *Bouquet of Indian Heritage : Research and Management*, (Vol. II, (ed.) Prasant Srivastava and Sanjaya Kumar Mahapatra, Delhi : Swati Publications, 2015 (pp. 487-492) (Co-author).
103. "Ekhonkar Samaj O Generation Gap", *Smaranika,* Kolkata : AG Block Dutga Puja Committee, 2007.(in Bengali).
104. "Management of Sustenance Activities in Island Environment", *Man in India*, Vol. 95, No. 3, 2015 (Jt.Author), Pp: 483-495.
105. "Narabali Pratha", in *Sharod Sharanika*, Salt Lake, Kolkata:, AG Block Durga Puja Committee, 2016 (in Bengali).
106. "Polarisation of Relations : Fusion, Fission and Mobility", in *The Indian Journal of Anthropology,* Vol. 4, No. 1, 2016 (pp. 51-74).
107. "Religious Life of Bastar Tribes with Special reference to Abujh Maria", in *Tribal Religions*, Vol. VII, Part. 13, (ed.), S. Shyamkishore Singh., New Delhi: Centre for Studies in Civilizations ,2017.
108. "Religions Beliefs among the Sundarban Tribes,"in *Tribal Religions*, Vol. VII, Part. 13, (ed.), S. Shyamkishore Singh., New Delhi: Centre for Studies in Civilizations,2017

109. "Religions Beliefs and Practices – a Cultural Space among the Toto Tribes of West Bengal" in *Tribal Religions*, Vol. VII, Part. 13, (ed.), S. Shyamkishore Singh., New Delhi: Centre for Studies in Civilizations,2017.

110. "Mishi-Muhu ba Echhe Mritiyu—Sapno Holeo Satiyee", (in Bengali), in *Sarod Suvechha*, (1424), Laheraisarai, Darbhanga (Bihar) : Binapani Club, 2017.

111. "Mishi-Muhu ba Echhe Mritiyu—Sapno Holeo Satiyee", in *Sarod Smaranika*, Salt Lake, Kolkata: AG Block Durga Puja Committee, 2017 (Reproduced by Request), 2017.

112. "Unanyer Epith—Opith", in *Sarod Suvechha,* Haltu, Kolkata: Haltu Nandibagan Sarbojanin Durgoutsav Committee (HNSDC), 2017.

113. "Denial of Social Justice", in *Bharitiya Adibasi O Loksanskriti : Bartaman Prekhit*, (ed) Buddhadeb Choudhury O Saktipada Haldar Narendrapur: Ramakrishna Mission Lokshiksha Parishad, Ramakrishna Mission Ashrama. (Jt. Author).Pp: 194—228.

114. "Concept of Diseases and Treatment among the Toto of Jalpaiguri District, West Bengal," in *South Asian Anthropologist*. Vol. 17, No. 2, 2017 (pp. 133-144).

115. "Samajik Danda", *Sarod Sankalan*, Salt Lake, Kolkata: AG Block Durga Puja Committee, 2018.(in Bengali).

116. "Unanyer Kantatar", (in Bengali), in *Naiya*, Utsav Sankhya, 2017 (Bengali Year, 1424).

117. "Atmasamikshya", (in Bengali), in *Naiya*, Utsav Sankhya, 2018 (Bengali Year, 1425)..

118. "Polarisation of Relation : Status Symbol", *Jr. of the Dept. of Anthropology*), North Bengal University Vol. 6, 2018 (pp. 1-6).

119. "Small Community and Large Industries : Food and other Resources of Dandami Maria of Bastar", in *Food an Power (Expression of Food Politics in South Asia*), (ed.), Kanchan Mukhopadhyay, New Delhi : Sage, 2020.

120. "Quest for Peace and Harmony : An Attempt of Social Audit of Changing Situation in Bastar",, in *South Asian Anthropologist*, Vol. 20, No. 1, 2020, Pp. 17-23.

121. "Conceptual Understanding of Diseases and treatment among Tribal People" ,in *Tribal Health : Perception and Realization (with special reference to Indian context*), (ed.), Awdhesh Naryan Sharma, Mauritius : Lap Lambert Academic Publishing, 2019., Pp: 83-102.

122. "Quest for Scheduled Tribe Status among the Pano or Kui Domanga – An Empirical Study," *Man in India*, Vol. 100, No. 1-2, Pp:1-21.

123. "Ïntroduction", in *Attributes of Culture: Reflection of Cultural Itineraries from a Multicultural Nation*, (ed) Amitabha Sarkar, Samira Dasgupta and et.al. New Delhi, Aayu Publication, 2016. Pp. 1-17.
124. Engraved Wooden Comb : Symbol of Love and an Excellence of Least Known Tribal Community of Bastar," (Co-author) in *Attributes of Culture : Reflection of Cultural Itineraries from a Multicultural Nation*, (ed) Amitabha Sarkar, Samira Dasgupta and et.al. New Delhi, Aayu Publications,2016. Pp: 145-150.
125. "Dush Avatar Tash – Artists and Art form and its Propagation through Tourism," (Co-author), in *Attributes of Culture : Reflection of Cultural Itineraries from a Multicultural Nation*, (ed) Amitabha Sarkar, Samira Dasgupta and et.al. New Delhi, Aayu Publication 2016, Pp. 217-228.
126. "Urskul : The Memorial Pillar : An Attribute of Dwimdling Tribal Culture of Bastar," in *Attributes of Culture* : *Reflection of Cultural Itineraries from a Multicultural Nation*, (ed) Amitabha Sarkar, Samira Dasgupta and et.al. New Delhi, Aayu, Publications, 2016, Pp. 328-340.
127. "Introduction," in *Little Traditions in a Culturally Pluralistic Nation*; (eds.), Amitabha Sarkar and Samira Dasgupta, New Delhi : Aayu Publications, 2018. Pp. 1-18.
128. "Occultism Practices among the Mal Paharia of Damin-i-koh," (Co-author), in *Little Tradition in a Culturally Pluralistic Nation* (eds.), Amitabha Sarkar and Samira Dasgupta, New Delhi : Aayu Publication, 2018, pp. 207-221.
129. "Dharamraj – a Little Tradition in Radh Bengal," in *Little Traditions in a Culturally Pluralistic Nation* (eds.), Amitabha Sarkar and Samira Dasgupta, New Delhi : Aayu Publication, 2018, pp. 295-303.
130. "Bondo – a Less known Tribal Group at the Highland Odisha," (Co-author), in *Little Tradition in a Culturally Pluralistic Nation*, (eds.), Amitabha Sarkar and Samira Dasgupta, New Delhi : Aayu Publication, 2018, pp. 350-356.
132. "Verrier Elwin (1902-1964)," in *Doyens of Indian Anthropology* (1920-2019), (eds.), Amitabha Sarkar and Samira Dasgupta, Delhi : Agam Kala Prakashan, 2019, Pp. 40-42.
133. "D.N. Majumdar (1903-1960)", in *Doyens of Indian Anthropology (1920-2019*), (eds.), Amitabha Sarkar and Samira Dasgupta, Delhi : Agam Kala Prakashan, 2019, Pp. 43-45.
134. "Minendra Nath Basu (1912-1976)", (Co-author), in *Doyens of Indian Anthropology (1920-2019*), (eds.), Amitabha Sarkar and Samira Dasgupta, 2019, Pp. 48-54.
135. "Dharani Sen (1909-1980)", in *Doyens of Indian Anthropology, (1920-2019),* (eds.), Amitabha Sarkar and Samira Dasgupta, 2019, Pp. 60-63.

136. "Shyama Charan Duba (25th July, 1922 – 4th Feb., 1996)", in *Doyens of Indian Anthropology (1920-2019*), (eds.), Amitabha Sarkar and Samira Dasgupta, 2019, Pp. 69-70.
137. "Probodh Kumar Bhowmick (1927-2003)", in *Doyens of Indian Anthropology (1920-2019),* (eds.), Amitabha Sarkar and Samira Dasgupta, 2019, Pp. 147-148.
138. "Biman Kumar Das Gupta (1st Ocotber, 1934 .....)," (Co-author) in *Doyens of Indian Anthropology (1920-2019*), (eds.), Amitabha Sarkar and Samira Dasgupta, 2019, Pp. 156-167.
139. "Biswanath Banerjee (1933-2009)," (Co-author), in *Doyens of Indian Anthropology (1920-2019*), (eds.), Amitabha Sarkar and Samira Dasgupta, Delhi : Agam Kala Prakashan, 2019, Pp. 177-181.
140. "L. K. Mahapatra (b. 1929 .....)," in *Doyens of Indian Anthropology (1920-2019*), (eds.), Amitabha Sarkar and Samira Dasgupta, Delhi : Agam Kala Prakashan, 2019, Pp. 189-190.
141. "Ram Dayal Munda (1939 – 2011)",(Co-author), in *Doyens of Indian Anthropology (1920-2019)*, (eds), Amitabha Sarkar and Samira Dasgupta, Delhi, Agam Kala Prakashan, 2019, Pp. 191-194.
142. Änthropology in Coming Days : New Approaches of Social/Cultural Anthropology"(Co-author), in *Doyens of Indian Anthropology (1920-2019*) (eds), Amitabha Sarkar and Samira Dasgupta, 2019, Pp. 195-197.
143. "Ïntroduction",in *Doyens of Indian Anthropology (1920-2019) Part-2*, (eds), Amitabha Sarkar and Samira Dasgupta, Delhi : Agam Kala Prakashan, 2020, Pp. 1-4.
144. "Bikash Raychaudhuri (1933- ...)",(Co-author), in *Doyens of Indian Anthropology (1920-2019) Part-2*, (eds), Amitabha Sarkar and Samira Dasgupta, Delhi : Agam Kala Prakashan, 2020, Pp. 67-74.
145. "Ämal Kumar Das (1934-1999)", in Doyens *of Indian Anthropology (1920-2019), Part-2,* (eds), Amitabha Sarkar and Samira Dasgupta, Delhi : Agam Kala Prakashan 2020, Pp. 75-87.
146. "Pranab Kumar Dasgupta (1934-2000)",in *Doyens of Indian Antghropology (1920-2019), Part-2*, (eds), Amitabha Sarkar and Samira Dasgupta, Delhi : Agam Kala Prakashan, 2020, Pp. 88-93.
147. "Pramode Kumar Misra (1936-...),", in *Doyens of Indian Anthropology (1920-2019), Part-2*, , (eds), Amitabha Sarkar and Samira Dasgupta, Delhi : Agam Kala Prakashan, 2020, Pp. 103-113.
148. "Manis Kumar Raha (1937- ...)", (Co-author), in Doyens *of Indian Anthropology (1920-2019), Part-2*, (eds), Amitabha Sarkar and Samira Dasgupta, Delhi : Agam Kala Prakashan, 2020, Pp. 114-121.

149. "Dipali Ghosh Danda (1939- ….)", (Co-author), in *Doyens in Indian Anthropology (1920-2019), Part-2*, (eds), Amitabha Sarkar and Samira Dasgupta, Delhi : Agam Kala Prakashan, 2020, Pp. 139-142.
150. "Study of Kinship Pattern and System," (Co-author), in *Doyens of Indian Anthropology (1920-2019), Part-2*, (eds), Amitabha Sarkar and Samira Dasgupta, Delhi : Agam Kala Prakashan, 2020, Pp 143-174.
151. "Cultural Notion : Anthropology of Culture of Space Dynamics among Indian Tribes – a tool of Community Development,"(Co-author), in *Doyens of Indian Anthropology (1920-2019), Part-2*, , (eds), Amitabha Sarkar and Samira Dasgupta, Delhi : Agam Kala Prakashan, 2020, Pp. 175-186.
152. "Study on Culture and Communication",(Co-author), in *Doyens of Indian Anthropology (1920-2019), Part-2*, (eds), Amitabha Sarkar and Samira Dasgupta, Delhi : Agam Kala Prakashan, 2020, Pp. 185-208.
153. "Ä Tool to view Social/Cultural Change in Anthropological Perspective", (Co-author), in *Doyens of Indian Anthropology (1920-2019), Part-2*, (eds), Amitabha Sarkar and Samira Dasgupta, Delhi : Agam Kala Prakashan, 2020, Pp. 213-231.
154. "Development of Social Thought", in *Retrospect of 100 years of Indian Anthropology, (1920-2019)* (Co-editor), New Delhi : Aayu Publications, 2020. Pp. 9-30.
155. "Role of Anthropological Knowledge in Social Auditing of Development Paradigm (Empirical Situation)",(Co-author), in *Retrospect of 100 years of Indian Anthropology (1920-2019)*, (Co-editor), New Delhi: Aayu Publications, 2020, Pp. 117-131.
156. "Question of Peace and Harmony – in the Eyes of an Anthropologist", in *Retrospect of 100 years of Indian Anthropology (1920-2019)*, New Delhi : Aayu Publications, 2020, Pp. 132-144.
157. "İntroduction", (Co-author), in *Doyens of Indian Anthropology (1920-2019), Part-3,* (ed), Amitabha Sarkar, Delhi : Agam Kala Prakashan, 2021, Pp. 1-8.
158. "Ranajit K Saha (1943- …)",(Co-author), in *Doyens of Indian Anthropology (1920-2019), Part-3*, (ed), Amitabha Sarkar, Delhi : Agam Kala Prakashan, 2020,Pp. 154-161.
159. "Hasan Ali (1945- …)",in *Doyens of Indian Anthropology (1920-2019), Part-3*, (ed), Amitabha Sarkar, Delhi : Agam Kala Prakashan, 2021, Pp. 166-168.
160. "Sekh Rahim Mondal (1951- …)," (Co-author), in *Doyens of Indian Anthropology (1920-2019), Part-3*, (ed), Amitabha Sarkar, Delhi : Agam Kala Prakashan, 2020, Pp. 184-197.

161. "Sumahan Bandyopadhyay (1974- …)",in *Doyens of Indian Anthropology (1920-2019), Part-3*, (ed), Amitabha Sarkar, Delhi : Agam Kala Prakashan, 2021, Pp. 220-232.
162. "Application of Anthropological Knowledge in Understanding Culture", (Co-author), in *Doyens of Indian Anthropology (1920-2019), Part-3*, (ed), Amitabha Sarkar, Delhi : Agam Kala Prakashan, 2021, Pp. 237-232.
163. "Verrier Elwin and Tallurmuttey—Concept of Earth Goddess among the Muria", in Glimpses into the World of Verrier Elwin (ed). K.M.Sinha Roy, New Delhi and Kolkata: Gyan Publishing House and Anthropological Survey of India, 2021, Pp: 107-115.

[**This apart, he has contributed 33 write-ups on various communities including SC and ST of Jharkhand of Bihar in Bihar Volume (Part one and two) in view of "People of India" project being a member of Anthropological Survey of India, Ministry of Culture, Govt. of India.**

People of India : Bihar including Jharkhand, Vol. XVI (Part – One and Two), (ed.), K.S. Singh, Calcutta : Anthropological Survey of India and Seagull Books, 2008].

3.10. Kaushik Sankar Bose (1962--)

Prof. Sumahan Bandhopadhyay.

An Industrious Biological Anthropologist

Kaushik Sankar Bose was born on 24th November,1962 in Kolkata to Mrs. Sabita Bose and Samir Kumar Bose. He belonged to the famous Bose family of central Kolkata. One of his grandfathers Dr. Kartik Chandra Bose was a pioneer in medical science research in India. His father, a biochemist/physiologist by profession had several international jobs which gave Kaushik to come across diverse ethnic groups of different nations. As a student, Kaushik possesses a brilliant track record. He passed the General Certificate of Education Ordinary Level Examination from University of Cambridge and General Certificate of Education Ordinary Level Examination from University of London in the years 1980 and 1981 respectively securing first division in both the examinations. He earned both the bachelor and master degrees in anthropology from Punjab University, Chandigarh. In both the levels, he stood first in the examinations. class. He was the recipient of a Commonwealth Scholarship (1990) and obtained his Ph.D. from Cambridge University in 1996. He was at Queens' College, Cambridge. Earlier he had obtained his Ph.D. degree from Panjab University, Chandigarh in 1992. He also worked as a Post-Doctoral Fellow at the Department of Nutrition and Dietetics, King's College London, during 1996-1997. He was awarded a D.Sc. degree by Vidyasagar University in 2016. He was recipient of a number of grants of which mention may be made of Ruggles Gates Grant for Doctoral Research by the Royal Anthropological Institute of Great Britain and Ireland and Parry Grant by Queens' College, University of Cambridge. He had received many fellowships and scholarships like Junior and Senior Research Fellowships from University Grants Commission, India and Commonwealth Scholarship. He has been the recipient of many medals including the Dewan Bahadur Wali Ram Taneja Gold

Medal (Panjab University) for attaining First Position in the Master of Science (Honours School) Examinations in Anthropology.

Professor Bose had several research collaborations with Indian as well foreign universities and institutions. In India, he has collaborated with faculties from at least ten institutes and universities. He has also foreign collaborations that include Unit for Bio-cultural Variation and Obesity (UBVO), University of Oxford, U.K.; Institute of Anthropology, Polish Academy of Sciences, Wroclaw, Poland; United States Agency for International Development (USAID), Washington, D.C., U.S.A.; Tufts University, U.S.A. and Family Health International (FHI) 360, Washington, D.C., U.S.A. He had visited Unit of Anthropology, Polish Academy of Sciences, Wroclaw, as an Indian National Science Academy (INSA) – Polish Academy of Sciences (PAS) Visiting Fellow. He has been the consultant in a National Centre of Science in Poland funded project entitled *"Prenatal maternal stress and growth and development of offspring, based on effects of tropical severe cyclone in India"*. He was also associated with a DFID (United Kingdom) funded research project entitled *"Effect of providing supplementary nutrition in improving the nutritional status of children at ICDS centres"*. Overall, Bose has supervised/undertaken 10 research projects.

He joined Vidyasagar University as Reader in 2002. Before that he was associated with the Department of Anthropology, University of Calcutta as a CSIR Senior Research Associate and later as a Lecturer. He served as the Head, Department of Anthropology, Vidyasagar University for two terms –2005 to 2007 and 2011 to 2013. He became a professor in 2010. He holds/held fellowships membership to as many as 16 societies or learned bodies or societies. He is a Fellow of Royal Society of Health (FRSH), U.K. In addition to this, he has been a fellow of Cambridge Philosophical Society. He is an International Fellow of Unit for Bio-cultural Variation and Obesity (UBVO), University of Oxford. At Vidyasgar University 16 researchers have obtained their Ph.D. degrees under his supervision.

He is the editor of the *Journal of Life Sciences* besides acting as a Member of the Editorial Board of several national and international journals. He is the Associate Editor of International Journal of Preventive and Public Health Sciences and BMC Pediatrics. He is also associated with Anthropology Open Journal as one of the Editors. He is in the editorial boards of 20 journals. Moreover, he acts as a reviewer for more than 50 national and international journals. He has numerous publications in national and international journals of high repute. He has about three hundred publications in journals. Some of these journals include *American Journal of Human Biology, International Journal of Anthropology, Bulletins et Memoires de la Societe d'Anthropologie de Paris, Annals of Human Biology, Acta Medica Auxologica, Anthropologischer Anzeiger, Collegium Antropologicum, Anthropological Science, Nature – Scientific Reports, Maternal and Child Nutrition, British Journal of Nutrition, HOMO, Anthropological Review and others.*

Prof. Kaushik Bose was among the pioneers who had shown, in detail, that South Asian migrants in the UK had significantly different adiposity patterns compared with native Caucasians. He had also demonstrated that there were distinct differences in the relationship of adiposity with risk factors for non-insulin dependent diabetes mellitus (NIDDM) and related metabolic disorders between these ethnic groups. He had hypothesized that there were *ethnic-specific* different threshold levels of adiposity and other variables regarding the risk for NIDDM and associated disorders.

On his return to West Bengal, he has investigated extensively on the problem of malnutrition (both over - as well as under -) among both sexes, in West Bengal, Orissa, Jharkhand, Punjab, Assam, Meghalaya, Gujarat and Andhra Pradesh. He was undertaken empirical research on pregnant women, lactating mothers, infants, pre-school children, children, adolescents and adults. Concurrently, he has continued with his research on the relationship between adiposity and risk factors for coronary heart disease (CHD) not only among the Bengalee population but also other ethnic groups in India.

Another important contribution of Bose has been the development of new anthropometric equations for the determination of body composition among Indian infants.

Bose along with colleagues has proposed new anthropometric cut-off points for the determination of low birth weight (LBW) among urban Bengalee women. He has also proposed new cut-off points for mid-upper arm circumference (MUAC) to determine nutritional status among adults belonging to different ethnic groups of India. Most significantly in a large international collaborative study involving several countries, he was involved in the determination a new MUAC cut-off point (24 cm) for MUAC at the global level.

Professor Bose has one book jointly written with Professor A.B. Das Chaudhuri (Das Chaudhuri and Bose, 2000). He has edited and co-edited 13 books on different aspects of health and nutrition, obesity, development, malnutrition among the children and tribal communities (Bose, 2005; 2006; 2008; Bose, et.al, 2016; Bose, et.al., 2018; Bose and Das,2020). It is pertinent to mention here that Bose has worked extensively on the problem of under nutrition among numerous tribal populations not only in West Bengal but also other regions of India. Recently, Bose has also focussed and published on the problem of *"dual burden of malnutrition"*.

Professor Bose is a prolific writer who has contributed enormously to the anthropological literature in the last three decades. It is herculean task for a biographer of Bose to refer to his each and every publication. A representative sample as given in the selected publications at the end of this article would indicate the nature of work he has done. He has substantially fulfilled the basic anthropological aim of understanding the variations across the ethnic groups around in India and outside. His studies carry enormous importance in the understanding the nutritional status of the people, particularly the tribal communities and weaker sections. Therefore, his works possess great pragmatic value in the betterment of health and nutritional status of the vulnerable sections of the population and tribal people.

Some of his Selected List of Publications are :

A. Articles :

1) Studies on Haemagglutinins in *Coprinus domesticus.*

   K. Bose and V. Bhalla.

   Indian Journal of Physical Anthropology and Human Genetics, 15 (3): 13-17, 1990.

2) A Survey of Haemagglutinins in Some Indian Seed Varieties and their Application in Characterising Adult and Cord Red Cells.

   K. Bose and V. Bhalla.

   South Asian Anthropologist, 11 (1): 15-18, 1990.

3) Anti - H Type Lectins in Two Varieties of Indian Mushrooms – *Helvellalacunosa* and Helvellamacropus.**K. Bose** and V. Bhalla.

   Panjab University Research Bulletin (Science), 41: 89-92, 1990.

4) *Geastrumarenarius*:A useful lectin for determining secretor types.

   Indian Journal of Physical Anthropology and Human Genetics, 16 (1 and 2): 29-36, 1990.

   K. Bose and V. Bhalla.

5) Haemagglutinins in Some Edible Varieties of Indian Mushrooms.

   K. Bose and V. Bhalla.

   In: *New Horizons in Human Biology*, pp 7-13, 1991. Eds: I.J.S. Bansal et al.

   New Delhi: Today and Tomorrow's Printers and Publishers.

6) Non-Insulin-Dependent Diabetes Mellitus and Obesity in Asians in UK. ---- Scope for Future Studies.

   K. Bose.

   Journal of the Royal Society for the Promotion of Health, 112 (6): 291-293, 1992.

7) Association of Truncal Subcutaneous Adiposity with Some Risk Factors of Type II Diabetes in Adult White and Migrant Pakistani Males.

   K. Bose and C.G.N. Mascie-Taylor.

   Journal of Human Ecology (Madrid), 4 (2/3): 301-310, 1995.

8) A Comparative Study of Generalised Obesity and Anatomical Distribution of Subcutaneous Fat in Adult White and Pakistani Migrant Males in Peterborough.

   K. Bose.

   Journal of the Royal Society for the Promotion of Health, 115 (2): 90-95, 1995.

9) Generalised Obesity and Regional Adiposity in Adult White and Migrant Muslim Males from Pakistan in Peterborough.

   K. Bose.

   Journal of the Royal Society for the Promotion of Health, 116 (3): 161-167, 1996.

10) Interrelationships of Age and the Body Mass Index with Risk Factors of Non-Insulin Dependent Diabetes in European and Migrant Asian Males.

    K. Bose and C.G.N. Mascie-Taylor.

    American Journal of Human Biology, 9: 291-296, 1997.

11) Ethnic Differences in Regional Adiposity between Adult Caucasian and Migrant Pakistani Males which are unexplained by Some Common Indicators of Lifestyles.

    K. Bose and C.G.N. Mascie-Taylor.

    International Journal of Anthropology, 12: 63-72, 1997.

12) The Association Between Age, Smoking, Physical Activity and Diet with Total Cholesterol in Adult Caucasian and Migrant Pakistani Males.

    K. Bose and C.G.N. Mascie-Taylor.

    Bulletins et Memoires de la Societe d'Anthropologie de Paris, 9: 267-278, 1997.

13) Coronary Heart Disease Among Migrant South Asians in Britain: An Overview.

    K. Bose.

    Journal of the Indian Anthropological Society, 32: 269-275, 1997.

14) Relationship of Body Mass Index, Regional Adiposity and Body Fat Distribution with Some Risk Factors of NIDDM in Adult Caucasian and Migrant Pakistani Males.

    K. Bose and C.G.N. Mascie-Taylor.

    Bulletins et Memoires de la Societe d'Anthropologie de Paris, 9: 279-290, 1997.

15) Conicity Index and Waist-Hip Ratio and their Relationship with Total Cholesterol and Blood Pressure in Middle-Aged European and Migrant Pakistani Men.

    K. Bose and C.G.N. Mascie-Taylor.

    Annals of Human Biology, 25 (1): 11-16, 1998.

16) Ethnic Difference in Adiposity and Body Fat Distribution Between Adult Caucasian and Migrant South Asian Men in East Anglia, England.

    K. Bose.

    In: *Physical Anthropology and Human Genetics: Contemporary Perspectives*, pp 7-23, 1998.

Ed: I.J.S. Jaswal. New Delhi: Asia Visions Publishers.

17) Relationship of Age and the Body Mass Index with Subcutaneous Adiposity in Adult European and Migrant South Asian Males Resident in Peterborough, England.

K. Bose.

Journal of Human Ecology, 10 (1): 41-45, 1999.

18) Body Fat Composition and its Relationship with Subcutaneous Adiposity in Adult Caucasian and Migrant Pakistani Men Resident in Peterborough, England.

K. Bose.

Journal of Human Ecology, 10 (1): 47-51, 1999.

19) Comparison of Anthropometric Characteristics Between Normotensive and Hypertensive Individuals Among a Population of Bengalee Hindu Elderly Men in Calcutta, India

A. Ghosh, **K. Bose** and A.B. Das Chaudhuri.

Journal of the Royal Society for the Promotion of Health, 120 (2): 100-106, 2000.

20) Age Trends in Anthropometric Characteristics Among an Elderly Population of Bengalee Hindu Men in Calcutta, India.

A. Ghosh, **K. Bose** and A.B. Das Chaudhuri.

The Mankind Quarterly, XLI (1): 71-90, 2000.

21) Body mass index, regional adiposity and central fat distribution among Hindu Bengalee girls: a comparative study of pre- and menarcheal subjects.

M. Bhadra, A. Mukhopadhyay and **K. Bose**.

Acta Medica Auxologica, 33 (1): 39-45, 2001.

22) Subcutaneous Adiposity and Relative Fat Patterning in Adult White and Migrant Asian Males in Britain.

K. Bose and C.G.N. Mascie-Taylor.

International Journal of Anthropology, 16 (1): 41-49, 2001.

23) Age and sex variations in adiposity and central fat distribution among elderly Bengalee Hindus of Calcutta, India.

A. Ghosh, **K. Bose** and A.B. Das Chaudhuri.

Annals of Human Biology, 28 (6): 616-623, 2001.

24) The Interaction of Waist-Hip Ratio and Conicity Index with Subcutaneous Adiposity in Two Ethnic Groups: Native British and Migrant Pakistani Men

K. Bose.

AnthropologischerAnzeiger, 59 (3): 275-282, 2001.

25) A comparative study of adiposity and central fat distribution of normotensive and hypertensive older Bengalee Hindu women of Calcutta, India.

    K. Bose and A.B. Das Chaudhuri.

    Collegium Antropologicum, 25 (2): 521-527, 2001.

26) Body Mass Index, Fat Distribution and Blood Pressure Among Post-Menarcheal Bengalee School Girls.

    K. Bose and A.B. Das Chaudhuri.

    Vidyasagar University Journal of Biological Sciences, 7: 1-8, 2001.

27) Age Variations in Adiposity and Central Body Fat Distribution Among 12-15 Year Old Bengalee Boys of Palta-Ichhapur, North 24 Parganas, West Bengal.

    K. Das, D. Mondal, **K. Bose** and A. Mukhopadhyay.

    Journal of The Department of Anthropology, University of Calcutta, 7 (1&2):162-168, 2001.

28) Age Trends in Adiposity and Central Fat Distribution Among Adult White Men Resident in Peterborough, East Anglia, England

    K. Bose.

    Collegium Antropologicum, 26 (1): 179-186, 2002.

29) Adiposity, central body fat distribution and blood pressure among young Bengalee adults of Kolkata, India: Sexual Dimorphism.

    M. Bhadra, A. Mukhopadhyay and **K. Bose**.

    Journal of Physiological Anthropology and Applied Human Science, 21 (6): 273-276, 2002.

30) Relationship between Anthropometric Measures and body composition among

    Bengalee Female University Students of Kolkata.

    K. Bose, A. Ghosh and A.B. Das Chaudhuri.

    Journal of Indian Anthropological Society 38 (1): 89-94, 2003.

31) Association of food patterns, central obesity measures and metabolic risk factors for

    Coronary heart disease (CHD) in middle-aged Bengalee Hindu men, Calcutta, India.

    Ghosh, **Bose, K**. and A.B. Das Chaudhuri.

    Asia Pacific Journal of Clinical Nutrition, 12 (2): 166-171, 2003.

32) Blood Pressure and Waist Circumference: An Empirical Study of the Effects of Waist Circumference on Blood Pressure among Bengalee Male Jute Mill Workers of Belur, West Bengal, India.

    K. Bose, A. Ghosh, S. Roy and S. Gangopadhyay.

Journal of Physiological Anthropology and Applied Human Science, 22 (4): 169-173, 2003.

33) Age variations in adiposity and body fat composition among older Bengalee Hindu women of Calcutta, India.

K. Bose and A.B. Das Chaudhuri.

Anthropologischer Anzeiger, 61 (3): 311-321, 2003.

34) Obesity among Punjabis of Kharagpur Town: Sex Differences.

N. Yadav, S. Roy, **K. Bose**, A. Mukhopadhyay and M. Bhadra.

Indian Journal of Biological Science, 9: 66-75, 2003.

35) Sex differences in anthropometric characteristics among 11-14 year old urban Bengalees of North 24 Parganas, West Bengal, India.

A. Mukhopadhyay, M. Bhadra and **K. Bose**.

Anthropologie, 42 (2): 137-140, 2004.

36) Central Obesity and Coronary Risk factors.

A. Ghosh, **K. Bose**, S. Chakravarti, A.B. Das Chaudhuri, J. Chattopadhyay, G. Dasgupta and S. Sengupta.

Journal of the Royal Society for the Promotion of Health, 124 (2): 86-90, 2004.

37) Association of adiposity with metabolic risk factors of coronary heart disease among Bengalee Hindu men of Kolkata, India: A comparison of three measures of central adiposity.

K. Bose and A.B. Das Chaudhuri.

In: *Selected Portrait – Position of Women, Aged and Weaker Section In Contemporary India.* Edited by: Ranjana Ray and Syamalkanti Sengupta. Pp. 320-330, 2004.

Kolkata: Classique Books.

38) Nutritional Status of Adolescent Bengalee Boys.

K. Bose and A. Mukhopadhyay.

Indian Pediatrics, 41 (6): 633, 2004.

39) Adiposity measures and their relationship with metabolic risk factors of coronary heart disease in Bengalee Hindu men of Kolkata, India.

A. Ghosh, **K. Bose**, S. Chakravarti, A.B. Das Chaudhuri, J. Chattopadhyay, G. Dasgupta and S. Sengupta.

Anthropological Science, 112 (2): 115-119, 2004.

40) Adult Bengalee Tuberculosis Patients and Controls: Comparison of anthropometric

characteristics and nutritional status.

S. Jana, **K. Bose**, A. Mukhopadhyay and M. Bhadra.

Indian Journal of Biological Sciences, 10: 21-29, 2004.

41) Anthropometric Assessment of Nutritional Status of Adolescents of Kolkata, West Bengal.

Mukhopadhyay, M. Bhadra and **K.Bose**.

Journal of Human Ecology, 18 (3): 213-216, 2005.

42) Anthropometric characteristics and nutritional status based on body mass index of

Bathudis: a tribal population of Keonjhar District, Orissa, India.

K. Bose and F. Chakraborty,

Asia Pacific Journal of Clinical Nutrition, 14 (1): 80-82, 2005.

43) Physical exercise, body mass index, subcutaneous adiposity and body composition among Bengalee boys aged 10-16 years, of Kolkata, India.

A. Mukhopadhyay, M. Bhadra and **K. Bose**.

AnthropologischerAnzeiger, 63 (1): 93-101, 2005.

44) The relationship of age, body mass index and waist circumference with blood pressure in Bengalee Hindu male jute mill workers of Belur, West Bengal, India.

K. Bose, A. Ghosh, S. Roy and S. Gangopadhyay.

AnthropologischerAnzeiger, 63 (2): 205-12, 2005.

45) Human Obesity: A Background.

A. Mukhopadhyay, M. Bhadra and **K. Bose**.

In: Human Obesity: A Major Health Burden.Journal of Human Ecology Special Issue Number 13. pp. 1-9. Edited by: K. Bose. Delhi: Kamla Raj Enterprise, 2005.

ISBN-81-85264-39-2.

46) Overweight and Obesity among adult Bengalee Hindu Women of Kolkata, India.

M. Bhadra, A. Mukhopadhyay and K. Bose.

In: Human Obesity: A Major Health Burden.Journal of Human Ecology Special Issue Number 13. pp. 77-83. Edited by: K. Bose. Delhi: Kamla Raj Enterprise, 2005.

ISBN-81-85264-39-2.

47) Differences in body composition between pre-menarcheal and menarchealBengalee Hindu girls of Madhyamgram, North 24 Parganas, West Bengal, India.

M. Bhadra, A. Mukhopadhyay and **K. Bose**.

Anthropological Science, 113 (2): 141-145, 2005.

48) Regional adiposity, body composition and central body fat distribution of 10-16 year oldBengalee boys of Nimta, 24 Parganas, West Bengal, India.

    A. Mukhopadhyay, M. Bhadra and **K. Bose**.

    Collegium Antropologicum, 29 (2):487-492, 2005.

49) Age trends in anthropometric characteristics among 6-9 year old Bengalee Hindu school girls of Kolkata, India.

    K. Bose, S. Bhattacharya, K. Basu, S. Ghosh, A. Mukhopadhyay and M. Bhadra.

    AnthropologischerAnzeiger, 63 (4): 439-448, 2005.

50) Anthropometric and Physiometric Assessment of Adult Dhimals of Naxabari, West Bengal.

    S. Datta Banik, **K. Bose** and S. Bisai.

    Indian Journal of Biological Sciences, 11: 26-39, 2005.

51) Rural Development: Some Health Aspects.

    M. Bhadra, A. Mukhopadhyay and **K. Bose**.

    In: *Perspectives of Rural Development: Problems and Prospects.*pp. 101-115, 2006. Edited By: R.K. Das, A. Basu and A. Guha. Kolkata and Midnapore: Indian Anthropological Society and Department of Anthropology, Vidyasagar University. ISBN 81-85525-05-6.

52) Anthropometric profile and chronic energy deficiency among adult Santal tribals of

    Jhargram, West Bengal, India: Comparison with other tribal populations of Eastern India.

    K. Bose, S. Banerjee, S. Bisai, A. Mukhopadhyay and M. Bhadra.

    Ecology of Food and Nutrition, 45 (3):159-169, 2006.

53) Presence of High Rates of Overweight and Obesity among Adult Marwaris of Howrah,

    West Bengal, India

    M. Das and **K. Bose**.

    Collegium Antropologicum, 30 (1): 81-86, 2006.

54) High prevalence of undernutrition among adult Kora Mudi tribals of Bankura District, West Bengal, India.

    K. Bose, S. Ganguli, H. Mamtaz, A. Mukhopadhyay and M. Bhadra.

    Anthropological Science, 114 (1): 65-68, 2006.

55) Age and sex variations in undernutrition of rural Bengalee primary school children of East Midnapore District, West Bengal, India.

    K. Bose, D. Bhunia, G. Paul, A. Mukhopadhyay and R. Chakraborty.

In: Culture, Ecology, Nutrition, Health and Disease. *Journal of Human Ecology Special Issue Number 14.* pp. 71-75. Edited by **K. Bose**. Delhi: Kamla Raj Enterprise, 2006.

56) The effect of maternal age and parity on birth weight among Bengalees of Kolkata, India.

S. Bisai, A. Sen, D. Mahalanabis,N. Datta and K. Bose.

In: Culture, Ecology, Nutrition, Health and Disease. *Journal of Human Ecology Special Issue Number 14.* pp. 139-143. Edited by **K. Bose.**Delhi: Kamla Raj Enterprise, 2006.

57) Nutritional status of adult Santal men in Keonjhar District, Orissa, India.

K. Bose, F. Chakraborty, K. Mitra and S. Bisai.

Food and Nutrition Bulletin, 27 (4):353-356, 2006.

58) Interrelationships of income, chronic energy deficiency, morbidity and hospitalization among adult male slum dwellers of Midnapore, West Bengal, India.

K. Bose, S. Bisai, P. Das, S. Dikshit and S. Pradhan.

Journal of Biosocial Science, 39 (5): 779-787, 2006.

59) Cut off point of maternal weight for low birth weight: Assessment by sensitivity versus specificity and regression equation.

S. Bisai, D. Mahalanabis, **K. Bose**, A. Sen and N. Datta In: Sudip Datta Banik, Saikat Kumar Basu and Amit Krishna De, editors. *Man and Environment: Global Concerns and Perspectives, pp. 65-80.*New Delhi: APH Publication Corporation, 2007. ISBN: 81-313-0170-2.

60) Age Variations in Anthropometric and Body Composition Characteristics and Underweight among Male Bathudis: A Tribal population of Keonjhar District, Orissa, India.

K. Bose, S. Bisai and F. Chakraborty.

Collegium Antropologicum (4): 771-775, 2006.

61) Body mass index and nutritional status of adult Savartribals of Keonjhar District, Orissa, India.

K. Bose, F. Chakraborty, S. Bisai, A. Khatun and H. Bauri.

Asia Pacific Journal of Public Health, 18 (3): 3-7, 2006.

62) Panchanan Mitra.

K. Bose.

Current Science, 91 (11): 1439, 2006.

63) Body mass index and chronic energy deficiency among urban slum dwellers of Kolkata, India: relationship with family income.

R. Chakraborty, **K. Bose** and S. Bisai.

International Journal of Anthropology, 21 (3-4): 209-215, 2006.

64) Low Birth Weight and Normal Birth Weight Newborns of Kolkata, India: Comparison of Some Maternal Risk Factors.

S. Bisai, D. Mahalanabis and **K. Bose**.

International Journal of Anthropology, 21 (3-4): 241-246, 2006.

65) Which measure of abdominal adiposity best relates with body mass index among older Bengalee Hindus of Kolkata, India ? A comparison of three measures.

K. Bose.

International Journal of Anthropology, 21 (3-4): 247-252, 2006.

66) Age and Sex Variations in some Anthropometric Parameters with reference to Undernutrition in

Rural Bengalee Primary School Children of East Midnapore District, West Bengal.

R. Chakraborty, A. Mukhopadhyay and **K. Bose**.

Journal of Indian Anthropological Society, 42 (2): 177-182, 2006.

67) Cut off point for Maternal Weight of Term Low Birth Weight Neonates Among Bengalees of Kolkata, India: Assessed by Two Methods. S, Bisai, N. Datta, D. Mahalanabis, K. Bose and A. Sen.

Indian Journal of Biological Sciences, 12: 10-22, 2006.

68) Maternal early second trimester pregnancy weight in relation to birth outcome among Bengalee Hindus of Kolkata, India.

S. Bisai, D. Mahalanabis, A. Sen, **K. Bose** and N. Datta.

Annals of Human Biology, 34 (1): 91-101, 2007.

69) Overweight and obesity among afluent Bengalee School Girls of Lake Town, Kolkata, India.

K. Bose, S. Bisai, A. Mukhopadhyay and M. Bhadra.

Maternal and Child Nutrition, 3 (1): 141-145, 2007.

70) Stunting, Underweight and Wasting among Integrated Child Development Services (ICDS) Scheme Children aged 3-5 years of Chapra, Nadia District, West Bengal, India:

K. Bose, S. Biswas, S. Bisai, S. Ganguli, A. Khatun, A. Mukhopadhyay and M. Bhadra.

Maternal and Child Nutrition, 3 (2): 216-221, 2007.

71) Age variations in overweight, obesity and hypertension among adult men and women of Dearah, Hooghly District, West Bengal, India.

S.K. Sadhukhan, **K. Bose**, A. Mukhopadhyay and M. Bhadra.

Indian Journal of Public Health, 51 (1): *59-61,* 2007.

72) Undernutrition among adult Dhimals of Naxalbari, West Bengal: Comparison with other tribes of eastern India.

S. Datta Banik, **K. Bose,** S. Bisai, M. Bhattacharya, S. Das, A. Jana and P. Purkait.

Food and Nutrition Bulletin, 28 (3): 348-352, 2007.

73) Adult Santal Males from Orissa and West Bengal: Comparison of Their Anthropometric Profile and Chronic Energy Deficiency

K. Bose and S. Bisai.

Studies of Tribes and Tribals, 5 (1): 65-69, 2007.

74) **Causes and Consequences of Obesity.**

K. Bose, M. Bhadra and A. Mukhopadhyay. In: V. Bhasin and M.K. Bhasin, editors. *Anthropology Today: Trends, Scope and Applications,* pp 223-240. Delhi: Kamla Raj Enterprise, 2007. ISBN: 81-85264-45-7.

75) Age variations in anthropometric and body composition characteristics and Undernutrition among female Bathudis: A tribal population of Keonjhar District, Orissa, India.

K. Bose, F.Chakraborty and S. Bisai.

AnthropologischerAnzeiger, 65 (3): 285-291, 2007.

76) Relationship of Income with Anthropometric Indicators of Chronic Energy Deficiency among Adult

Female Slum Dwellers of Midnapore Town.

K. Bose, S. Bisai, P. Das, S. Dikshit and S. Pradhan.

Journal of Human Ecology, 22 (2): 171-176, 2007.

77) Comparison of Nutritional Status Between Tuberculosis Patients and Controls: a Study from North 24 Parganas District in West Bengal, India.

K. Bose, S. Jana, S. Bisai, A. Mukhopadhyay and M. Bhadra.

Malaysian Journal of Nutrition, 13 (2): 131-139, 2007.

78) Utility and efficacy of utilizing body mass index and percent body fat in the evaluation of nutritional status among university students.

S. Bisai, **K. Bose** and D. Ghosh.

Indian Journal of Biological Sciences, 13: 27-32, 2007.

79) Concept of Human Physical Growth and Development.

K. Bose.

In: Fundamentals in Human Genetics and Human Growth. Chapter 5.

http://hdl.handle.net/123456789/243, 2007.

80) Extreme Levels of Underweight and Stunting Among Pre-Adolescent Children of Low Socioeconomic Class from Madhyamgram and Barasat, West Bengal India.

K. Bose, S. Bisai, J. Chakraborty, N. Datta and P. Banerjee.

Collegium Antropologicum, 32 (1): 73-77, 2008.

81) Body composition of two tribal populations of Keonjhar, Orissa, India: A Comparison.

K. Bose, S. Bisai, F. Chakraborty, A. Khatun and H. Bauri.

The Internet Journal of Biological Anthropology, Volume 1, Number 2, 2008.

82) Nutritional Status of Rural Adolescent School Children in Paschim Medinipur, West Bengal.

K. Bose and S. Bisai.

Indian Pediatrics, 45 (6): 515-516, 2008.

83) Undernutrition among Integrated Child Development Services (ICDS) Scheme Children aged 2-6 years of Arambag, Hooghly District, West Bengal, India: A serious public health problem.

G.C. Mandal, **K. Bose**, S. Bisai and S. Ganguli.

Italian Journal of Public Health, 5 (1): 28-33, 2008.

84) Body mass index and chronic energy deficiency among adult male Lodhas and Bhumijs: A comparison with other tribal populations of West Bengal, India.

K. Bose, S. Bisai, P.S. Mondal and M. Ghosh.

Journal of Public Health, 16 (2): 117-121, 2008.

85) Prevalence of undernutrition among rural adolescents of West Bengal, India.

K.Bose and S. Bisai.

Journal of Tropical Pediatrics, 54 (6): 422-423, 2008.

86) Nutritional Stress in Kora Mudis of Two Districts in West Bengal India - A Comparative Statement.

S. Bisai, **K.. Bose**, A.. Khatun, S. Ganguli, P. Das, S. Dikshit, S. Pradhan and Mishra, T.

In: Saikat Kumar Basu and Sudip Datta Banik (editors). Environment Pollution and conservation: Global issues and Policies. APH Publication Corporation, New Delhi, 2008, Chapter XIX, pp 379-389.

87) Anthropometric characteristics and nutritional status of adult Oraon men of Gumla District, Jharkhand, India.

R. Chakraborty and **K. Bose.**

TheInternet Journal of Biological Anthropology, Volume 2, Number 1, 2008.

88) Anthropometric characteristics and nutritional status of rural school children.

K. Bose, S. Bisai and S. Mukherjee.

The Internet Journal of Biological Anthropology, Volume 2, Number 1, 2008.

89) Body Mass Index and Chronic Energy Deficiency among adult Tribal populations of West Bengal:

A Review.

S. Bisai and **K. Bose.**

In: *Health and Nutritional Problems of Indigenous Populations. Tribes and Tribals Special Issue Number 2.* pp. 81-94. Edited by **K. Bose**. Delhi: Kamla Raj Enterprise, 2008

90) Sexual Dimorphism and Age variations in Anthropometry, Body Composition and Nutritional Status among Kora Mudi Tribals of Bankura, West Bengal, India.

S. Bisai, **K. Bose,** S. Ganguli, H. Mumtaz, A. Mukhopadhyay and M. Bhadra.

In: *Health and Nutritional Problems of Indigenous Populations. Tribes and Tribals Special Issue Number 2.* pp. 103-109. Edited by **K. Bose**. Delhi: Kamla Raj Enterprise, 2008.

91) Central adiposity measures of Bengalee male slum dwellers.

R. Chakraborty and K. Bose.

International Journal of Body Composition Research, 6 (3): 122-126, 2008.

92) Prevalence of Undernutrition of Lodha Children Aged 1-14 Years of Paschim Medinipur District, West Bengal, India.

S. Bisai, **K. Bose** and A. Ghosh

Iranian Journal of Pediatrics, 18 (4): 323-329, 2008.

93) Nutritional Status of Lodha Children in a Village of Paschim Medinipur District, West Bengal.

S. Bisai, **K. Bose** and A. Ghosh.

Indian Journal of Public Health, 52 (4): 203-206, 2008.

94) Prevalence of underweight and stunting among school children in West Bengal

K. Bose and S. Bisai.

Indian Journal of Pediatrics, 75 (12): 1271, 2008.

95) Evaluation of equations for fat-free mass based on anthropometry in infants and young children in South Asia.

B. Sen, D. Mahalanabis, S. Shaik, A.V. Kurpad and **K. Bose.**

British Journal of Nutrition, 101 (4): 543-549, 2009.

96) Relationship of family income and house type to body mass index and chronic energy deficiency among urban Bengalee male slum dwellers of Kolkata, India.

R. Chakraborty, **K. Bose** and S. Bisai.

HOMO - Journal of Comparative Human Biology, 60 (1): 45-57, 2009

97) Height and Weight as a Simple Indicator for Assessment of Undernutrition among rural Bengalee Pre-School Children of Chapra Block, Nadia District, West Bengal.

S. Biswas, **K. Bose,** A. Mukhopadhyay and M. Bhadra.

In: *People of Contemporary West Bengal*.pp. 380-384. Edited by: D.K. Adak, A. Chattopadhyay and P. Bharati. New Delhi: Mohit Publications, 2009.

98) Under-nutrition among slum children aged 3-6 years in Midnapore town, India.

S. Bisai, **K. Bose** and S. Dikshit.

The Internet Journal of Biological Anthropology, Volume 2, Number 2, 2009.

99) Underweight and stunting among slum children of Midnapore, india

S.Bisai, **K. Bose,** and S. Dikshit.

Journal of Pediatrics and Child Health, 45: 161-162, 2009.

100) Very high prevalence of thinness using new international body mass index cut off points among 5-10 year old school children of Nandigram, West Bengal, India

R. Chakraborty and **K. Bose.**

Journal of Research in Medical Sciences, 14(2): 129-133, 2009.

101) Undernutrition in the Kora Mudi tribal population, West Bengal, India: A Comparison of body mass index and mid-upper-arm circumference.

S.Bisaiand**K. Bose.**

Food and Nutrition Bulletin, 30 (1): 63-67, 2009.

102) Central Adiposity, Body Mass Index and Percent Body Fat among Bengalee Hindu Male Slum Dwellers of Dum Dum, West Bengal, India.

R. Chakraborty and **K. Bose**.

Open Obesity Journal, 1: 32-37, 2009.

103) Undernutrition among adult Bengalees of Dearah, Hooghly District, West Bengal: Relationship with educational status and food habit.

K.Bose, S. Bisai, S. Sadhukhan, A. Mukhopadhyay and M. Bhadra.

AnthropologischerAnzeiger, 67 (2): 121-128, 2009.

104) Mid-upper arm circumference as a measure of nutritional status among adult Bengalee male slum dwellers of Kolkata, India: relationship with self reported morbidity.

R. Chakraborty, **K. Bose,** and S. Bisai.

AnthropologischerAnzeiger, 67 (2): 129-137, 2009.

105) Age-Related Anthropometric Changes and Undernutrition among Middle Aged and Older Savar Tribal Females of Keonjhar District, Orissa, India.

S. Bisai, **K.Bose,** A.Khatun, and H. Bauri.

Journal of Life Sciences, 1 (1): 21-26, 2009.

106) Body mass index and blood pressure among adult Bengalee male slum dwellers of Kolkata, India.

R. Chakraborty, **K.Bose**and S. Bisai.

Journal of Public Health, 17 (5): 301-308, 2009.

107) Assessment of Overall Prevalence of Undernutrition Using Composite Index of Anthropometric

failure (CIAF) among Preschool Children Of West Bengal, India.

GC. Mandal and **K.Bose**.

Iranian Journal of Pediatrics, 19 (3): 237-243, 2009.

108) Thinness Among Rural Children in Bengal.

G.C. Mandal, **K. Bose** and S. Bisai.

Indian Journal of Pediatrics, 76 (8): 817-819, 2009.

109) Receiver operating characteristics (ROC) curve estimation of low birth weight based on maternal third trimester weight among women of Kolkata, India.

S. Bisai, N. Datta, **K. Bose**, D. Mahalanabis and A. Sen.

Collegium Anthropologicum, 33 (3): 725-728, 2009.

110) Prevalence of Thinness among Rural Bengalee Pre-school Children in Chapra, Nadia District, West Bengal, India.

S. Biswas, **K. Bose**, S. Bisai and R. Chakraborty.

Malaysian Journal of Nutrition, 15 (2): 155-164, 2009.

111) Use of mid-upper arm circumference as a measure of nutritional status and its relationship with self reported morbidity among adult Bengalee male slum dwellers of Kolkata, India.

R. Chakraborty, **K. Bose** and S. Bisai.

In: Shane J Ellsworth and Reece C Schuster (editors), Appetite and Nutritional Assessment. Nova Science Publishers, Inc, New York, 2009; 377- 385

112) Undernutrition among Bauri Pre-School Children of Nituria Block, Purulia District, West Bengal, India.

S. Dasand **K. Bose**.

Journal of Life Sciences, 1 (2): 85-89, 2009.

113) High prevalence of stunting among Integrated Child Development Services (ICDS) Scheme Children aged 1-5 years of Chapra Block, Nadia District, West Bengal, India.

S. Biswas, **K. Bose** and A. Mukhopadhyay.

The Internet Journal of Biological Anthropology, Volume 3, Number 2, 2009.

114) Anthropometric Characteristics and Nutritional Status of Bauri Pre-School Children of Nituria Block, Purulia, West Bengal.

S. Das and **K. Bose.**

The Internet Journal of Biological Anthropology, Volume 3, Number 2, 2009.

115) Leanness among Early Adolescents in Two Rural Schools of Two Districts in West Bengal.

S. Bisai and **K. Bose**.

Indian Journal of Public Health, 53 (4): 235-236, 2009.

116) Assessment of undernutrition by mid-upper arm circumference among Pre-school children of Arambag, Hooghly District, West Bengal, India: An observational study.

G. C. Mandal and **K.Bose**.

The Internet Journal of Paediatrics and Neonatology, Volume 11, Number 1, 2009.

117) Report on "anthropometric failure" among rural 2-6 years old Indian Bauri caste children of West Bengal.

S. Das and **K.Bose**

Anthropological Review, 72: 81-88, 2009.

118) Prevalence and trends in Overweight and Obesity among Bengalee Adults of Kolkata Metropolitan Area, West Bengal, India.

M. Bhadra, A. Mukhopadhyay and **K. Bose**.

In: Rashmi Sinha and Satwanti Kapoor (editors), Obesity – A Multidimensional Approach to Contemporary Global Issue. Dhanraj Book House, New Delhi, 2009; 120-128.

119) Use of mid-upper arm circumference as a measure of nutritional status and its relationship with self reported morbidity among adult Bengalee male slum dwellers of Kolkata, India.

R. Chakraborty, **K. Bose** and S. Bisai. In: Jacob K. Levine (editor), Low Incomes – Social, Health and Educational Impacts. Nova Science Publishers, Inc, New York, 2009; 207-215.

120) Prevalence of undernutrition among pre-school children of Chapra, Nadia District, West Bengal, India, measured by composite index of anthropometric failure (CIAF).

S. Biswas, **K. Bose**, A. Mukhopadhyay and M Bhadra.

AnthropolgischerAnzieger, 67 (3):269-279 79, 2009.

121) Evaluation of thinness among urban Bengalee adolescents of Midnapore, India: Using new international BMI cutoffs.

S. Bisai, R. Khongsdier and **K. Bose.**

Indian Journal of Biological Sciences, 15: 49-55, 2009.

122) Body mass index and body fat among adult Bengalee male slum dwellers in West Bengal, India.

R. Chakraborty, **K. Bose**, R. Khongsdier and S. Bisai.

Obesity Research and Clinical Practice, 3 (3): 141-148, 2009.

123) Mid-upper Arm Circumference Based Undernutrition among Bengalee Children of Chapra, West Bengal, India.

S. Biswas, **K. Bose**, A. Mukhopadhyay and M. Bhadra.

Iranian Journal of Pediatrics, 20 (1): 77-82, 2010.

124) Prediction Equations for Body-fat Percentage in Indian Infants and Young Children Using Skinfold Thickness and Mid-arm Circumference.

B. Sen, **K. Bose**, S. Shaikh and D. Mahalanabis.

Journal of Health, Populationand Nutrition, 28 (3): 221-229, 2010

125) Sex differences in the effect of birth order and parents' educational status on stunting: A study on Bengalee preschool children from Eastern India.

S. Biswas and **K. Bose**.

HOMO – Journal of Comparative Human Biology, 61(4):271-6, 2010.

126) Prevalence of underweight, stunting and wasting among urban poor children aged 1-5 years of West Bengal, India.

S.Bisai, T. Ghosh and **K. Bose.**

International Journal of Current Research, 6: 39-44, 2010.

127) Lean Body Mass in Indian Infants and Young Childrenand Variation by Sex.

B. Sen, **K. Bose** and D. Mahalanabis.

Journal of Life Sciences, 2 (1): 27-35, 2010.

128) Total body water and fat-free mass: evaluation of equations based onbioelectricalimpedanceanalysis in infants and young children in India.

B. Sen, D. Mahalanabis, A. V. Kurpad, S. Shaikh and **K. Bose**.

British Journal of Nutrition, 104: 256–264, 2010.

129) Nutritional Status of Pre-School Children: A Major Global Health Challenge.

G.C. Mandal and **K.Bose.**

In: Anthropology Today: Trends and Scope of Human Biology, pp 33-42.

Edited by M.K. Bhasin and Charles Susanne. Delhi: Kamla Raj Enterprises, 2010. ISBN-81-85264-52-X.

130) Body Mass Index and Chronic Energy Deficiency among Adult Santals of Purulia District, West Bengal, India.

S. Das and **K. Bose.**

International Journal of Human Sciences, 7 (2): 488-503, 2010.

131) Very High Prevalence of Thinness among Kora-Mudi Tribal Children of Paschim Medinipur District of West Bengal, India.

S. Bisai, T. Ghosh, G. K. De and **K. Bose**.

*E Journal of Biological Sciences,*3 (1): 43-49, 2010.

132) A Longitudinal growth study of weight among Lodhaand Non-Lodha infants and young children of Lodhasuli, West Bengal, India

N. K. Sinha, S. Das, K.Boseand D.K.Nandi.

Antrocom, 6 (2):135-140, 2010.

133) Prevalence of Overweight and Obesity among Bengalee Adolescents in Midnapore Town, West Bengal, India.

S. Bisai, R. Khongsdier, **K. Bose**, A. K. Bhunia, D. Mahalanabisand S. Koziel.

International Journal of Current Research, 10: 74-83, 2010.

134) Undernutrition among the Rural Preschool Children (ICDS) of Arambag, Hooghly District, West Bengal, India, Using New Head Circumference Cut-Off Points.

G. C. Mandal and **K. Bose**.

International Journal of Current Research, 10: 7-11, 2010.

135) Assessment of Undernutrition Among Bauri Pre-School Children of Nituria Block, Purulia District, West Bengal, India.

S. Das and **K. Bose.**

Journal of the Department of Anthropology, University of Calcutta, 12 & 13: 42-46, 2010.

136) The utility of a new index for adiposity among pre-school children.

S. Biswas and **K.Bose**

Malaysian Journal of Nutrition, 16 (3): 447-450, 2010.

137) MUAC-based Nutritional Status of 2-5 Years Old Bauri Caste Preschool Children of Purulia, West Bengal.

K. Bose and S. Das.

Journal of Indian Anthropological Society, 45: 301-306, 2010.

138) Stunting among rural Bengalee Children from ICDS Centres of Patashpur-II Block, East Midnapur, West Bengal, India.

G.C. Mandal**, K. Bose** and A. Acharya.

Indian Journal of Physical Anthropology and Human Genetics, 29. (1-2): 99-107, 2110.

139) Association between place of delivery and undernutrition.

S. Biswas and **K. Bose**.

Nutritional Segment, 1 (1): NS1540, 2010.

140) A Longitudinal study of weight gain among Santal and Non-Santal infants of Kankabati Gram Panchayat, West Bengal, India.

A. Sarkar, A. Samanta, N.K. Sinha, P. Samanta, S. Das and **K. Bose**.

Indian Journal of Biological Sciences, 16: 29-33, 2010.

141) Proposed New Anthropometric Indices of Childhood Undernutrition.

K. Bose and G.C. Mandal.

Malaysian Journal of Nutrition, 16(1): 131-136, 2010.

142) Prevalence of thinness among Santal preschool children using new Body Mass Index cut-off points.

S. Das and **K.Bose.**

Journal of Anthropology. Article ID: 602782, 4 pages.

doi:10.1155/2011/602782, 2011.

143) Growth Pattern and Prevalence of Underweight and Stunting Among Rural Adolescents.

S. Bisai, **K. Bose,** D. Ghosh and K. De.

Journal of NepalPaediatric Society, 31 (1): 17–24, 2011.

144) Effect of social factors on nutritional status among rural Bengalee preschool children from Eastern India.

S. Biswas, **K. Bose** and S. Koziel.

International Journal of Human Sciences, 8 (1): 289-300, 2011.

145) Impact of social class on body fatness among rural pre-school Bengalee Hindu children of Arambagh, West Bengal, India.

G. C. Mandal, **K. Bose** and S. Koziel.

HOMO – Journal of Comparative Human Biology, 62 (3): 228-236, 2011.

146) Use of waist circumference and its optimal value to identify obesity inrelation to hypertension: across-sectional study among adult male slumdwellers of Eastern India

R. Chakraborty, **K. Bose** and S. Koziel.

Italian Journal of Public Health, 8 (2): 137-148, 2011.

147) Waist circumference in determining obesity and hypertension among18–60 years old Bengalee Hindu male slum dwellers in Eastern India.

R. Chakraborty, **K. Bose** and S. Kozieł.

Annals of Human Biology, 38 (6): 669-675, 2011.

148) Body Mass Abdominal Index: A New Index for Adiposity among Pre-school Children.

S. Das and **K. Bose**.

IbrahimMedicalCollege Journal, 5 (1): 9-12, 2011.

149) Use of mid-upper arm circumference in determining undernutrition and illness in rural adult Oraon men of Gumla District, Jharkhand, India.

R. Chakraborty, **K. Bose** and S. Koziel.

Rural and Remote Health 11 (online),2011: no. 1754. Available from: http://www.rrh.org.au

150) Prevalence of thinness using new international cut-off points among Santaltribal children and adolescents of Purulia District, West Bengal, India.

S. Das and **K.Bose.**

Sri Lanka Journal of Child Health, 40(3):105-110, 2011.

151) Anthropometric assessment of Nutritional Status among College Women of Midnapore, West

Bengal, India.

S. Mandal, N. K. Sinha, P. Samanta, S. Das and **K. Bose**.

International Journal of Life Science and Pharma Research, 1 (1): L81-L87, 2011.

152) Prevalence of Undernutrition and Wasting among 3-6 Year Old Children in East Midnapore, West Bengal, India.

G.C. Mandal, **K. Bose** and A. Acharya.

Humankind, 7: 129-138, 2011.

153) Is body adiposity index a good measure of nutritional status ? A study among two adult tribal populations of Pashim Medinipur, West Bengal, India.

K. Bose, B. Debsarma and S. Das.

Science Journal of Sociology and Anthropology, 1: 1-4, 2011.

154) New reference values of body mass index for rural pre-school children of Bengalee ethnicity.

K. Bose, S. Biswas and S. Bisai.

Science Journal of Sociology and Anthropology, 1: 5-9, 2011.

155) Leanness among pre-school children of Bali Gram Panchayat, Arambag, West Bengal, India.

G.C. Mandal and **K. Bose.**

Science Journal of Sociology and Anthropology, 1: 10-11, 2011.

156) Measuring fatness among rural pre-school children using a new index of abdominal adiposity.

G.C. Mandal and **K. Bose**.

International Journal of Child Health and Human Development, 4 (3): 309-315, 2011.

157) Effect of Number of Rooms and Sibs on Nutritional Status among Rural Bengalee Preschool Children from Eastern India.

S. Biswas and **K. Bose.**

Collegium Antropologicum, 35 (4): 1017-1022, 2011.

158) Assessment of Nutritional Status by Anthropometric Indices in Santal Tribal Children.

S. Das and **K. Bose.**

Journal of Life Sciences, 3 (2): 81-85, 2011.

159) Thinness Among Hill Kharia Children and Adolescents of Purulia Using Body Mass Index Cut-Off Points.

S. Das and **K. Bose**.

Research and Reviews: A Journal of Health Professions, 1 (2-3): 31-36, 2011.

160) Does Educational Attainment Affect Nutritional Status? A Study amongUnderprivileged Adults of Six Districts of West Bengal, India.

S. Biswasand**K. Bose.**

In: *Undernutrition: Effects, Causes and Management*, pp. 87-98. Edited by: Jason E. Lee. New York: Nova Science Publishers, 2011.

161) Prevalence of Thinness among Rural Bengalee Muslim School Children from Eastern India.

P. R. Mondal, S. Biswas and **K. Bose.**

In: *Undernutrition: Effects, Causes and Management*, pp. 99-110. Edited by: Jason E. Lee. New York: Nova Science Publishers, 2011.

162) Prevalence of Pre-hypertension and Hypertension among University-Going Adult Bengalee Males and Females.

S. Das, **K. Bose** and S. Datta Banik.

Journal of the Department of Anthropology, CalcuttaUniversity, 14 (1): 205-215, 2011.

163) Biological effects of economic transition in Poland.

S. Koziel and **K. Bose**.

In: *Public Health Yearbook.* Edited by: JoavMerrick;pp. 351-374. New York: Nova Science Publishers, 2011.

164) Body composition characteristics among rural Bengalee children of Integrated Child Development Services scheme from Eastern India.

S. Biswas and **K. Bose.**

International Journal of Body Composition Research, 9 (3): 95-100, 2011.

165) Nutritional Status of Tribal Children of Paschim Medinipur District of West Bengal.

A. Khatun, S. Ganguli, **K. Bose** and S. Bisai.

In: *Indigenous People in India: Identity, Empowerment and Discontent.* Edited by: Dipak K. Midya. pp. 128-136.New Delhi: APH Publishing Corporation, 2012.

166) Gender discrimination in undernutrition with mediating factors among Bengalee school children from Eastern India.

P.R. Mandal, S. Biswas and **K. Bose**.

HOMO – Journal of Comparative Biology, 63 (2): 126-135, 2012.

167) Double burden of malnutrition among urban Bengalee adolescent boys in Midnapore, West Bengal, India.

S. Bisai, R. Khongsdier, **K. Bose** and D. Mahalanabis.

Nature Precedings.

http://dx.doi.org/10.1038/npre.2012.7106.2, 2012.

168) Critical nutritional stress among adult tribal populations of West Bengal and Orissa, India.

S. Bisai and **K. Bose.**

Nature Precedings.

http://dx.doi.org/10.1038/npre.2012.7068.2, 2012.

169) Age trends in thinness among Birhor children and adolescents of Purulia: a primitive tribe of West Bengal, India.

S. Das, M. Mahata and **K. Bose**.

Asian Journal of Biological and Life Sciences, 1 (1): 58-60, 2012.

170) Age variations in anthropometric and body compositioncharacteristics among adult Bauri females of PaschimMedinipur, West Bengal, India.

S. Das, T. Chowdhury and **K. Bose**.

Scholarly Journal of Scientific Research and Essay Writing, 1(2):16-24,2012.

171) Comparison of Body Composition Among Rural Preschool Children of Purulia, West Bengal, Using Two different Equations.

S. Das and **K. Bose**.

Human Biology Review, 1 (3): 222-234, 2012.

172) Nutritional Status Based on Anthropometry Of Tribal Preschool Children In Paschim Medinipur District of West Bengal, India.

S. Bisai, **K. Bose**, T. Ghosh, G.K. DE, R. Khongsdier, S. Koziel, D. Mahalanabis and P. Mallick.

International Journal of Innovative Research and Development, **1** (3): 61-79, 2012.

173) Etiological Factors, Assisted Reproduction and Pregnancy Outcome: A Retrospective Observation Among Infertile Couples.

A.K. Ray, S. Bisai, **K. Bose**, S. Ray, M. Raychoudhury and J. Bhattacharya.

In: *Human Health: A Biocultural Synthesis,* pp. 200-210. Edited by: Subir Biswas. New Delhi: Concept Publishing Company, 2012.

174) Body mass index percentiles for rural Bengalee pre-schoolchildren aged 2-6 years, in comparison with the WHOreference and other studies.

S. Das, S. Bisai, S. Datta Banik and **K.Bose**.

Acta BiologicaSzegediensis, 56(1):25-30,2012.

175) Age and Sex Variations in Body Mass Index and Chronic Energy Deficiency among Adult Santals of Purulia District, West Bengal, India.

S. Das and **K. Bose**.

In: *New Trends in Body Mass Index Research*, pp. 81-96. Edited by: Alard Vermeulen and Edme De Smet. ISBN: 978-1-61942-430-2.New York: Nova Science Publishers, 2012.

176) Nutritional deprivation among Indian tribals: A cause for concern.

S. Das and **K. Bose**.

Anthropological Notebooks, 18 (2): 5-16, 2012.

177) Nutritional status based on anthropometry of tribal children of Paschim Medinipur district, West Bengal.

S. Ganguly, A. Khatun, S. Bisai, S. Das and **K. Bose**.

In: *Bio-Cultural Development of Scheduled Tribes: Policies and Issues,* pp. 125-133. Edited by: P.K. Misra, H.K. Bhat and K.K. Misra. ISBN: 978-81-316-0534-9. New Delhi: Rawat Publications, 2012.

178) Nutritional Profile of Preschool Children: A Review.

S. Das and **K. Bose**.

Anthropologist 14, (5): 467-472, 2012.

179) Inter Generational Growth Trend and Nutritional Status Among Adult Bengalee Women of Paschim Midnapore, West Bengal, India.

S. Das, S. Chakraborty and **K. Bose.**

International Journal of Anthropology, 27 (4): 275-285, 2012.

180) Impact of Age and Body Mass Index on Pregnancy Outcome: A Retrospective Study among Primary and Secondary Infertile Couples of Ranchi, Jharkhand.

A.K. Ray, R.N. Sahu, S. Maity, S. Bisai, **K. Bose**, S. Ray, M. Roychoudhury, D. Ray and J. Bhattacharya.

In: *Dimensions of Anthropological Research in India,* pp. 70-81. Edited by: Jayanta Sarkar, ArabindaBasu and Ajit K. Singh. Kolkata: Indian Anthropological Society, 2012.

181) Mid-Upper Arm Circumference Based Undernutrition in SAHAI Families: A Study among Adults of Six Districts of West Bengal.

S. Biswas and **K. Bose**.

In: *Dimensions of Anthropological Research in India,* pp. 82-95. Edited by: Jayanta Sarkar, ArabindaBasu and Ajit K. Singh. Kolkata: Indian Anthropological Society, 2012.

182) Anthropometric Status among Primary School Children of Migrated Santals of Bali Gram Panchayat, Arambag, West Bengal.

G.C. Mandal and **K. Bose.**

In: *Dimensions of Anthropological Research in India,* pp. 96-110. Edited by: Jayanta Sarkar, ArabindaBasu and Ajit K. Singh. Kolkata: Indian Anthropological Society, 2012.

183) Comparison of Body Adiposity Indices in Predicting Blood Pressure and Hypertension among Slum-Dwelling Men in Kolkata, India.

R. Chakraborty and **K. Bose.**

Malaysian Journal of Nutrition, 18 (3): 319-328, 2012.

184) Prevalence of thinness among rural pre-school children of East Midnapore, West Bengal, India.

G.C. Mandal, A. Acharya and **K. Bose**.

Asian Journal of Biological and Life Sciences, 1 (3): 181–185, 2012.

185) Significant influence of parity on thinness among preschool children of Arambagh, West Bengal, India.

G.C. Mandal and **K. Bose**.

In: *Human Malnutrition: Twin Burdens of Undernutrition and Overnutrition,* pp. 239-244. Edited by: Kaushik Bose. New York: Nova Science Publishers, 2012.

186) Nutritional Profile of adult Birhors of Purulia: A Particular Vulnerable Tribal Group of West Bengal, India.

S. Das, M. Mahata and **K. Bose.**

Asian Academic Research Journal of Multi-Disciplinary, 1 (5), 271-278, 2013.

187) Adiposity and Health Status among Adult Male Mundas and Oraons of Paschim Medinipur, West Bengal, India.

S. Das, B. Bebsharma and **K. Bose.**

Journal of Anthropology. Article ID: 324264, 7 pages.

http://dx.doi.org/10.1155/2013/324264, *2013.*

188) Nutritional status of rural Bengalee girls aged 10-18 years of Salboni, Paschim Medinipur, West Bengal, India.

K. De, S. Das, **K. Bose** and R. Chakraborty.

*Asian Journal of Biological and Life Sciences,*2 (1): 68-72, 2013.

189) Anthropometric characteristics and age at menarche of rural Bengaleeadolescemts of Nadia District, West Bengal, India.

S. Biswas, P.R. Mondal and **K. Bose**.

North Bengal Anthropologist, 1: 29-36, 2013.

190) Relative fat distribution in relation to menarcheal status among Bengalee Hindu girls of West Bengal, India.

M. Bhadra, A. Mukhopadhyay, R. Chakraborty, **K. Bose,** S. Koziel and S. Ulijaszek.

*Journal of Natural Science, Biology and Medicine,*4 (2): 369-373, 2013.

191) Mid-upper arm circumference for age and undernutrition among 2 to 6 year old Bauri and Santal children of Purulia, West Bengal, India.

S. Das, S. Datta Banik and **K. Bose.**

Human Biology Review, 2 (4): 359-372, 2013.

192) Overall burden of under-nutrition measured by a Composite Index in rural pre-school children in Purba Midnapore, West Bengal, India

A. Acharya, G.C. Mandal and **K. Bose**.

Anthropological Review, 76 (1): 109-116, 2013.

193) Sibling Composition and Household Room Sharing are Associated with Menarcheal Status among Rural Bengalee Girls of West Bengal, India.

S. Biswas, S. Koziel, R. Chakraborty and **K. Bose.**

Human Biology, 85 (4): 607-618, 2013.

194) Measuring Fatness Among Rural Children of Bengalee Ethnicity: An Alternative Way.

G.C. Mandal and **K. Bose.**

In: *India: Health and Human Development Aspects,* pp. 437-446. Editor: Joav Merrick. New York: Nova Science Publishers, 2014. ISBN: 978-1-62948-784-7.

195) Anthropometric Assessment of Nutritional Status of Adult Hill Kherias of Purulia District, West Bengal.

S. Das and **K. Bose.**

In: *Human Ecology in an Era of Globalization and Urbanization: Anthropological Dimensions,* pp. 381-390. Editors: K. Sinha and K. Sharma. New Delhi: Global Research Publications, 2014.

196) Defining malnutrition in India: how much is too little, how much is too much ?

R. Chakraborty and **K. Bose**.

*Current Science,*106 (5): 670-672, 2014.

197) Sexual Dimorphism in Blood Pressure and Hypertension among Adult ParengiPorjas of Visakhapatnam, Andhra Pradesh, India.

I.Arjun Rao, A. C. Venugopal N. Pulamaghatta,S.Das and **K. Bose**.

Journal of Anthropology, Volume 2014, Article ID 374649, 5 pages http://dx.doi.org/10.1155/2014/374649, 2014.

198) Impact of Age and Socio-Economic Status on Waist Circumference among Male Urban Slum-Dwellers Near Kolkata, West Bengal, India.

R. Chakaborty and **K. Bose.**

In: *Health Consequences of Human Central Obesity,* pp.151-162. Edited By: **K. Bose** and R. Chakraborty. New York: Nova Science Publishers, 2014

199) Comparisons of the effects of food supplementation programmes of ICDS centres and primary schools at Bali Gram Panchayat, Arambagh, West Bengal, India.

G.C. Mandal, **K. Bose** and S. Koziel.

International Journal of Sociology and Social Policy, 34 (3/4): 232-246, 2014.

200) Thinness among primary school children of the migrated Santals of Arambag, West Bengal, India.

G.C. Mandal and **K. Bose.**

International Journal of Food Safety, Nutrition and Public Health, 5 (1): 46-53, 2014.

201) Blood Pressure and Hypertension among Adult Savara Tribals of Visakhapatnam, Andhra Pradesh, India: A Public Health Concern.

I.Arjun Rao, A. C. Venugopal N. Pulamaghatta,S.Das and **K. Bose**.

Afro Asian Journal of Anthropology and Social Policy; 5(1):96-101.2014.

202) Anthropometric failure among the Santal preschool children of Purulia, West Bengal, India.

S. Das S. Datta Banik and K. **Bose**. 2015

In: Human Growth: The mirror of the society, pp. 243-253, Chapter 13. Edited By: M. Sikdar. New Delhi: BR Publishing Corporation, New Delhi. ISBN: 978-9-35050-200-6

203) Association of ABO blood groups with malaria: A study from Bilaspur, Chhattisgarh, India.

H.S. Singh, P.K. Das, S. Das and **K. Bose.**

*Research,*1: 976, 2014.

*DOI:*http://dxdoi.org/10/rs.en.1.976

204) Opportunity for Natural Selection among Bhuiyans:A Tribal Population of Keonjhar District, Odisha, India.

B.K. Kuiti and **K. Bose**.

Weekly Science 2 (5) :DOI : 10.9780/ 2321-7871/1202013/53, 2014.

205) Association of second to fourth digit length ratio (2D:4D) with some anthropometric measurements: acomparison between Polish and Indianyoungadultsaged 18-25 years.

R. Chakraborty, T. Mukherjee, S.Jana, S. Koziel, K. Boryslawskiand**K. Bose**.

Human BiologyReview, 3 (4):315-326,2014.

206) Maternal Education, Reported Morbidity and Number of Siblings are Associated with Malnutrition among Lodha Preschool Children of Paschim Medinipur, West Bengal, India

S. Bisai, D. Mahalanabis, A. Sen and **K. Bose**.

International Journal of Pediatrics, (Supplement 6), 2, (.4-2, Serial No.11): 13-21, 2014.

207) Prevalence of hypertension among adults of Midnapore, West Bengal, India: A comparison between sexes.

H.S. Singh, P.K. Das, P.J. Mishra, S. Das and **K. Bose**.

Elixir Biosciences, 77: 29144-29147, 2014.

208) Ethnic-Specific Prevalence of Thinness among Bengalee Youths of Midnapore, West Bengal, India.

S. Das, S. Panda and **K. Bose**.

Research Journal of Pharmaceutical, Biological and Chemical Sciences, 6 (1):1374-1380, 2015.

209) Growth and Nutritional Status of 2 to 6 years old Santal and Bauri Children in Relation with Mother's Education.

S. Das, S. Datta Banik and **K. Bose.**

In: *Health and Tribes in India: Challenges and Opportunities, pp.*235-245. Edited by: K. N. Dash.

New Delhi: Sarup Book Publishers Pvt. Ltd, 2015.

210) Adult tribal malnutrition in India: an anthropometric and socio-demographic review.

S. Das and **K. Bose.**

Anthropological Review, 78 (1): 47-65, 2015.

211) Socio-demographic Profile and Nutritional Status of Gond tribals from Melnadih village, Chhattisgarh.

H. S. Singh, P. K. Das, S. Das, S. Datta Banik and **K. Bose.**

American Journal of Advances in Medical Science. 3(1): 19-21, 2015.

212) Assessment of undernutrition among male Bhumijs of West Bengal, India: A comparison of body mass index and mid-upper arm circumference.

M. Ghosh and **K. Bose**.

Human Biology Review, 4 (2), 140-149, 2015.

213) Selection intensity and its opportunity among Santal women of Keonjhar, Odisha, India

B. Kuiti, S.Das and **K. Bose**.

International Journal of Advances in Scientific Research, 1 (04): 203-210, 2015.

214) Fluctuating asymmetry of hand and foot dimensions among University girl-students from Bilaspur, India

S. Datta Banik, M. Gritlahre, S. Das and **K. Bose**.

Human Biology Review, 4 (4): 378-386, 2015.

215) Body Composition Charts among Older Bengalees of Purba Medinipur, West Bengal, India: Implications for Health.

B. Kuiti and **K. Bose.**

International Journal of Preventive and Public Health Sciences, 1 (4): 2-6, 2015.

216) Prevalence of double burden of malnutrition among urban school going Bodo children aged 5-11 years of Assam, Northeast India.

N. Mondal, B. Basumatary, J. Kropi and **K. Bose.**

Epidemiology, Biostatistics and Public Health, 12 (4): DOI: e11497-1-e11497-10, 2015.

217) Predicted weight with different body segments and its use in nutritional assessment among older Bengalees of PurbaMedinipur District, West Bengal

B. Kuiti and **K. Bose.**

Human Biology Review, 5 (1): 34-52, 2016.

218) Predictive equations for height estimation using knee height of older Bengalees of Purba Medinipur, West Bengal, India.

B. Kuiti and **K. Bose**.

Anthropological Review, 79 (1): 47 – 57, 2016.

219) Is the Effect of Age on Diastolic Blood Pressure Modified by the Age at Migration ? A Study Among the Adult Male Slum Dwellers in Eastern India.

R. Chakraborty, S. Koziel and **K. Bose.**

In: *Biological Implications of Human Mobility*.pp.27-40. (Editors: S. Koziel, R. Chakraborty and **K.Bose**). New York: Nova Science Publishers, 2016. ISBN: 978-1-63485-644-7.

220) Prevalence of Undernutrition Among Five Tribes of West Bengal, India.

S. Das and **K. Bose.**

In: *Nutrition and Health Among Tribal Populations of India:* A Biocultural Approach. pp. 159-170. Edited by: N. Mondal and J. Sen. New Delhi: B.R. Publishing Corporation, 2016. ISBN: 9789350502976.

221) Relationship of cephalic Index with some anthropometric variables among the rural preschool children of West Bengal, India.

G.C. Mandal, A. Acharya and **K. Bose.**

Human Biology Review, 5 (3): 296 – 308, 2016.

222) Selected Socio-demographic Correlates of Nutritional Status among BhainaTribal Female Children and Women of Pendra Block, Chhattisgarh.

S. Das, M. Ghritlahre, H.S. Singh, S. Datta Banik and **K. Bose.**

South Asian Anthropologist, 16 (1): 19-26, 2016.

223) Neck circumference as a screen measure of overweight/obesity among Indian adults.

N. Mondal, J. Sen, **K. Bose,** R. Timungpi, M. Kathar and S. Hanse.

Anthropological Review, 79 (3): 354 – 363, 2016.

224) Assessment of body composition of Bengalee boys of Binpur, West Bengal, India, using a modified Hattori chart method.

S. Pratihar, B. Kuiti and **K. Bose.**

Sri Lanka Journal of Child Health, 45 (3): 177–183, 2016

225) Does ethnic heterogeneity lead to ethnic variation in nature of relationship between central adiposity measures and coronary disease risk factors among Indians.

K. Bose.

Journal of Indian AnthropologicalSociety, 50: 199-200, 2016.

226) In Memorium: Deba Prasad Mukherjee, 1933-2015.

K. Bose.

Journal of Indian Anthropological Society, 50: 207-208, 2016.

227) Age and sex variations in anthropometric characteristics of Muslim adolescents of North 24 Parganas, West Bengal,

A. Khatun, A. Mukhopadhyay and **K. Bose.**

Human Biology Review, 5 (4): 456-464, 2016.

228) Anthropometric and body frame size characteristics in relation to body mass index and percentage body fat among adult Bengalee male brick-kiln workers from Murshidabad, West Bengal, India.

S. Datta Banik, M. Ghosh and **K. Bose.**

AnthropologischerAnzeiger, 73 (4): 313-321, 2016.

229) High prevalence of undernutrition among male brick kiln workers of Murshidabad District, West Bengal, India: A comparison of body mass index and mid-upper arm circumference.

M. Ghosh and **K. Bose.**

Al Ameen Journal of Medical Sciences, 9 (4): 265-271, 2016.

230) Estimation of stature from hand and foot dimensions among university girl-students in Bilaspur, Chhattisgarh, India.

S. Datta Banik, S. Das, **K. Bose** and M. Gritlahre.

Anthropologie, LIV/3: 291-297, 2016.

231) Socio-economic and demographic correlates of stunting among adolescents of Assam, North-east India.

M.S. Rengma, **K. Bose** and N. Mondal.

Anthropological Review, 79 (4): 409-425, 2016.

232) Nutritional Status and Menarcheal Age of Rural Adolescent Girls of Salboni Block of Paschim Medinipur, West Bengal, India.

K. De and **K. Bose.**

International Journal of Experimental Research and Review, 6: 35-40, 2016.

233) Adiposity and body composition in relation to physical activity status among Muslim adolescents of North 24 Parganas, West Bengal.

A. Khatun, A. Mukhopadhyay and **K. Bose.**

Journal of Indian Anthropological Society, 51: 168-176, 2016.

234) Impact of pubertal age on nutritional status among 18-23 years females of Bilaspur, Chhattisgarh, India.

M. Ghritlahre, S. Das and **K. Bose.**

In: Health, Nutrition and Hygiene: The Dynamics of Social Ecology in India. pp. 183-189. (Editors: N.K. Sinha, M.K. Patsa, R. Das and P. Samanta). Midnapore: Shreelipi Publisher, 2016. ISBN: 978-81-930138-1-6.

235) Anthropometric characteristics of rural primary school children of Hooghly District, West Bengal, India.

S. Pal and **K. Bose**

Human Biology Review, 6 (1): 30 – 46, 2017.

236) Statistical association of adiposity measures with body composition among adult brick-kiln workers of Murshidabad District, West Bengal, India.

M. Ghosh and **K. Bose.**

Proceedings of the International Conference on Bioinformatics and Biostatistics for Agriculture, Health and Environment, 154-159, 2017.

ISBN: 978-984-34-0996-6.

Edited by: M.A. Hoque, M.A. Khalek, A.S.M.A. Mamun and M.M. Rahman. Dhaka: Prime Minister's Office.

237) Nutritional status among children and adolescents aged 6–18 years of Kolam tribe of Andhra Pradesh, India.

K. Bharthi, M. Ghritlahre, S. Das and **K. Bose.**

Anthropological Review, 80 (2):13–23, 2017.

238) Cut-off point estimation of neckcircumference to determine overweight andobesity among Asian Indian adults.

N. Mondal, R. Timungpi, M. Kathar, S. Hanse, S. Teronpi, A. Timung, **K. Bose** and J. Sen.

Epidemiology, Biostatistics and Public Health, 14 (2): DOI:10.2427/12310, 2017.

239) Socio-Economic and DemographicCorrelates of Overweight and Obesity:A Study on the Karbi Women of Assam,Northeast India.

N. Mondal, R. Timungpi, J. Sen and **K. Bose.**

Anthropology Open Journal, 2 (2): 31 – 39, 2017.

240) Determining a Global Mid-Upper Arm Circumference Cutoff to Assess Underweight in Adults (Men and Nonpregnant Women).

A.M. Tang, M. Chung, K. Dong, C. Wanke, P. Bahwere, **K. Bose**, R. Chakraborty, K. Charlton, S. Hong, P. Nguyen, C. B. Patsche, M. Deitchler and Z. Maalouf-Manasseh.

USAID Food and Nutrition Technical Assistance III Project (FANTA) FHI 360, 2017. Washington, DC, USA. .

241) Growth Pattern of School Going Children of Medinipur Districts of West Bengal, India.

B. K. Kuiti, I. Dash, M. Jana, S. Pratihar and **K. Bose**.

Journal of Life Sciences, 9 (1): 18-27, 2017.

242) Body Composition of Rural Children Aged 2-6 Years of BengaleeEthnicity from Arambagh, West Bengal, India.

G. C. MandalandK. **Bose**.

Journal of Life Sciences, 9 (1): 48 – 54, 2017.

243) Nutritional Assessment of Adult Male Munda and OraonTribals of Paschim Medinipur, West Bengal, India.

K. Bose, B. Debsharma and S. Das. In: Development among the Tribal and Minority Societies.pp. 315-322. (Editors: S. Bhui, M. S. Das and P. C. Coomar). New Delhi: Gyan Publishing House, 2017.

ISBN: 978-9351-282-42-6.

244) Prevalence of undernutrition among Bengalee preschool childrenof Sundarban, South 24 Parganas, West Bengal, India. S.P. Giri, S. Biswas and **K. Bose**.

Human Biology Review, 6 (4): 284-300, 2017.

245) Very High Prevalence of Thinness AmongRural Bengalee Preschool Children ofIntegrated Child Development Service(ICDS) Scheme of Sagar Island, South 24Parganas, West Bengal, India.

S.P. Giri, S. Biswas and **K. Bose.**

Anthropology Open Journal, 2 (2): 54-60, 2017.

246) Evaluation of Undernutrition Using International Cut-offs among 2-12 Years Children of Midnapore and Purulia, West Bengal, India.

S. Das, H. Suraj Singh, B. Tiwari and **K. Bose**. In: Child Health in India, pp. 1-12. (Editors: B. Das, M. Talukdar and A.J. Bharati). New Delhi: Omsons Publications, 2017. ISBN: 978-93-81981

247) Relationship between temperament and fatness in 11-year-old children and 17-year-old adolescents from Wrocław,

S. Koziel, R. Chakraborty and **K.Bose.**

HOMO - Journal of Comparative Human Biology, 68: 479–486, 2017.

248) Assessment of Nutritional Status among Muslim Adolescents of Deganga, North 24 Parganas, West Bengal. A. Khatun, A. Mukhopadhyay and **K. Bose**.

Journal of Life Sciences, 9 (2): 98-103, 2017

249) Body Composition among Rural BengaleePreschool Children of Integrated Child Development Service (ICDS) Scheme of Sagar Island, South 24 Parganas, West Bengal, India.

S. P. Giri,S. Biswasand **K. Bose**.

Journal of Life Sciences, 9 (2): 111-117, 2017.

250) Assessment of Nutritional Status among 2 to 12 Years Children of Two Districts in West Bengal, India.

S. Das, M. Ghritlahre, B. Tiwari and **K. Bose.**

Journal of Life Sciences, 9 (2): 118 – 125, 2017.

251) Anthropometric Characteristics and Nutritional Status of Adult Sabars of Bankura District, West Bengal.

M. Ghosh, S. Bhandari and **K. Bose.**

Human Biology Review, 7 (1), 71-83, 2018.

252) Sexual dimorphism in central obesity among adult rural adults of Ghatal Block, Paschim Medinipur, West Bengal, India.

M. Chanak and **K. Bose.**

Human Biology Review, 7 (2): 183-204, 2018.

253) The validity of mid-upper arm circumference as an indicator of low BMI in population screening for undernutrition: a study among adult slum dwellers in eastern India.

P. Das, A. Khatun, **K. Bose** and R. Chakraborty.

Public Health Nutrition, 21 (14): 2575-2583, 2018.

254) The Paradox of "Double Burden"" of Malnutrition in India.

N. Mondal, **K. Bose** and J. Sen.

In: Malnutrition: A Double Burden, pp. 267-269. (Editors: N. Mondal, **K. Bose** and J. Sen). New Delhi:

B.R. Publishing Corporation, 2018. ISBN: 978-9-38758-742-7.

255) Global MUAC Cutoffs for Adults: A Technical Consultation Report. USAID Food and Nutrition

Technical Assistance III Project (FANTA) FHI 360, 2018. Washington, DC, USA.

256) Assessment of nutritional status by compositeindex of anthropometric failure (CIAF): a study among preschool children of Sagar Block, South24 Parganas District, West Bengal, India S, Biswas, S.P. Giri and **K. Bose.**

Anthropological Review, 81 (3): 269-277, 2018.

257) Relationship between Anthropometric Measures and Body Composition Parameters in Adult Brick Kiln Workers of Murshidabad District, West Bengal.

M. Ghosh and **K. Bose.**

Journal of Life Science, 10(2): 107-115, 2018.

258) The Concept of Composite Index of AnthropometricFailure (CIAF): Revisited and Revised

B.K. Kuiti and **K. Bose.**

*Anthropology – Open Journal,*8: 3(1): 32-35, 2018.

259) Syndrome X: Common determinants of cardiovascular disease and non-insulin dependent diabetes mellitus.

M. Das and **K. Bose**.

Journal of the Department of Anthropology, Calcutta University, (18): 1-13, 2018.

260) Syndrome X: Some Common Determinants Worldwide.

M. Das and K. Bose.

In: Obesity and Syndrome X: A Global Public Health Burden, pp. 273-289. (Editors: M. Das and

K. Bose). New York: Nova Science Publishers, 2019. ISBN: 978-1-53614-669-1.

261) Nutritional Assessment by Composite Index of Anthropometric Failure among School Going Children of Purba Medinipur, West Bengal, India.

P. Khanra, S. Biswas and **K. Bose**.

Human Biology Review, 8 (1), 66-76, 2019.

262) Socio-Demographic Characteristics and Prevalence of Under Nutrition among Adult Sabars of Bankura District, West Bengal, India

S. Bhandari, M. Ghosh and **K. Bose.**

International Journal of Advancement in Life Sciences Research, 2 (1): 1-10, 2019.

263) The Assessment of Nutritional Status Using Mid-Upper Arm Circumference among Bengalee Preschool Children of Sagar Island, South 24 Parganas, West Bengal, India.

S.P. Giri, S. Biswas and **K. Bose**.

Journal of Life Sciences, 11 (1-2): 1-6, 2019.

264) Prevalence of Under nutrition among Santal Preschool Children of Two Districts of West Bengal, India B. Mahapatra, J. Dey, S. Pal and **K. Bose**.

Human Biology Review, 8 (2), 179-196, 2019.

265) Physical Growth Assessment among Indigenous Karbi Children of Assam, India: Comparison of WHO, CDC and NHANES Growth References.

N. Mondal, H. Rongpi and **K. Bose.**

In: Growth And Nutritional Studies: Perspective from North East India, 85-107. (Editors: S. Sengupta and D. Dutta). New Delhi: Gyan Publishing House, 2019. ISBN: 9788121214933.

266) Central obesity and hypertension among rural adults of Paschim Medinipur, West Bengal, India.

M. Chanak and **K. Bose.**

Anthropological Review, 82 (3): 239-252, 2019.

267) Mid-Upper Arm Circumference as an Indicator of Undernutrition among Old Age Home and Community Based Elderly in Punjab, India

K. Singh, S. P. Singh, G. Kaur and **K. Bose**.

Care Weekly, Published online September 1 6, 2019, http://dx.doi.org/10.14283/cw.2019.5.

268) Association of body mass index and upper arm body composition with depressive symptoms in old age home and family based elderly.

K. Singh, S.P. Singh, G. Kaur and **K. Bose**.

HOMO – Journal of Comparative Human Biology, 70 (2): 155-162, 2019.

269) Mid-upper arm based nutritional status and body fat pattern among adult Mahalis of Bankura District, West Bengal, India.

K. Bose, M. Ghosh, S. Bhandari and B. K. Kuiti.

Man in India, 99 (3-4): 189-203, 2019.

270) Co-existence of High Levels of Undernutrition and Hypertension among Sabar Males of Purulia, West Bengal, India: A Paradox

K. Das, K. Mukherjee, M. Chanak, S. Pal, S. Ganguli,S. Bagchi and**K. Bose**.

International Journal of Advancement in Life Sciences Research, 2(4) 38-47, 2019.

271) Thinness among rural primary school children of Hooghly District, West Bengal, India.

S. Pal and **K. Bose.**

North Bengal Anthropologist, 7: 85-102, 2019.

272) Comparison ofAge-Related Anthropometric Changes Among Elderly Punjabi Males Residingin Old-Age Homes withThose Residing withTheir Families.

K. Singh, S.P. Singh, G. Kaur and **K. Bose.**

Journal of Anthropological Survey of India, 2020.

DOI: 10.1177/2277436X20905923.

273) Factors Affecting Thinness amongChildren of Purba Medinipur, West Bengal.

P. Khanra, **K. Bose** and J.R. Ghosh

In: Contemporary Issues in Childhood Malnutrition, 169 -184. (Editors: J.R. Ghosh and K. Bose). New York: Nova Science Publications, 2020, ISBN: 9781536173482.

274) Malnutrition and Childhood Infections.

J.R. Ghosh and **K. Bose.**

In: Contemporary Issues in Childhood Malnutrition, 195 -206. (Editors: J.R. Ghosh and K. Bose). New York: Nova Science Publications, 2020, ISBN: 9781536173482.

275) Prevalence of Malnutrition among Rural Bengalee Children of Hooghly District, West Bengal, India.

S. Pal and **K. Bose**.

In: Malnutriiton: Prevalence, Risk Factors and Outcomes, 43 – 72. (Editor: Azizur Rahman).

New York: Nova Science Publications, 2020, ISBN: 9781536175974.

276) Age Trends in Under-nutrition among Sabar Males of Purulia,West Bengal, India.

K. Das, K. Mukherjee, M. Chanak, S. Pal, S. Ganguli,S.S. Bagchi and **K. Bose.**

Journal of Human Ecology, 70(1-3):110-117, 2020.

277) Age Variations and Sexual Dimorphism in Linear BodySegments among Children Aged 2-6-Years of BengaleeEthnicity from Arambagh, West Bengal, India.

G.C. Mandal and **K. Bose**.

Anthropology – Open Journal, 4(1): 15-19, 2020.

278) Ethnicity and Syndrome X.

M. Das and **K. Bose**.

In: Ethnicity and Syndrome X. Chapter 1, pp. 1 – 14. (Editors: Mithun Das and Kaushik Bose).

New York: Nova Science Publications, 2020, ISBN: 978-1-53618-042-8.

279) Prevalence of Undernutrition, Obesity and Hypertension among Adult Shabars and Mahalis of Bankura District of West Bengal, India.

S. Bhandari, S. Biswas, M. Ghosh, B. K. Kuiti and **K. Bose**.

In: Ethnicity and Syndrome X. Chapter 7, pp. 113 – 128. (Editors: Mithun Das and Kaushik Bose).

New York: Nova Science Publications, 2020, ISBN: 978-1-53618-042-8.

280) Undernutrition using Anthropometric Indices among the Bhumij Pre-school Children of West Bengal, India.

B. Mahapatra, S. Pal, **K. Bose** andG. Sahoo.

International Journal of Statistical Sciences, 20 (1): 1–18, 2020.

281) Prevalence and Sex Specific Determinants of Stunting among Rural Primary School Children of Hooghly District, West Bengal, India.

S. Pal and **K. Bose.**

International Journal of Statistical Sciences, 20 (1): 67–86, 2020.

282) Global mid-upper arm circumference cut-offs foradults: a call to action.

Z. Maalouf-Manasseh, S. Remancus, E. Milner, L. Fenlason,T. Quick, C.B.Patsche, **K. Bose**, S. Collins, M. Ververs,S. Walia, J. Escobar-Alegria, M. Chung and A. M. Tang.

Public Health Nutrition, 2020. DOI:10.1017/S1368980020000385.

283) Determining a global mid-upper arm circumference cut-off to assess underweight in adults (men and non-pregnant women).

A. M. Tang, M. Chung, K. R. Dong, P. Bahwere, K. Bose, R. Chakraborty, K. Charlton, P. Das, M. Ghosh, M. Hossain, P. Nguyen, C.B. Patsche, T.Sultana, M. Deitchler and Z.Maalouf-Manasseh.

Public Health Nutrition, 2020.

DOI: https://doi.org/10.1017/S1368980020000397.

284) Socio-Economic and Demographic Influences on Body Mass Index and Thinness among Rural Tribal Adolescent Boys of Kharagpur, West Bengal, India.

P.K. Roy, G.C. Mandal and **K. Bose**.

Saudi Journal of Life Sciences, 5(9): 170-175, 2020.

285) Factors affecting anthropometric failure in urban Bengalee children of Purba Medinipur, West Bengal, India.

P. Khanra, R. Chakraborty and **K. Bose**.

Human Biology Review, 9 (4): 309-327, 2020.

286) Mother's education level is associated with anthropometric failure among 3- to 12-year-old rural

children in Purba Medinipur, West Bengal, India

P. Khanra, K. Bose and R. Chakraborty.

Journal of Biosocial Science, 2020.

doi:10.1017/S0021932020000577.

287) Prevalence of Thinness among tribal preschool children of West Bengal: An assessment measured by BMI Cut Off Points.

B. Mahapatra and **K. Bose.**

Antrocom – Online Journal of Anthropology, 16 (2): 213-222, 2020.

288) Nutritional status among rural tribal adolescent girls of Kharagpur, Paschim Medinipur, West Bengal.

S. Biswas, M. Chanak and **K. Bose.**

North Bengal Anthropologist, 8: 61-86, 2020.

289) Thinness and its association with socio-economic and demographic factors among rural tribal adolescent girls of Kharagpur, West Bengal, India

S. Biswas, G.C. Mandal and **K. Bose**.

Human Biology Review, 10 (1): 1-4, 2021.

290) Age Trends in Anthropometric Characteristics and Nutritional Status among Adult Mahali Females of Bankura District, West Bengal, India.

K. Bose, S. Bhandari, M. Ghosh, B.K. Kuiti, S. Pal and S. Pratihar.

In: West Bengal: Economic , Political and Social Issues. Chapter 3, pp. 81-98.
(Editor: Rihanu Bowell). New York: Nova Science Publishers, 2021, ISBN: 978-1-53619-258-2.

291) Age Variations and Sexual Dimorphism in Adiposity and Body Composition among Tribal Adolescents of Kharagpur, West Bengal, India.
G. C. Mandal, S. Biswas, P. K. Roy and **K. Bose**.
Anthropological Researches and Studies, 11: 65-77, 2021.

292) Ethnic heterogeneity in body composition patterning and CVD risk factors: a multi-ethnic study of Asian Indian Tribes.
G. K. Kshatriya, M. Das and **K. Bose.**
Ethnicity and Health, 2021.
https://doi.org/10.1080/13557858.2021.1910626.

293) The effect of a natural disaster on handgrip strengthin pre-pubertal Indian children exposed to a severe cyclone during the prenatal and early postnatal growth.
S. Kozieł, R. Chakraborty, **K. Bose,** Z. Ignasiak, A. Gomula and N. Nowak-Szczepanska.
Nature – Scientific Reports, 2021.
https://doi.org/10.1038/s41598-021-86845-4.

294) The use of Sitting Height Index of Build to determine undernutrition among rural Bengalee preschool children of West Bengal, India.
G. C. Mandal and **K. Bose.**
Anthropologie, LIX/2, 171 -177, 2021.

295) Composite index of anthropometric failure (CIAF): A better indicator of overall burden of undernutrition among primary school children.
G. C. Mandal and **K. Bose.**
Sri Lanka Journal of Child Health, 2021; **50**(2): 194-199, 2021.

296) Long Antiquity Of Low Resting Metabolism And Recent Shift To Sedentary Lifestyle Leading To Cardiovascular Disease Risk Among South Asians: A Multi-Ethnic Study Of
Asian Indian Tribes. G. K. Kshatriya, M. Das and **K. Bose.**
Journal of Cardiovascular Disease Research, 12(3): 1175-1190, 2021.

B. Book:

1. *A Review of Studies on Central Fat Distribution Among Indians.*
A.B. Das Chaudhuri and **K. Bose**.
Kolkata: *Salmoli Publications*, 2000.

C. Edited Books:

1) *Human Obesity: A Major Health Burden.* Delhi: *Kamla Raj*, 2005. ISBN: 81-85264-39-2.
2) *Ecology, Culture, Nutrition, Health and Disease.* Delhi: *Kamla Raj*, 2006. ISBN: 81-85264-42-2.
3) *Health and Nutritional Problems of Indigenous Populations.* Delhi: *Kamla Raj*, 2008. ISBN: 81-85264-48-1.
4) *Human Malnutrition: Twin Burdens of Undernutrition and Overnutrition.* New York: *Nova Science Publishers*, 2012. ISBN: 978-1-62417-043-0.
5) *Health Consequence of Human Central Obesity*. (Co-Editor: R.Chakraborty). New York: *Nova Science Publishers*, 2014. ISBN: 978-1-63321-152-0.
6) *Panorama of Development: Challenges Ahead.*(Co-Editors: A. Guha and F. Chakraborty). New Delhi: *Concept Publishers*, 2014. ISBN:9789351250180.
7) *Biological Implications of Human Mobility.* (Co-Editors: S. Koziel and R. Chakraborty). New York: *Nova Science Publishers*, 2016. ISBN: 978-1-63485-644-7.
8) *Malnutrition: A Double Burden.* (Co-Editors: N. Mondal and J. Sen). New Delhi: B.R. Publishing Corporation, 2018. ISBN: 978-9-38758-742-7.
9) Obesity and Syndrome X: A Global Public Health Burden. (Co-Editor: M. Das) New York: Nova Science Publishers, 2019. ISBN: 978-1-53614-669-1.
10) *Contemporary Issues in Childhood Malnutrition.* (Co-Editor: J.R. Ghosh). New York: Nova Science Publishers, 2020. ISBN: 9781536173482.
11) *Ethnicity and Syndrome X.* (Co-Editor: M. Das) New York: Nova Science Publishers, 2020. ISBN: 978-1-53618-042-8

CHAPTER 4

BASIC CONCEPTS OF CULTURE ECOLOGY

Dr. Samira Dasgupta.

Culture and environment play significant symbiotic role for human adaptation. Majority of Indian tribes are nurtured in forest environment. The wild flowers blossom infusing the air with their enchanting sweet smell. The tribal are born in the forest, grown in the forest and also die in the forest. Infact forests govern their way of life and culture. Quite naturally indigenous ecological knowledge system is embedded in such human population who is eking out his survival strategy and existence from such ecological niche for his survival and sustenance. The ecological survival of the Indian subcontinent is ultimately linked to the preservation of forest; more than 80 million tribal people of India are still dwelling in the forest. Empirical studies on the isolated and self contained primitive communities taken up by anthropologists have helped in the development of the methods and concepts in the social anthropology. Study of the primitive communities appears to its students to be of practical importance at this age of globalization in India where many primitive people still adhere to their traditional patterns of living, recalling the days of the lithic period (Dasgupta, 1994).

It is already established that ecology plays a vital role in conditioning the culture, life style of a community and the geographical situation of a locale is responsible in shaping the needs, customs, behavior and mental make up of the people. In different ecological settings, different types of cultural traits are expected to be established with distinctive economy, social organization and religious beliefs and practices as the people had to coalesce with the nature to eke out their existence. In one hand it is believed that the environment determines a culture (Ratzel, 1882, Semple, 1911) and on the the other hand it is expected that the environment limits a culture (Kroeber, 1969, Toynbee, 1947, Forde, 1934- reprinted in 1979). Nobody can ignore the impact of environment on life and culture and the inter-relation and inter-dependence between man and his environment. In this regard my personal view is to support the view of Boas (1888) that the culture of the Eskimos who are settled in the arctic environment could not be the same had they lived in an arid zone, is quite tenable. Steward (1955) has also argued that the inter-relationship of a culture, technology and its environment must be studied and analyzed. Steward further asserts that we must look into the nature and degree of exploitation of the available resources by a specific culture. This also naturally leads us to know about the process of cultural adaptation which remains main contention of J.Steward's theme of **'Cultural Ecology'(**Dasgupta, 1994).

Both Wissler (1926) and Kroeber (1939) have explained the inter-relationship between man and his ecology in terms of culture area and human and environmental traits. Steward (1955, 1968), in his concept of Cultural ecology, mentioned that there is a close relationship between the eco-system and some parts of culture which he had termed as culture –core. He further stated three fundamental procedures of cultural ecology—

(a). the relationship between environment and exploitative or productive technology,

(b). the behavior pattern involved, in the exploitation of a particular area by means of particular technology,

(c). the extent to which the behavior pattern entailed in exploiting the environment affect others aspects of culture.

An american anthropologist Clifford Geertz (1968) followed Steward's concept of cultural ecology as a reason of great demographic disparity that exists between Java and the outer islands of Indonesia. Evans-Pritchard (1940)-a leading British social anthropologist showed that there is a relationship between the settlement pattern of the Nuer pastoralists of the Sudan to the seasonal changes in resource availability. Further, Marvin Harris (1966) in his work, following Steward's concept of cultural ecology, refers to the techno-environmental determinism. According to him cultural evolution occurs through the technological means of adaptation to the environment. He asserts that all forms of culture including the religious beliefs are determined by the relationship between technology and environment. Sahlin (1969) showed that human beings have sufficient capacity to adapt the ecology for the sake of their existence. In words of Redfield (1955) , "man and nature are the twin-agents of the perennial revolution that shapes the face of the earth". Sidney Mintz (1956), Eric Wolf (1957) and Morton Fried (1959), in some of their works showed how culture ecology links emic phenomena with the etic conditions of nature. Anderson (1973) thinks that cultural traits or structures could be understood by analyzing socio-cultural environmental adaptations.

Vayda and Roy Rappopart (1968) suggested that attention should be given on the relationship of a specific human population to specific eco-system in studying culture ecology. An eco-system consists of all the living organisms and non-living environmental elements such as soil, water, climate etc. which interact with each other within a spatially defined area.

Barth (1969) in his study of ecological relationship of ethnic groups in Swat, North Pakistan stated that the distribution of population in a specific ecological niche is dependent on how a particular community is able to exploit it.

In India Vidyarthi (1963) through his studies among the' Maler' divided the tribal communities into four cultural types on the basis of their ecological setting, analytically he described how nature guides man's culture.

Mann (1981) has shown in his study "Animism , economy, ecology and change among Negrito hunters and gatherers" that the inter-relatedness of ecology with economy, religion and social life of Onge tribe of Little Andaman Island.

Morab (1981) examined Vidyarthi's concept of nature-man-spirit complex in his study—"The Soliga : A Study in ecology, society and religion of a Hill tribe in South India" and came to the conclusion that there is a harmony between ecology, economy and society.

Before going into detail let us allow describing the development of the school of cultural adaptation through ecological anthropology.

II

Human ecology, most broadly speaking as the study of human interactions with the environment.

In this lecture alternative conceptual models of human relations with the environment are being described in the historical order in which they have appeared in the scientific literature.

Although largely described among social scientists, classical and early modern theories of environmental influence on human affairs i.e. **determinism** and **possibilism**, are often employed by historians like Arnold J. Toynbee, who advocates a possibilist stance in his book---*A Study of History*.

The **model of Cultural ecology** proposed by Julian Steward is still the guiding paradigm for many among us but in recent years it has been challenged by the **Ecosystem- based model** first proposed by Andrew P. Vayda and Roy A . Rappaport.

The individual making characteristic is the focus of **Actor-based model** of human ecology and the **systems model of human ecology** stresses investigation of interaction between human social systems and ecosystems based on their reciprocal exchange of energy, materials and information (i.e. the human social system is seen as being linked to its ecosystem through the interchange of energy, materials and information).

III

Origin of Human Ecology

- Since early days there have been many attempts to explain events in terms of environmental influences on human behavior. Astrology represents one early system of thought relating environmental forces i.e. stars / planet, to human actions.
- With modern scientific thought the ancient Greek Philosophers recognized that man was both influenced by nature and a force for change in the environment. It was suggested, for example,that the different forms of political organization of the Greek city states and the eastern empires reflected the influence of climate on the personalities of their citizens.
- This theme later was developed by **Montesquieu** and other French writers of the Enlightment and advocated in recent times by the American Geographer **Samuel Huntington**.
- The ecological **Catastrophe writing** during **1880's by George P. Marsh, entitled 'Man and Nature or, Physical Geography as Modified by Human Action'.**
- It was only with the development of geography and anthropology as scientific disciplines in the later part of 19th century that human

/ culture ecology became the subject of systemic study. The first theoretical approach is Environmental determinism.

IV

Ecological anthropology may be defined as the study of the relations among the population dynamics, social organization and culture of human population and the environment in which they live (Orlove, 1980). "It presents the development of ecological anthropology, not as a smooth accumulation of information and insights, but as a series of stages" (Orlove, 1980). "The first stage is characterized by the work of Steward and White, the second is termed neo-functionalism and neo-evolutionism and third one is called processual ecological anthropology" (Orlove, 1980).

The German-Austrian continental diffusionists are considered superior to British School in their outlook, methodology and ideology. Freidrich Ratzel was one of such scholars in German School. He was basically zoologist but soon he turned towards geography and then to anthropology. He wrote many volumes on anthropo-geography. German School of diffusion owes its origin to Ratzel. He made a clear-cut distinction between territorial geography and social geography, which he called as anthropo-geography. According to him, environment plays an important adaptive role. He was nevertheless convinced that people were more influenced by one another than by factors of climate and terrain.

"Anthropologists in America led by Boas questioned the unilinearity of the evolutionary thought and the assumption of progress inherent in evolution". (ibid, 1980). The American diffusionists received idea from their German friends and, therefore, it is said that in the American Culture Area Theory of diffusion was influenced by the Museum Methodology of German School of Diffusion. Boas, the father of American ethnology, was born and educated in Germany. German diffusionists were followers of Cultural Circle School or Cultural Historic School, talked about complex form of diffusion of culture but they failed to explain as to why diffusion took place. Here American diffusionists attempted to solve this question. On the basis of empirical researches, they discredited the universal sequences established by the classical evolutionists. They were of view that the empirical researches were evident to refer to that give and take of culture traits and culture complex had taken place through the medium of transport and communication. In order to show the diffusion of cultural traits and complexes, the American diffusionists devised a methodology known as culture area approach. They did not analyze cultural diffusion prevalent all over the world at the same time; instead, they divided the world into different cultural areas on the basis of geographical regions. They were of the opinion that geographical aspects of culture could not be ignored in the study of culture area. Thus, according to them, the concept of culture area reveals geographical area of cultural similarities. Under the influence of geographical categories, the American Museum of Natural History, New York and the Field Museum, Chicago decided simultaneously to use geographical categories instead of evolutionary trends in the museum, in order to get better insight by the museum visitors. The teachers of Boas were trained physicists and mathematicians from whom he learnt many theoretical concepts and applied them in anthropological field. He joined an arctic expedition of Baffinland, North America, as a geographer in 1883-84. With the passage of time, a definite central theme "historical particularism" has come to be associated with Boasion period.

The scholars accepted the interest in cultural process and change but looked more prudently for details of each case of cultural change, examining whether traits were diffused or independently invented and how they were reworked by each culture that adopted them. The school that they formed was named historical particularism. In fact, ecological anthropology emerged from the Boasian School of Historical Particularism.

Steward's work in ecological anthropology due to contact with noted geographer Carl Sauer led him to examine the effect of environment on culture. His method of cultural ecology signifies materialist emphasis. This method entails the study of the relation between certain feature of the environment and certain traits of the culture possessed by the people living in that environment. Within the environment, Steward emphasized the quality, quantity and distribution of resources. The aspects of culture that he examined most closely were technology, economic arrangements, social organization and demography, although he also included other aspects. Steward stressed the fact that the environment influenced only certain elements of a culture, which he termed the 'culture-core".

"Leslie White's relation to Boasian tradition was somewhat different. White shared Steward's emphasis on culture as the unit of analysis and his interest in cultural evolution, his partitioning of culture into technological, social and ideological components gave him a materialist stance generally similar to Steward's. White was more concerned with the broad details of evolution than with specific adaptations, however, he also directed relatively little attention to the influence of environment on particular cultures. Instead he emphasized levels of energy use as the determinant of cultural evolution" (Orlove, 1980).

There are certain fundamental differences in the approaches of White and Steward. The former may be called universal evolutionist who defined cultural evolution culturally (and not biologically) while the later was a multilinear evolutionist who adopted a functional approach to comprehend the interrelationship of ecology, technology and other aspects of culture. White's primary thrust has been on 'technology' whereas Steward's major emphasis has been on 'ecology'. Nevertheless, both represent an American trend to reconsider the importance of evolutionism in the post-1935 era.

In the second stage of ecological anthropology there are two main trends: (i) neo-evolutionists who claimed both White and Steward's were correct, and (ii) neo-functionalists who claimed that they were both wrong.

The neo-functionalists established a series of evolutionary stages and used the notions of specific and general evolution to accommodate Steward's method of cultural ecology to White's work on unilinear evolution (ibid, 1980).

Marvin Harris and the early work of Andrew Vayda and Roy Rappaport represent the neo-functionalist school. The term 'neo-functionalism' signifies "the social organization and culture of specific populations as functional adaptations which permit the populations to exploit their environments successfully without exceeding their carrying capacity" (ibid, 1980). "In general, neo-functionalists explain specific aspects of social organization and culture in terms of functions which they serve in adapting local populations to their environments" (ibid, 1980).

Both neo-evolutionists and neo-functionalists have examined the mechanisms which link social structure and culture to the environment.

Apart from the neo-evolutionist and neo-functionalist schools, a different approach in the arena of ecological anthropology has begun to emerge. This work will be called "processual ecological anthropology". The use of the term "process" refers to the importance of diachronic studies in ecological anthropology and to the need to examine mechanism of change. The term "processual ecological anthropology" signifying current developments in the field does appear to be new. Important trends are: (a) the examination of the relation of demographic variables and production system, (b) the response of populations to environmental stress, (c) the formation and consolidation of adaptive strategies which follow Barth's early work on the use of the concept of the niche, and (iv) new work in Marxism, including the emerging interest of anthropologists in political economy and structural Marxism (Orlove, 1980).

A number of comprehensive treatments of environmental thinking in anthropology and the environment vs. culture controversy have been complied by cultural anthropologists who have found that an ecological approach is fruitful both in research and teaching

(Anderson, 1973; Hardesty, 1977, Vayda and Rappaport, 1968). The framework for these reviews has been provided by some contrasting major schools of thoughts or conceptual approaches, viz., environmental determinism, environmental possibilism, cultural ecology of Steward, and current ecological anthropology including actor-based model, eco-system-based model, ethno-ecology and systems-ecology model, etc.

Environmental Determinism

In this concept, it is said that environment of a particular area determines its culture directly. The founders of this concept are Ratzel (1889), Semple (1911), etc. They all believed that humans were completely the product of their environment that is, human culture and behavior were caused directly by environmental influences. For example, the British were a nation of seafarers because they were an island dwelling community surrounded by seas ; the Arabs were monotheistic Muslims because living in the vast empty desert turned their minds towards a single God ; the Eskimos were primitive nomads because the harsh conditions of their arctic habitat forbade their development into a complex civilization and so on.

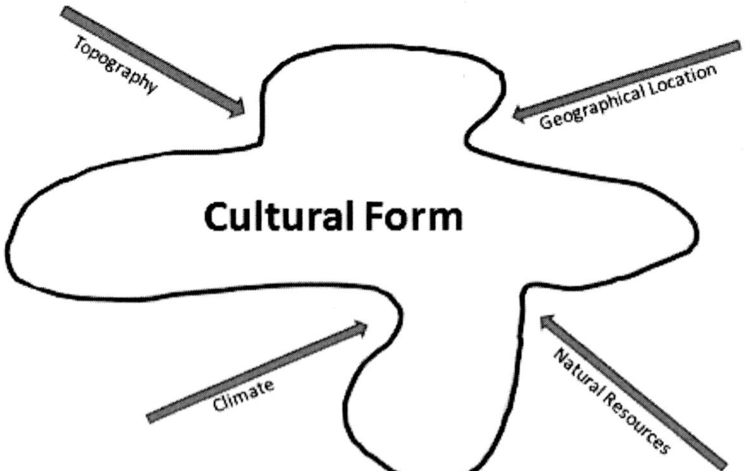

The Model of Environmental Determinism

Environmental Possibilism

In this concept, environment limits the possibilities of cultural development but not directly determines the culture of a particular area. Kroeber (1939), Toynbee (1947) and Forde (1934) are the believers of this thought.

Its proponents asserted that while the environment did not directly cause specific cultural developments, the presence or absence of specific environmental factors placed limits or such developments by either permitting or forbidding their occurrence. Thus island peoples could be seafarers but residents of Inner – Mongolia could not be ; inhabitants of temperate regions might practice agriculture, but those living in arctic latitudes could not. The value of the possibilist approach was perhaps best cited by the American Anthropologist A.L.Kroeber who showed that the Indians of northwestern North America could not adapt maize cultivation from their southern neighbours because the frost- free growing season in their region was shorter than the four months required time for the maize plant to attain maturity. Their environment thus limited the ability of their culture to evolve in an agricultural direction.

The British Anthropologist Daryll Forde concluded in his book *–Habitat, Economy and Society (1934)* which was perhaps the last major scientific exploration of Possibilism, " **between the physical environment and human activity there is always a middle term, a collection of specific objectives and values, a body of knowledge and belief, in other words, a cultural pattern".**

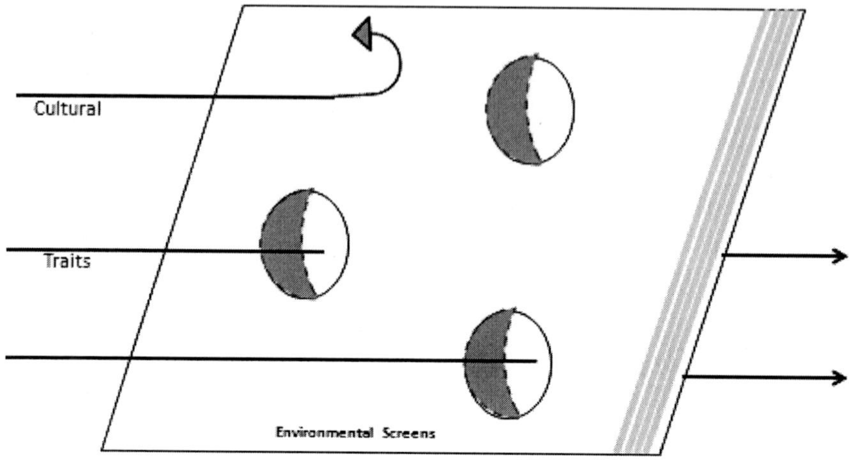

The Model of Environmental Possibilism

The Concept of Culture Ecology

The founder of the concept is Steward (1955). Ecological anthropology emerged from Boasian school of historical particularism. According to Steward, the interaction between environment and technology is related with the core of culture, which includes the population structure, economy, and socio-political structure. Before Steward, all the scientists used to limit their concept on the material culture. Geertz (1963) and Harris (1966) also followed the model of cultural ecology developed by Steward.

(** **According to Steward** ***Culture Core means those feature of a culture that are most closely related to subsistence***).

Steward experience of field work among the SHOSHONE hunters and gatherers in the Great Basin of North America had led him to recognize that ecological adaptation had played at least as significant a role as diffusion in the formation of Shoshone culture. It was Steward view that not all aspects of Shoshone culture, could be explained in ecological terms –many traits were present as simply the accidental result of diffusion from neighbouring tribes—but that only some elements, which he labeled as ' Culture Core ', had adaptive significance. He gave special emphasis to the relationship between technology and the environment in his model of Cultural ecology.

The implicit feed-back conception in this concept –"how the adaptation to the physical environment had an influence on other features of culture and to determine whether similar adjustments occur in similar environments and to trace these historically through a succession of very unlike periods".

Therefore, the method of cultural ecology then involved the analysis of :

1. The interrelationship between environment and exploitative or productive technology
2. The interrelationship between **behavior** patterns and exploitative technology,
3. The extent to which those "behavior" patterns affect other sectors of culture

C. The Model of Cultural Ecology (J. Steward)

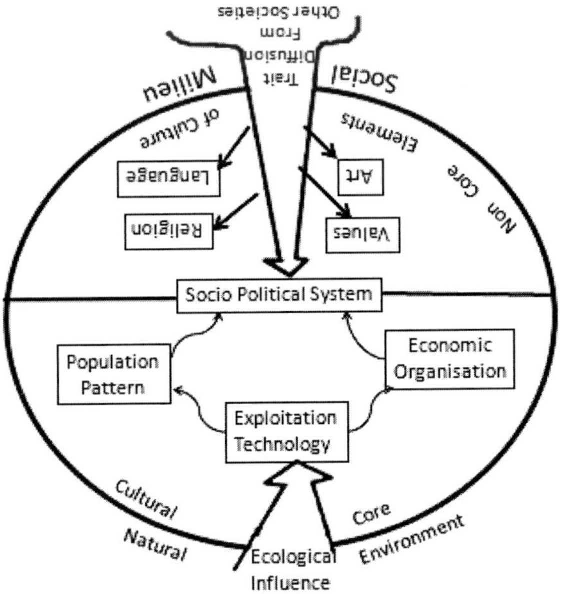

Andrew Vayda and Roy Rappaport (1968) while recognizing the importance of Steward's contribution, have criticized his approach as being inadequate.

Cultural Ecosystemicism by Geertz, Clifford (1963) approach influenced many cultural ecologist and prehistory. Here interdependence of culture and physical factors is the primary postulate.

Cultural Ecosystemicism

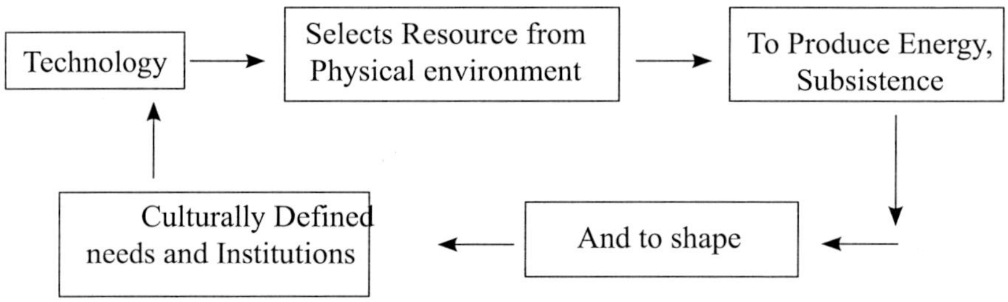

The fundamental weakness of the concept of the cultural ecology is revealed in the work of Marvin Harris—an American anthropologist who has incorporated this approach into studies of what he refers as ' **techno-environmental determinism'**, means, technological means of adaptation to the environment is the prime mover of cultural evolution. In his paper " **The Cultural Ecology of India's Sacred Cattle"(1966)** Harris argues that, contrary to the accepted view that Hindus keep excessive numbers of useless cattle because of their religious belief that cattle are sacred, these cows are actually extremely important to the economic welfare of the poor peasants , helping them to make maximum use of the scarce resources of their environment. Therefore, he concludes, the religious beliefs must have been caused by **techno-environmental** factors.

Ecosystem-based Model

Vayda (1968, 1969) and Rappaport (1968) suggested that instead of studying how cultures are adapted to the environment, attention should be focused on the relationship of specific human population to specific ecosystem. In their view, human beings constitute simply another population among the many populations of plants and animal species that interact with each other with the non-living components (climate, soil, water) of their local ecosystem. Thus, the ecosystem, rather than culture, constitutes the fundamental unit of analysis in their conceptual framework for human ecology.

The ecosystem based model of human ecology is illustrated by Roy Rappaport's well known book--- *Pigs for the Ancestors* (1968) in which he attempted to demonstrate how the religious rituals practiced by the Tsembaga tribal group of New Guinea functioned to maintain their population in balance with the available resources of their environment. Religion, an institution that Steward had largely excluded from his concept of ecologically adaptive cultural core, was seen by Rappaport as playing a key regulatory role in relations between the Tsembaga population and the other components of their eco system.

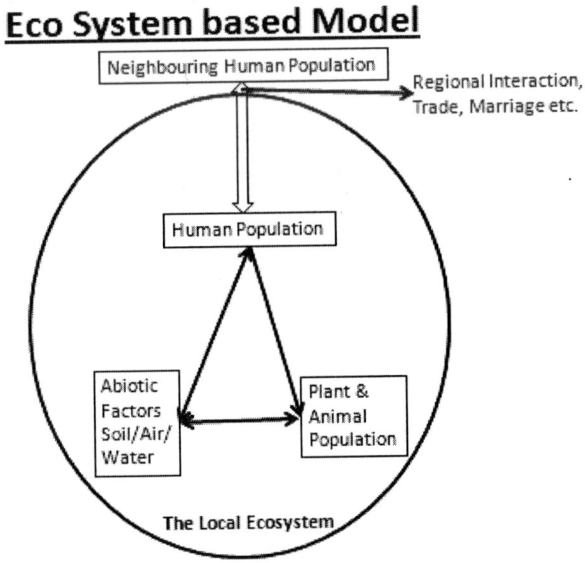

Actor-based Model

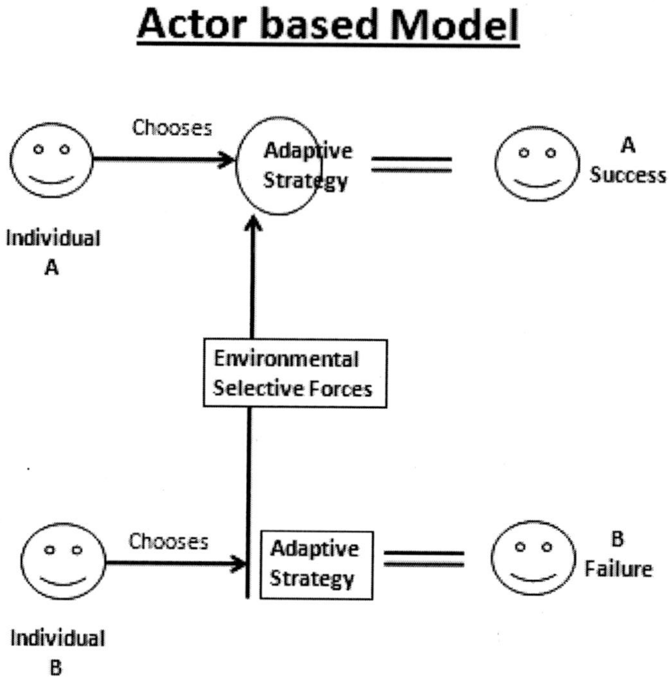

The adaptation occurs primarily at the individual level rather than at the level of group, population and social system. The founder of this model is Benjamin Orlove (1980). This model emphasized the process by which the people make decision about how to interact with their environment.

In the case of human society, environmental adaptation is seen as occurring not as the result of natural selection on the cultural or social system level but rather as the result of the thousands of individual decisions about how best to interact with the environment. Individuals are assumed to be making choices constantly about how to exploit available resources while coping with environmental hazards. Those who make the "correct " choices will survive and prosper ; those who choose less wisely will be selected against.

The actor-based model of human ecology is thus one of limited applicability. It can reveal a great deal about why individuals within a particular social system make the particular choices about interactions with the environment that they do, but cannot explain why their social system presents them with particular choices it does. **Hence, System Model of human ecological approach emerged.**

System Model

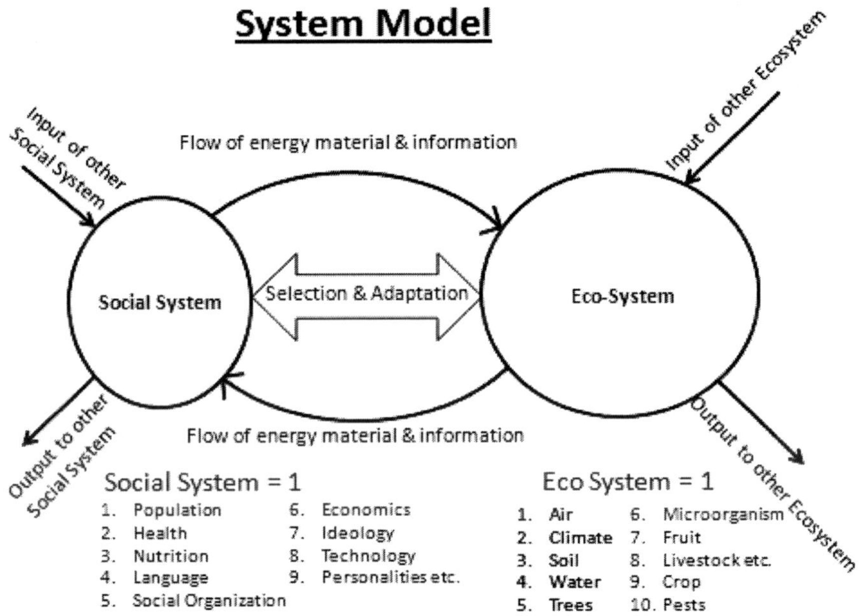

A major scientific development in recent years has been the formulation of "General System Theory", which is concerned with the general properties of the structures and functions of systems as such rather than with their specific contents; adaptation and selection through interaction between ecosystem and social systems (Greetz, 1963; Rambo, 1983). Ecosystem includes water, soil, climate, flora, fauna, fish, pet livestock, crops, trees etc, and social system includes social organization, nutrition, health, population, technology, economy, religious values, language etc. In the system model of human ecology, both the social system and the ecosystem with which the population interacts retain their integrity as systems, with each changing its structural configuration according to its internal dynamics.

Geertz believes that the concept of the ecosystem or ecological system is the constant interplay between culture , biology, and environment. Theoretically, the ecological system is a **dynamic set of relationships between living and non-living things through which energy flows** and materials cycle and because of which other problems of survival are worked out.

Thus, **System ecology is the study of systemic relationship between living and non- living things.**

Ethno-ecology

The differences between the approach and philosophy adopted by ethno-ecology and by systems ecology orientation in anthropology are so great as to make it appear, perhaps, inappropriate to discuss them under the same heading. **Ethno-ecologist has produced detailed and excellent data on how people in different societies categorize their environment** (Conklin, 1954; Frake, 1962). Vayda and Rappaport (1968) also are in favour of an ethno-ecological approach. Ethno-ecology is essentially a research strategy and a number of anthropologists who have used an etic and systematic theoretical orientation have sought to introduce rigour into their fieldwork by adopting in part an ethno-ecological approach (Knight, 1974).

New Ethnography

In the post-1950 era, the anthropologists have been more interested in cognitive anthropology or structural anthropology or new ethnography. The major thrust has been to understand the structure of the culture and to know about the cognitive structuring of the culture. In the formation of culture or the structure of the culture, geography has influenced immensely and therefore, a thorough assessment of cognitive aspect of ecology has been found to be useful for the study of culture. In this, the **new ethnography has relied more on the insiders cognition than an outsiders interpretation**. This often is called as ethno-science.

References

Anderson, James N 1973. "Ecological Anthropology and Anthropological Ecology", in Hand Book of Social and Cultural Anthropology (ed). John J. Honigmann, Chicago: Rand Mc nally & co.

Barth, Fredrik 1969. "Ecologic relationship of Ethnic groups in Swat, North Pakistan", in Environment and Cultural Behaviour, (ed). Andrew P. Vayda, New York : The Natural History Press.

Bennett, John W. 1976. The Ecological Trasition: Cultural Anthropology and Human adaptation, New York: Pergamon Press Inc.

Boas, Franz 1888. The Central Eskimo, Washington: Smithsonian Institution.

Conklin, H.C. 1954. A"An Ethno-ecological Approach to shifting Agriculture," New York Academy of Sciences, Transactions, Vol. 17, No.2. pp.133-42.

Dasgupta, Samira 1994. Birjia: Society and Culture (A Study in Cultural Ecological Perspective), Calcutta : Firma KLM Pvt. Ltd.

Ellen , Roy 1982 Environment, Subsistence and System: : The Ecology of Small Scale Social Formation, Cambridge : Cambridge University Press

Evans-Pritchard, E.E. 1940. The Nuer, New York : Oxford University Press.

Forde, G.D. 1934 (reprinted in 1979). Habitat, Economy and Society, London: Methuen & Co. Ltd.

Frake, C.O. 1962. "Cultural Ecology and Ehnography", American Anthropoligist, Vol. 64.

Geertz C. 1963. Agricultural Involution: The Process of Ecological Change in Indonesia, Berkeley, Univ. of California Press.

Hardesty, D.L. 1977. Ecological Anthropology, New York : John Wiley & Sons

Knight, C.G. 1974. "Ethno-Science as a Research Paradigm; in Language in Anthropology, (ed). W.C. Mecormack and S.A. Wurm, Mouton: The Hague.

Kroeber, A.L. 1939. Cultural and Natural areas of Native North America, Berkeley: University of California Press.

Kroeber, A..L. 1969. "Relations of Environmental and Cultural Factors", in Environment and Cultural Behaviour (ed). Andrew P.Vayda, New York : The Natural History Press.

Mann, R.S. 1981. "Animism, Economy, Ecology and Change among Negrito Hunters and Gatherers", in Nature Man Spirit Complex in Tribal India (ed). R.S.Mann, New Delhi: Concept Publishing Company.

Morab, S.G. 1981. "The Soliga: A Study in Ecology, Society and Religion of a Hill Tribe in South India", in Nature Man Spirit Complex in Tribal India (ed). R.S.Mann, New Delhi: Concept Publishing Company.

Morton H. Fried. 1959. Readings in Anthropology, New York: Crowell.

Rambo, A.Terry 1983 "Conceptual Approaches to Human Ecology", Research Report, No.14, Honolulu Hawaii : East-West Environment and Policy Institute.

Ratzel. F. 1899 (Orig. 1882). Anthropogeographic, Stuttgart: J.E. Engelhorn.

Redfield, Robert. 1955. The Little Community, Chicago: Chicago University Press.

Sarkar, Amitabha and Samira Dasgupta, 2000. Ethno-Ecology of Indian Tribes : Diversity in Cultural Adaptation, Jaipur and New Delhi: Rawat Publications.

Semple, E.C. 1911. Influences of Geographic : On the Basis of Ratzel's System of Anthropo-Geography, New York: Henry Hott.

Steward, J.H. 1955. Theory of Culture Change, Urbana : University of Illinois Press.

Steward, J.H., Robert A.Manners, Eric R.Wolf, Elena Padilla Seda, Sidney W. Mintz and Raymond L. Schecle. 1956. The People of Puerto Rico : A Study in Social Anthropology, Urbana : University of Illinois Press.

Toynbee, A.J. 1947. A Study of History (abridgement of Vol. I—VI), New York: Oxford University Press.

Vayda, A.P. and R.A. Rappaport. 1968. " Ecology: Culture and Non-cultural", in Introduction to Cultural Anthropology (ed). J.A. Clipton, Boston: Houghton Mifflin Co.

Vidyarthi, L.P. 1963. The Maler: Nature-Man-Spirit Complex, Calcutta: Book Land.

Wissler, Clark. 1926. The Relation of Nature to Man in Aboriginal America , New York: Oxford University Press.

Wolf, E.R. 1957. ' Closed Corporate Communities in Mesoamerica and Java', in Southwestern Journal of Anthropology, Vol.13. No.1.

CHAPTER 5

STUDY OF TRADITIONAL KNOWLEDGE FOR SUSTAINABLE DEVELOPMENT (EMPIRICAL OBSERVATION ON ASUR)

Dr. Samira Dasgupta and Dr. Amitabha Sarkar.

Indigenous or Traditional Knowledge (I.K or T.K.) refers to the unique, traditional, local knowledge existing within & developed around the specific condition of women & men indigenous to a particular geographic area. The development of TK/IK systems, covering all aspects of life, including management of natural resources have been a matter of survival to the people who generated these systems. It is based on experience, often tested over centuries and adapted to local culture, environment & dynamics. Other names for TK/1K are local knowledge, folk knowledge, indigenous technical knowledge and traditional ecological knowledge.

Rural people have an intimate knowledge of many aspects of their surroundings and their daily life is governed as per the dictum of such knowledge. Over centuries, people have learned how to grow food and to survive even in difficult environments. They possess knowledge of varieties of crops to cultivate in a same plot considering the nature of soil and its water retention capacity, when to sow and weed, which plants, tubers and mushroom are poisonous and which can be used for medicine,(i.e. particular part of the plant), how to cure diseases and how protect or preserve their environment in harmonious manner and in sustainable fashion.

This TK/IK covers a wide range of subject such as agriculture, food preparation, education, institutional management, natural resource management, health care and many other allied disciplines.

IK is stored in people's memories and activities and is expressed in the form of stories, songs, folklore, proverbs, dances, myth, cultural values, beliefs, rituals, community laws, local language and taxonomy agricultural practices, equipment, materials, plant species and animal breeds. IK is shared and communicated orally by specific examples and through culture. It may be noted that IK is not confined to tribal groups or the original inhabitants of an area; it is not even confined to rural people, rather any community may possesses indigenous knowledge –among the rural / urban / settled / nomadic / and migrants too.

Learning from IK can improve understanding of local conditions and provide a productive context for activities designed to help the communities. Yet IK is still an underutilized resource in the development activities. Special efforts are needed to understand, document and disseminate IK for preservation, transfer or adoption elsewhere.

The holders of indigenous/traditional knowledge and initial conservers of biodiversity in rural India remain marginalized and poor while on the other hand those who use their heritage knowledge bank and material in commercial way through bio-technological enterprises are not only rich but well established in society. Now time has come to recognize the primary conservers of biodiversity for possessing and maintaining this knowledge bank over generations.

In order to understand the difference between IK and TK, the working definition following Kamal. K. Misra (2007) is taken into consideration. While defining indigenous knowledge, he has listed the following characteristics:

Indigenous knowledge is local and culture-specific; it is orally transmitted through imitation and demonstration; it is the consequence of practical engagement in everyday life and is constantly reinforced by experience, trial and error and deliberate experiment; it tends to be empirical and empirico-hypothetical rather than theoretical in the strict sense; it is 'people's science' and is asymmetrically distributed in a population; the organization of indigenous knowledge is essentially functional, denotative 'know-how' geared to practical response and performance; and it is holistic, integrative and situated within broader cultural traditions.

Traditional Knowledge and indigenous knowledge are often used as synonyms. However, indigenous knowledge is more confined to a group or locality, while traditional knowledge can be indigenous or non-indigenous for the practicing community. Hence, we would prefer the term Traditional Knowledge. Knowledge, which is collectively held from experience and transmitted inter-generationally is defined as TK. It is expressed through environmental knowledge;

a. Knowledge on the natural environment,
b. Knowledge on human modified environment.

Knowledge on social environment includes knowledge on self and others including knowledge about social organization and conflict management (legal knowledge), agricultural knowledge, knowledge on health and hygiene, traditional technical knowledge (TTK) religious knowledge, cultural interpretations of landscape etc. Some of this knowledge remains secret to their custodians, while many other forms of knowledge are expressed in public domain and shared within and beyond the boundary of the community. Thus traditional knowledge is holistic, comprehensive, context sensitive, culturally compatible, environmentally viable and located within broader cultural traditions of the practicing communities. It is generally transmitted orally and through body centric performances and conservation ethics are often part of traditional knowledge.

Traditional Knowledge for Sustenance among the Asur

Human society is dynamic and it's culture is expressed through tangible and intangible forms. In the tangible forms of culture one can observe and even touch the objects while the intangible forms of culture can be felt through one's empathy and expressed through folklore, myth, riddle, and also through performing art forms etc. These are all included in intangible expression of a culture. Through all those tangible and intangible forms the indigenous knowledge and traditional knowledge are described.

Though apparently the term traditional knowledge (TK) and indigenous knowledge (IK) are synonymous to each other but in course of our empirical study among various communities of India it has emerged that there lies very subtle difference between these two. Traditional knowledge (TK) is a holistic Knowledge of a community for his sustainable living while indigenous knowledge (IK) is usually very much local knowledge embedded in the community of a particular geographical terrain and very much unique to specific cultural group.

"Since the early 1990's, IK has been a fertile ground for research, exploring the ways in which it is stored in peoples memories and activities and expressed in stories, songs folk lore, proverbs, dances, myths, cultural values, beliefs, rituals, community laws, local languages and taxonomy, agricultural practices, equipments, materials, plant species and animal breeds etc. Attention is also being paid to how it is shared and communicated orally with specific examples and through culturally accepted ways of communication."(Misra, Kamal Kant; 2007).

Perhaps the most important outcome of the research on IK is to document the best practices and to replicate them in other places and communities. But there are many inherent problems in this exercise in this age of patenting, bio- piracy and Intellectual Property Rites (IPR). (ibid, 2007).

It is important to study indigenous knowledge as it is the local knowledge and the people (both permanent settlers and migrants) of a particular place have their own traditional knowledge. Now how the people of that particular region are adjusting to the local ecological condition responsible for growing of socio-economic life of that particular region applying either of or both traditional knowledge and indigenous knowledge suitable to a particular situation, is to be exnaustively examined.

In the present study the authors have done their work among the Asur-a primitive tribe of Chotanagpur area of Jharkhand state of India. They live in the Netarhat Plateau, in the midst of forest of Gumla and Latehar Districts at 3600 feet height above sea level, where it is very difficult to reach. Among their villages some are Jovipat, Lodapat, Amtipani, Chhattasarai, Bhatthi pat/Bhatipat, Naoatola, Kujam, Chapakona, Chotongpat, Kone, Komepat, Gorapahar, Khairipat, Sakhuapani, Polpolpat, Ramjharia, Pirhapat, Chakdipa, Kotia, Sonaitangar, Garhatoli, Kulhukona, Tiluwari, Dokapat, Lopungpat, Bijapat Bhariapat, etc. These all are situated in Gumla District. In Latehar district, Husumbu is the only one village where Asurs live. Here the investigators are interested to see how far the Asur are adjusting to their local niche with the help of local or indigenous knowledge even after they had to shift to other economic pursuits leaving their own traditional callings of iron smelting and slash and burn cultivation. Here it is necessary to mention that they have not totally forgotten or abandoned their own traditional knowledge rather they also apply it when and where it is necessary, applicable and also suitable.

There are several opinions on the term Asur. Leuva (1963: 3) was with opinion that they have similarities with Ashur in Assyria mean 'powerful people'. There is mention of Asur in several places of Rigveda, Upanishad and even in the epic Ramayana where they were mentioned as great builders. They also opine that they are the descendants or children of Asur of Ramayana who were cursed by Ravana originally their forefather and the king of Lanka to become dull and worthless as they fought against Ravana taking the side of Ram and also for killing their own brother, who was with Ravana. They are sure that due to his curse they are in the present state without any progress in a miserable condition.

Roy Bahadur S.C. Roy (1926) wrote that the Asur are divided into three sections namely Soikia Asur or Agaria, Birjia and Asur (Dasgupta; 1994). They also introduce themselves as Bir Asur. They claim that they are superior among the three groups and very strong and well-built just like Hanumanji and they call Birjias as Bandar whom they give a very low status. They told that they were originally the inhabitants of Patan of Sarguja district of Chhattishgarh. They used to do iron smelting work as their traditional calling where they used young Sal trees to generate heat (about 1500 degree Celsius) to melt stone containing iron-ore. One-day the king of Patan got irritated with the smoke of that burning wood and ordered his chiefs to drive out all the Asurs from his, state. As a result, they were forced to leave the place and migrated to nearby Gumla and Palamau region and ultimately settled to the Netarhat Plateau of the region.

The Asur informants told that once upon a time they were in dispute resulting to fight with their Oraon neighbours in the issue of their land. As a result they were defeated and had to leave their land and habitat and ultimately forced to leave Sarguja and settlein their present habitat at Netarhat Plateau.

According to 1991 census the Asur are 10712 in number and their literacy rate is 10.66. Traditionally they are iron smelter. Along with iron smelting, they also used to do slash and burn cultivation. Hunting and collection from jungle were also very much important. Gradually they had to shift from iron smelting and slash and burn cultivation to settled cultivation. They had totally left iron smelting but could not totally stop slash burn cultivation. Hunting became an occasional and primarily a festive phenomenon. At present along with settled cultivation they do collection of various edible roots, fruits, tubers, mushroom, seeds etc and several non-edible items for their materialuse.

They are an endogamous community having atleast sixteen exogamous totemistic clans. Some of those are Indwar, Beng, Toppo, and Tiyigo etc. The tradition of child marriage in the community is presently replaced by adult marriage. As usual like their other neighbouring tribes they are very much afraid of the malevolent deities roaming in their vicinity. To keep them quiet they resort to several rituals and magical performances. Along with those, several benevolent deities are also there who they believe are their protecting deities. Though they have totally stopped iron smelting work but could not stop *Sansikutasi* ritual attached with their iron smelting work.

The present in-depth empirical study was carried out at Sakhuapani village of Bishunpur block of Gumla district, Jharkhand. It is a more or less uniethnic Asur village. In the northern outskirt of the village there are bauxite mines where a few villagers are involved as wage earners. On the east of the village, there is a village named Jovipat, in west Dumberpat and at the south Amtipani and Ramjhoria villages are situated. Infact all the mentioned villages are situated in Gumla district. For substantiating our empirical observation we also collected quantitative data from Dodhikona tola of Husumboo village; it is a multi-ethnic village under Mahuadanr block of Latehar district. In addition to this, we also collected data from Ramjhoria and Jovipat villages.

The Asur villages are found situated either on *pat* or table land area or in *garha* or gorge area, such as Ramjhoria village is situated at gorge. There are altogether 25 Asur villages with a total 755 families in Bishunpur block of Gumla district and found chiefly in Jovipat, Dumberpat panchyat. It is also reported that altogether 1188 Asur families live in Gumla district and they are distributed in Ghaghra, Bishunpur, Chainpur, and Dumbri and Raidih blocks of the district.

The village Sakhuapani is about 35 Km away from Netarhat-the base camp of our present investigation. The village roads are jeepable but kutchha. There is no electricity. For drinking water they depend on well and a tube well. There is one *anganbari* school and a residential secondary school, which is purely for tribal boys. There is one Asur teacher in the school who hails from this village, named, Tipun Asur. On the southeast corner of the village hillock there is *sarna* (Sacred grove). Apparently the soil condition of the village is full of laterite. There is no primary health centre in the village while these are available in Netarhat and in the block headquarter of Mahuadanr, and Bishunpur block. The nearest hat or weekly market is at Dumberpat on Saturday, it is hardly 4 Km. away on foot through forest and hill slopes, and at Netarhat on Wednesday, which is about 35 Km away. Jovipat village hat is on Thursday, about 22 km away and Banari hat is on Monday and Friday which is at the foot hills of Netarhat and is about 30 km away. The bus stoppage from the village is about 10 Km away.

Methodology:

The investigators employed standard anthropological techniques in collecting the empirical data, that is, door-to-door approach for household survey, which is followed by collection of genealogies. This not only helped them to have a good rapport in the village but also to get authentic data from the informants who enthusiastically, curiously and very joyfully without any hesitation gave data on change of occupation, marriage distance, nature of marital alliance and impact of developmental programmes. All these are easily ascertained through this method. Apart from this, group interviews as well as focused interviews were done along with verification and authenticity of collected data. Fieldwork was carried out from December.2008 to January 2009.

A demographic profile among the Asur of Sakhuapani village is presented in order to understand the Sex Ratio, level of Literacy, family Size, nature of their families, marital status and Economic pursuits of Asur which clearly give significance of instability in their economic life and till date forest plays a key role in their subsistence activities. Inspite of the total change over from traditional economic pursuit of **iron smelting** work to **settled agriculture** in this plateau it does not provide their bare subsistence throughout the year and they are compelled to involve themselves in other locally available subsidiary means of livelihood and this is clearly depicted in the table of economic pursuit.

It appears that main economic pursuits among the Asur are Agriculture, Collection. Wage labour, Service, Household work, and Cattle herding. But not a single economic pursuit is sufficient for their subsistence and therefore they are compelled to involve in other economically gainful activities as subsidiary economic pursuits. Infact occupational opportunity in this plateau plays a major role among the Asur for their survival. It is also revealed from the data that collection still plays a key role in their economic life. Of the total population 376, only 133(35.38%) persons are involved in various economic pursuits for maintaining their livelihood. It is also observed that only 43(11.43%) persons are involved in local bauxite mines as wage earners and from this avenue they earn cash directly.

Tangible heritage: Use of traditional knowledge for sustenance by using local resources.

The Asur are a tribe living in forest environment. Their cultural life is styled in relation to their local environment, that is forest environment. In each and every aspect of their life forest has some contribution. They use Sal or Karange twig as tooth brush. According to them it helps to keep the teeth clean and healthy. If there is any toothache, carries or any gum trouble and even bad smell in mouth the bitter tasted sap of the twig helps to get rid of all the troubles.

They use locally available mud called as *gilli hans or nakra hans* as soap to clean their body and head hair. If the scalp is affected by the attack of lice (*siku*) or dandurf (*chitu*) then this mud is very useful to get rid of all these problems. They clean and wash their clothes and utensils with ash of sal twig. They use plates and bowls madeof sal tree leaves along with metal utensils.

(i) Their traditional knowledge in Preparation of Haria/Hadia

Haria is part and parcel of their life and culture and for preparation of *haria* they primarily depend on local resources, and the knowledge they acquired from their forefathers.

At first they cook rice. Then it is spread on floor with dense starch till it gets cold. After it gets cold, they mix powdered *ranu* with it and keep the rice mixed with *ranu* in a mud handi and close the opening tightly with sakhoa leaves for seven days during cold season and for three days in hot summer season. Then they open the pitcher and verify whether the rice got fermented. After it is fermented they pour water, stir the whole substance and take it for consumption. According to them haria sometimes works as a substitute of food. They do not feel hungry quickly, get energy and it reduces the exhaustion of their hectic daily work. As it is prepared by rice it is full with carbohydrate.

Ranu is a substance used to help in fermentation. It is prepared with fruit of Koriya plant. It also works as digestive. To prepare *ranu*, according to some of them they collect a variety of shrub called as *jhilmilia* along its roots, then grind the whole shrub and dry it. Then they mix the substance with rice powder. In this way they prepare *ranu.*

(ii) Folk Classification of Soil (hans):

According to them there are several varieties of soil with their different works found in their vicinity. Those are as follows: -

Safed hans- It is white coloured glazy soil also known as *chuhi hans.* They collect it from jungle, and use it to anoint the floor and walls of house after plastering.

Karia hans- Black coloured soil collected from jungle and *don*-1type of land. They use it in construction of floor and wall.

Jarra hans- It is yellow in colour used in house construction collected from *don*-1 and *tand*-1 type of land. It is told that after its collection they shatter/ smash it with feet. After it is satisfactorily smashed they mix cow dung with it and then plaster the walls and floor with the mixture. After an interval of two to three days when those become dry, they paint those with black soil. This process helps to strengthen the construction, and they claim that their construction is stronger than cement.

Gilli hans /Nakra hans- Used as soap.

(iii) Traditional knowledge in House construction.

They construct their houses at a higher place on uneven rock, sometimes at a slope, after selecting the place through some magical performances. Wooden log, bamboo, *khapra* of local soil, unbaked brick, (sometimes replaced by Bauxite), different types of *hans* and cow dung are needed. The central pole of the house is necessarily a fully matured thick *sal* wooden log. According to them their practical experience, taught them that the central pole should be strongest as it is responsible to keep the house structure totally balanced and carries the maximum weight of the roof. They prefer *sal* wood and if not then *gambhar* wood and bamboo poles as other supporting poles. They keep some holes at the base of the house just at the point of maximum slope. It is told that as the land is slanting, sometimes there may be some seepage or accumulation of water there inside the room .To take out the water from the room, they keep holes at the base of the hut at the slanting from where automatically water comes out. Otherwise the construction will get weak. They prefer to construct their houses either east facing as at the eastern side Sing Bonga – their supreme deity rises every day early in the morning, or south facing, as they believe it should keep connection with their own original kingdom at the southern direction as they have learnt from their ancestors. Actually the cause behind it is probably to get fresh air that got linked with the myth.

(iv) Source of water

To dig well they select a place with big trees. They follow the direction of the roots. They are of opinion that the roots of a tree always go towards the water sources. In this way they ascertain the water source in the village. It is their source of traditional knowledge to find out the level of underground water in the village. Moreover, there are persons among them who possess a unique technique to identify underground water source through two bamboo sticks holding by their hands. The two sticks are tied together at one end. The open end of the two sticks are kept on both sides of the shoulder and hold by hands on two sides and the tied portion is kept in front of him and he proceeds forward. He says that during his walk, once he feels some vibration and in further proceeds, the sticks are attracted towards the ground and comes very close to the ground where he stops. This is the point where water is available. When such a person was asked how he identifies the place He answered that he feels vibration just like the waves of water. Again, the sticks points out the actual point of water source, and never he failed. He is very much in demand also by the neighboring villages.

(v) Folk Classification of forest based on need for survival:

1. Reserve Buru - Government reserve forest; villagers are not allowed to collect any MFP (Minor Forest Produce) from this area
2. Bakash Buru--The forest areas outside the reserve forest from where collection of fuel wood and cattle grazing are allowed.
3. Ghanghor Buru- It is a deep forest and some portion of which is declared as reserve forest. In this forest they generally go for collection of edibles, medicinal plants and materials of daily use. In this forest there are several *sarnas* (sacred grove) such as *Kadleta Sarna, Sarhul Sarna, Kara Sarna* etc. Kadleta Sarna is a small reserve forest, while *Sarhul Sarna* is a bigger one. There is another

sarna named *Kara Sarna.* In all the *sarnas* they go for rituals associated with the *sarna* such as in twelve years they perform Kara festival when they offer a *kara* (buffalo) to the spirits (both malevolent and benevolent) to appease them. After the ritual is performed, they leave the buffalo in the forest and return. They are tabooed to fell wood and collect even dry wood in the *sarnas.* They are allowed to do collection outside the *sarnas.* In this way their beliefs helps in conservation of their forest.

4. Patdara Pat-It is also a very big reserve forest.

(vi) Survival Strategy: Folk Classification of neighbouring hillocks in terms of availability of water (their traditional knowledge)

1. Dnari Kona-At the eastern side of the village Sakhoapani the hill is situated. Their own Sarna is situated in this place where their own deities reside. They fell wood in this jungle leaving aside the place of their own Sarna and it's surroundings. They very often go to this hill for collection, as it is full with several varieties of tubers and other edible items.
2. Gurdari Dnari – It is situated at the western side of the village. Here also several of their benevolent and malevolent spirits reside. One of those is Barham bhut. Its shadow is also dangerous which brings diseases and sometimes-even death. In this hill one very interesting thing is that there is a point where water is available throughout the year but due to the fear of several bhuts they hardly go to the place only except certain rituals and worships.
3. Icha Dnari- situated at the northern direction. Here in this pahar, water is available throughout the year. They are not tabooed to fell wood in this area.
4. Burha/ Mandav Dnari kona- it is situated at the southern side of the village. Here a very dangerous evil spirit named

Kara darha resides. They are tabooed to fell wood in this hillock.

Adaptive Strategy for Maintenance of Livelihood: Use of Traditional Knowledge in Economic Life

Traditionally they are iron smelters and slash and burn cultivators. Hunting and collection were the subsidiary occupations.

Iron Smelting- They had their own traditional knowledge for identification of particular stone (rich with iron) and also of extraction of iron. They used to extract iron from a special type of stone having two varieties. These were collected from the area named Banstoli. The name of those two varieties of stone are *bichi tuku* and *karia tuku*. Bichi *tuku* is deep chocolate/ brown/ liver coloured and of best quality very rich with iron content. Another variety of stone is *karia tuku,* which is black in colour. It is told that for iron smelting their traditional knowledge taught them to fell and burn green young *sal* trees to generate heat for melting of stone. (This particular variety of fuel is needed to extract iron because it can generate 1500 degree Celsius temperature that was essential for iron extraction.) They used to construct mud *bhatti* (furnace) near water sources, as after melting, water is needed to cool the melt. Agricultural implements, domestic articles, and tools of daily use were prepared with that iron.

Traditional Knowledge for Slash and burn cultivation- They used to clear a vast patch of land and fell wood not from the base but leaving atleast two feet from the base. The felled woods were then kept in that land for drying. After drying those were burnt into ashes. Then they used to wait till shower comes. After shower the land is ready for broadcasting and they used to spread seeds. Sometimes some holes were dug in that land and a few seeds were sown in each of the dug holes. After three to four months when the crop were ripen those were harvested. It is told that generally they used to do slash and burn cultivation for three successive years in a particular patch of land, then leave it as fallow land for a long time

,atleast fifteen to twenty years, to replenish nutrients and by this time the land regains its fertility and there are again big trees grown and the land gets ready for slash and burn cultivation.

At present they have totally abandoned Iron smelting. Slash and burn cultivation is done in insignificant form. Among Hunting and collection, hunting became an occasional event.

Now Plough cultivation became their primary occupation. Collection has got a very important position in their life.

Hunting and collection: They have different types of traps such as *sim funda* to catch jungle fowl, *kutunga funda*- a variety of noose trap to catch hare and porcupine. They have knowledge about how an animal will be attracted towards a trap and easily will be caught. As for an example ,hares are very fond of salt, to trap it they dig a hole at the side of the road and fit a trap there. The villagers who pass by the side of the hole urinate there. The salt of urine is accumulated in the hole. Being attracted by it's smells hares come to taste the salt and fall down in it and are automatically trapped.

There are several indigenous techniques to catch birds where traditional knowledge, which they have acquired over generation, is also applied.

Collection is done primarily by women They are efficient to detect the place from where they will get various types roots fruits and tubers. Their traditional knowledge taught them to identify the place from where *kanda* (tuber) is available observing it's plants/ creepers grown on the soil. They do not dig up the whole portion but leave a portion of it for growth for future.

Table–5:1: Annual Calendar of Collection of Minor Forest Produce (MFP) required for sustenance among the Asur

Month in Local dialect (E.E.)	Collection of Forest Materials						
	Root/ Tubers	Shoot	Leaves/ Vegetables	Flowers	Fruits	Seeds	Mushroom
1	2	3	4	5	6	7	8
Chait (March-April)	-	-	Munga Sag	Mahua	Ber	-	-
Vaisakh (April-May	Gethi, Nakoa, Pitharu, Daru, Kulu, Baiyaug, Baser	-	Koenar Sag, Amit Sag, Munga Sag, Jirkan Patta, Futkal Sag, Tend Patta*	Moreja, Mahua	Amba, Jamun, Kathar, Papra, Piyar, Tend, Chihar, Mahulain, Pethu, Kachnar	-	-
Jaith (May-June)	Do	-	Fudina Sag, Chirkani Sag, Rote Sag, Munga Sag, Jirkan, Patta, Koenar Sag, Tend Patta*	Moreja, Mahua	Dumbar, Amba, Gular, Kathar, Kusum, Jamun, Porhu, Tut	Sakhoa, Dori, Karanj	-
Ashad (June-July)	Do	-	Munga Sag, Matha Sag, Katai Sag, Boro Sag, Futkal Sag, Koenar Sag	Mahua	Satalu	Do	Various types of edible mushroom
Sawan (July-August)	Do	Karil	Munga Sag, Boro Sag, Kena Sag, Seliar Sag, Dail Sag, Futkal Sat	-	Karonda Satalu	-	Do
Bhado (August-Sept.)	Do	Do	Do	-	Do	-	Do
Aswin/ Kuar (Sept.-October)	Do	Do	Munga Sag	-	Do	-	-

Kartick (October-Nov.)	Sakhina/ Sakar Kanda	-	Kohra Sag, Laua Sag, Munga Sag	-	Kohra, Gongra	-	-
Aghan (November-December)	-	-	Munga Sag	-	-	-	-
Pus (December-January)	-	-	Munga Sag	-	-	-	-
Magh (January-February)	Pitharu, Nakoa, Gethi	-	Do	Jirkan Kachnar	Bayer	-	-
Fagun (February-March)	-	-	Do	Mahua flower	Ber	-	-

*Except Tend Patta (Bidi leaves all are food items)

They also collect wood *moreja patta* (by which they used to prepare string), Mahulain Patta and Juru Patta (for preparing rain coat and Chopi or hat) Khajur leaves (to prepare mat) and Kher grass (for thatching) throughout the year.

Application of Traditional knowledge: Folk Taxonomic classification of MFP being edible items:

They have several types of tubers of various taste and edible value. Some of those such as *gethi* and *pitharu* are of bitter taste. To remove the bitter taste they keep it in a basket after slicing it in a flowing water source overnight. Next day they take it, boil atleast for two to three times changing water and then after washing in fresh water they cook it.

They identify the *putu* (a variety of tuber taste like potato) in the forest by observing the upper surface of soil in naked eye; If it is broken then there are chances to get *putu* either *jait putu* (black) and *chhaira putu* (white). These grow in forest and hills. The colour of young *chhaira putu* is white and when it grows old becomes black in colour. They take the young one. Jait *putu* is tastier and they cook it with chicken. They eat several varieties of *jait putu* and among those *mani putu* is very tasty.

They have varieties of leafy vegetables (sag) such as *koenar sag* (collected from jungle), *bathua* (in cultivable land), *futkal* (in the homestead land), *kado/ losar sag* (in jungle), *puru sag* (in jungle). They sometimes cook the *sag* only by boiling in water. They take it adding salt only. Puru sag is very tasty and they take it mixing with *dal* (pulses).

Varieties of *khukrie*s (mushroom) grow in their vicinity such as *sarki lom, utur, bharwali, patka* (of bitter taste), *burbhu, ad,* and *bans khukri*. Those grow in forest and hills. They can easily identify what type of mushroom they can consume and which one is poisonous.

Indigenous Knowledge in view of perception of time as well as picking up of mahua:

The *mahua* flower is available during the summer months. Everyday it starts falling from tree early in the morning and it is continued till 12 noon to 1p.m.by which they identify the time. The flower falls under the tree where throughout the day leaves are fallen and accumulated, from where it is difficult to pick up the flower. To avoid the difficulties, at night they do control firing so that they can easily pick up the flower fallen on the ash, early in the morning. Mahua is a precious and important item in their daily life and culture.

Traditional knowledge to use local natural resources for economic activities:

Grass:

They have identified several varieties of grass growing in their vicinity. (a) Among those *kher* grass is very necessary which grows on the contour bunding in the cultivable land, on the pathway of the hillocks and slopes or tarai. They use those to make cattle shed, poultry and piggery. Some of those are used to shed their huts also. These are used as fodder for the cattle. (b) Another variety is *kash* grass. These are also grown in the contour bunding. Their cattle eat the smaller, younger one while the larger one is used to prepare *kumni* (fishing trap). (c) Where there is soft and wet mud, *dub* grass is grown there. Their cattle are fond of this. (d) *chhiner* –another variety of grass when it is young, their cattle consume it otherwise it has no use. (e) They have another variety of grass known as *kush* grass used for preparation of broom.

Bamboo (*mand*):

Two varieties of *mand* are there. Those, which they collect from jungle, are known as *jungle bans/mand* and the other one is *gaon mand*. It is told by them that they prefer *gaon mand* to jungle *mand* because of its strength and durability. They use jungle *mand* as a substitute for *gaon mand*

Fishing

They do fishing in garha river- a streamlet in the western side and dhardhari nadi (streamlet) in the eastern side. They say that fishes are available in good quantity in the month of Bhado (Aug- Sept). During winter they get fishes of smaller size, and also large headed hamru fish (hanku). During summer, they get prawn of smaller size, lathi or puti, bhumig and aind hanku. During rainy season they set varieties of traps such as dander to catch large and kumbi for small fishes. They can locate path and signature of movement of fishes in water beside the land. It helps them to understand whether there is fish or not in the water. Sometimes they take manjhua, a variety of leaves, dry it and then grind it; then the powder is mixed with molasses and after binding a portion of it for at least two days put the substance in a streamlet where they have identified the presence of fish. The fishes get intoxicated and float on the river and become easy to catch. They use fenka jal or danra jal in this fishing. They buy the thread of net from the market and in fenka jal they attach 100 to 150 weights of led at the net's open portion to increase its weight, which is necessary during fishing to keep it stable in water after throwing. The increase in number of weight and closer fitting of those is advisable and helpful for fishing.

They tell that where they get large fishes, small fishes are not available as the bigger ones swallow the smaller ones.

Cultivation

Settled plough cultivation is their primary occupation now. Primarily they have two varieties of land namely *tand* (dry or non-irrigated) and *don* (wet) land. These two are again divided into several divisions depending on their quality (whether even or uneven), position, irrigated or non-irrigated, water retention capacity etc .As for example, a portion of land of the *tand* variety situated at slope is known as *telengtar*. A brief chart is given where a structure of their land holding along with their choice of cereals production is given in order to understand their embedded knowledge in this regard which they have learnt from their neighbours like the tribal group- the Oraon, Munda and Nagesia.

Ploughing- They start cultivation with ploughing. They plough a land for four times. They refer it *char chas and* **each of such *chas* has its own significance as per their wisdom**. Those are as follows:

When a cultivator observes lightning at the southeastern side of the sky he understands that the time of ploughing has come and he gets ready to go to the field for first ploughing. The first ploughing is known as *chairabu* or *farin*. It is done just before or after first shower. The first ploughing is done to crack the hard soil and to break the lumps and also to uproot all the grasses grown in the field. In this ploughing, the land is cracked through which the cold air and the water pass from surface to the lower portion of soil to make it soft and wet.

After first ploughing, they leave the land for two to three days

The second ploughing is known as *dograibu* or *dobar*. If one has done first ploughing from east to west, then second ploughing is done from north to south.

Third ploughing is known as *tibrai abu* or *teghar*. They plough to prepare land thoroughly. All the weeds are uprooted and those are ultimately decomposed, the insects are killed. The land is loosened

CLASSIFICATION OF CULTIVABLE LAND AS PER WATER RRETENTION CAPACITY IN THE LAND

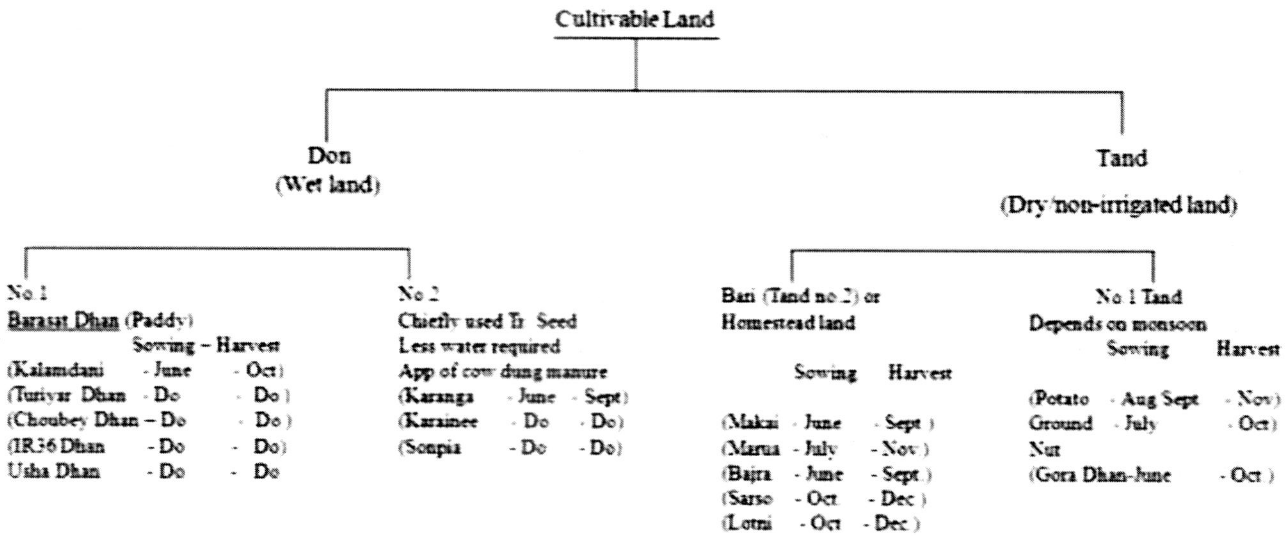

and made ready for cultivation. During ploughing lumps of cow dung are broken and mixed with land.

The fourth ploughing is known as *choukhaibu* or *chanbar*. In this ploughing broadcasting or spreading of the seeds is done. After each and every ploughing they leave the land for three to four days to give time for decomposition. Through ploughing the soil gets loosened so that air, water and sunlight easily can penetrate. The rotation of the soil of upper level to lower level and the soil of lower level to upper level along with the grasses, decomposed insects and cow dung is done which are also very necessary to increase the fertility of the plot.

After rain, they again do ploughing to prepare the muddy, cultivable land ready for transplantation. This is known as *paltai abu*. In cultivation through transplantation, more water is needed and for retaintion of water according to their wisdom *paltai abu* is needed. It is told that they get more products in the method of transplantation than broadcasting.

Their Traditional Knowledge in Storing of seeds-.

They store the seed either in an earthen pitcher or prepare a container by *juru* leaves called as *potom* and after keeping seeds in it; it is tightly covered with straw. According to them till the next summer season, they are tabooed to touch the pot. Otherwise, they believe that, the seeds will be damaged or spoiled by insects. The pot is kept inside the *ora-bhitar* (the room where the souls of their ancestors, regarded as their guardian deities are established), where the outsiders are not allowed to enter. In case of earthen pitcher, they plaster cow dung outside the container. Sometimes they store seeds in bamboo baskets. The inner and the outer portion of the container are plastered with cow dung. The mouth of the basket is open. It is told by other informants that sometimes to protect the seeds from damp and insects they bring out the seeds in open space of the courtyard in sunlight. The seeds eaten or half eaten by insects are fanned away and the unaffected are stored again. They prefer to use their traditional seeds but those cannot fulfil their need. So they are compelled to purchase seeds such as *chobe, karenga, sita, kaveri, kalinga* and *sita* etc. from block.

Traditional Knowledge involves in preparation of land for sowing:

Prior to seed sowing, they add fertilizer in their land. Among the fertilizers cow dung is preferred. To prepare cow dung as fertilizer they have to decompose the cow dung. At first they dig out big holes and accumulate cow dung in those holes till those are completely filled up. It is done in the month of May and kept till it gets rotten. After that they dig out all those and add to the cultivable land. They also use D.A.P. and other inorganic manures during transplantation. They also use urea for quick growth of plant.

Traditional Knowledge for Irrigation in the terrace land:

Generally their lands of *tand* 1 and 2 and *don* 1 are completely dependent on rain. Irrigation from nearby streamlets is done in don1 type of lands by preparing canals. Again it is told that as the villages are situated at the hilly slope there is no need to channalise or drain out the village waste water, which also carries a lot of organic materials and a good source of fertility. Generally don1 and sometimes tand 2 type of land gets such water. Excess water in case of plots of lands separated by contour bundings flows from one plot to its immediate next plot situated at slightly lower level. To channelise the excess water from one plot to its next plot at lower level they keep hole on that side. In this way all the plots from upper level to lower level are automatically irrigated and at the same time excess water cannot harm the crop.

Traditional Knowledge to protect the plant, soil erosion and various phases of cultivation:

When a plant grows above 6 inches of water level, there are chances of its getting infected by insects. Upto 6 inches the insects cannot climb or stay on the plant. So they always are careful in this issue.

In case the insects affect a plant; they apply D.D.T. and other insecticides purchased from shops.

Boundary is needed especially in Bari land attached to their homestead land to check the loss of soil or soil erosion. They plant different types of fruit giving plants such as *papita* (papaya), *tamrash* (guava), *kathal* (jackfruit), jojo (tamarind), in the boundary to check soil erosion and at the same time it gives them a little economic support adding to their food chart. Again the bio-degradable wastes from homestead land comprising of vegetable waste, poultry waste, piggery waste and the waste water from kitchen and other places of hut are accumulated in the bari land which ultimately are decomposed and very useful for the increase of fertility of the land.

Weeding or *hnerera* is done during rainy season after transplantation. They say that if weeding is not done in proper way and there are weeds, then the paddy will not grow properly. When they see that the paddy grains are black in colour they understand that the crop did not get sufficient food in the form of juice and as a result this is ill nourished because the weeds along with the cultivable items share the nutrients of the land. To avoid it and to give sufficient nourishment, weeding is compulsory. In paddy cultivation, they plant a bunch of plant consisting of three to four plants in a same hole in transplantation. They avoid planting more as the plants then will be also week as from a single area they have to extract their food. The crops and cereals produced in the lands are mentioned in the chart/ table.

Mixed cultivation- They cultivate *makai* and *bajra at* the same time in the same plot of *bari* land. They sow the seeds of *makai* in lines and at the same time they broadcast the seeds of *bajra* in that land. The plants of both the varieties grow simultaneously but grow with separate identity of plant, fruits etc.

When they cultivate *arhar* with urid/marua/kurthi or surthi they plant arhar in between the other plants. The *arhar* plants grow taller than the other plants so one can easily identify it.

General characteristics of some plants- It is told that *marua* can also grow in rough rocky area, if the chemical fertilizer is added but for it's cultivation muddy soil is preferred. They broadcast *kurthi* in a much dispersed manner, as they do not want thick growth of the plant, as this is a creeper. If they grow thick in a plot then the creepers will grow clumsy and interlocking with each other. As a result the product will not be sufficient. Kurthi can grow in non-irrigated, rocky area full with pebble. Its roots are very strong, can pass through the rocky substance. Gondli cannot grow on rocky area instead soft muddy soil is needed. But *arhar* can grow in both the conditions in *tand* 1 and *tand*-2 types of land. Jatengi grows in *tand* land by broadcasting method. A large quantity of seeds is broadcast. As the grains are very small in size, to get more product they broadcast in such a fashion that the plants grow in bunch and very dense. The paddy of smaller size ripens quickly. In *bari* land they cultivate *jino*r (*maka*i or maize) and after it's harvest they cultivate *sarso*. Along with *sarso* at the same time in the same plot they cultivate *alu* (potato) and *muli*. They cultivate these in broadcasting method.

After the crop and cereals get mature, they do cutting. Each and every item has it's own time for cultivation. After cutting they keep the harvested crop in the field in the sun for drying. After those become dry, they take the grain /cereal from the whole plant by threshing or beating the harvested crop/cereal.

During harvesting, they do not cut from the base or uproot the whole plant but cut leaving at least 10 inches to 1 foot from the base in the land. These are left in the plot for natural decomposition and transformation to fertilizer. These are dried in sun, decomposed in rain and ultimately get mixed with the mud. Their cattle that graze in the land after harvest also feed on these. When the cattle graze in such a land it is profitable for a cultivator by thir droppings, which ultimately become manure and add to their land. In this way the cultivator is benefited. All these add to the soil fertility.

The straw is a very important item used as fodder for their cattle. They separate *pual* (straw) by a wooden stick with spikes. Those are stored in a side of their field and in rainy season are stored in a corner of living room.

The husk is mixed with fodder of their pigs. And some are burnt into ashes to manure the field.

Traditional Knowledge for Extraction of oil from jatengi- They extract oil from *jatengi*, which is used to cook vegetables. To extract oil from *jatengi*, at first they grind the grains. Then those are kept in a bamboo basket, and then the opening of the basket is tightly closed with a fine cloth. After that they keep the basket turned upside down on a container. The container has a small opening and it is filled with water. The water is then boiled and when it reaches the boiling point, the vapour comes out and passes up to *jatengi* through the cloth. After sometime when the vapour comes out from the basket they understand that the seeds are ready for oil extraction and immediately they bring out the jatengi and press to extract oil.

Folk Classification of their domesticated animals and birds being tangible heritage:

Along with their other movable and immovable properties, domesticated animals and birds give a family a very important position not only in their society but also as necessary and compulsory items in their daily life and in their ritual occasions. Among those the most important to them is chicken, as it is needed not only for their consumption but also as a compulsory and necessary item as an important offering for their rituals. Next to chicken, pigs are very important. A person's economic condition is judged by his pig holdings. In fact it is needed in any feast associated with their life cycle and other festive occasions. Next position is hold by goat-specially the he goat. They can earn a good amount by selling them. They also consume the meat and in some of their rituals it is sacrificed. Cow and bullock holds the lowest position among them It is told that bullock is only needed in ploughing. Rest of the time these have no utility but they have to fed and taken care of throughout the year. To them, cow is only important for the rearing of it's calves. They do not drink milk as it is regarded as the gift of Heavenly father as food for its calves. They are tabooed to milk the cow. They do not eat beef and it has no importance in their ritual life.

Conservation of forest

There is much scope for utilising traditional knowledge for sustainable development. TK has an important role to play to restore and conserve the biodiversity of village forests. They have several ideas for the preservation and conservation of bio-diversity of flora and fauna. Some of those are given below-

Whenever they fell trees in the jungle, they do not cut it from its bottom but leaving at least 2 feet height. They do not cut it straight but oblique or slanting. They say that in straight cutting, the tree cannot survive but when it is cut in a slanting way it definitely survives and after rains more than one tree grows from the same tree along the original one. Again in felling of trees, they always use axe instead of saw as saw damages the tree and it dies.

They never uproot the roots and tubers totally but leave at least a small portion beneath the ground for future growth.

Their cattle graze in jungle. The cow dung and droppings of other animals are transformed into manure, which is very useful and necessary item for forest growth.

Their customary laws tabooed them to fell several trees especially of sacred groves locally known as *sarna*, which are regarded as the abode of their deities. Their deities stay there, play, sing, swing in the trees. Always they have to keep the place pure with sanctity. They are tabooed to spit or urinate and their women are never allowed to visit a sacred grove. The male members can visit there but nobody is allowed to fell wood even the dry one and to cut a branch or pick up a flower or fruit or even a small twig fallen on the floor. If anybody does it even by mistake, their deities will be very angry and will send tiger or any jungle animal or an evil spirit to cause harm to the guilty person and his family. They perform several of their rituals in the *sarnas*. Rest of the period they do not disturb the place. They have several *sarnas* in several hills and forests of their vicinity Under Gurderi Panch; there is their biggest *sarna*, named as **Gurderi Sarna**. Expect this there are several other smaller *sarna* such as **Raiyat Sarna, Deheri Sarna**, etc. As mentioned earlier there are several *sarnas* in different hills and forests and are named as per the name of the place or mountain. Several economically valuable trees and plants such as Sakhoa, Durri, and Bel etc. are found in those *sarnas* but felling of those is not allowed. If a person cuts a tree in a *sarna* (to them this is an offence to the deities as they stay there) they are sure that within a few months the man will die and several persons of the village may also die. Those places are strictly kept undisturbed and sanctity is maintained as those places are only the abode of their deities.In this way by their customary laws and ritual bindings, conservation of forest is done.

They have several evil spirits roaming in the jungle. There are places meant for those. They go to the forest but avoid visiting those places so chances of collection and felling of trees there are nil and as a result conservation of forest is done.

They are tabooed to eat new fruits of the season and harvest before offering them to their deities and ancestors through rituals. They have to wait till the performance of the ritual on a particular date, fixed for it. Otherwise they have a belief that tiger will come out of the jungle and kill the offender or the person will suffer from stomachache or any stomach problem within this period of time and by this time the product gets fully matured and ready for further growth of new ones.

They are tabooed to consume or even kill the animals of their totems, which also helpthem for their protection of those animals.

Intangible heritage: Cognisance of environment and their beliefs:

1. They understand that summer season is coming with the singing of *Kuhi Charai* (cuckoo).
2. When new leaves come in the Sal trees, it signifies that summer is coming.
3. With the falling of *pipal* leaves and coming of new leaves they get indication that summer is coming.
4. The blooming of flower of jackfruit, mango, *mahua, and palash* and with the performance of *Basant Panchmi* (aritual- newly introduced through village residential school) also indicates that the summer is approaching.
5. With the performance of *Basant Panchmi* they believe that the season of cold has come to its last phase. **Haria** gradually will become very tasty.
6. When they see that soft Sal leaves became large and hard then they understand that summer is at it's last stage and rainy season is coming.
7. When Daona/ Daonaha- a bird sings then they believe that rainy season is coming.
8. When *jhingur* (a kind of insects) cries or the drone of the cricket is loud in jungle –generally in May, they know that within a few days rain will come.
9. Frog'scroaking also indicates for heavy shower.
10. If there is lightning at the southeastern side of the sky, then a cultivator understands that rain is coming and he gets ready with his plough to go to his field.
11. Heavy sweating also is an indicator of rains
12. Black ants locally known as *sunumuig* or *lormui* (bigger variety of ant) with their food and eggs going in a line is a very good indication of rain.
13. When Sarai/Sal seeds get fully matured and fall from tree, it is an indication of end of summer season.

14. With the performance of Sohorai in the month katic (Sept- Oct) winter season comes.
15. Haria becomes tasteless, as cold climate is not suitable for fermentation.
16 They feel the change of climate with the change of wind.
17 If there is *badri* (cloud) at the east, then there are chances of rains. If badri is seen at the west side, then rain will not come quickly but it will take time. If *badri* is seen at the southern side then rain will come from south, .It is told that it hampers the crop; it is believed that the rain from south brings salty water and it damages the plant and the produced cereal will be tasteless. The rain from north is good news to the cultivators as it is favourable for production of crops. If rains from south occur during katic, then immediately the cultivator cuts the crop to prevent the damage.
18. If wind blows from west to east, it is not good for their health and disease comes with it. Wind from east to west indicates that rain may come. Wind from north to south is very good for their health but wind from south to north brings rain and after that the weather will be very hot and they may be attacked by *loo (*heat wave*)*. Their crops and cereals will be damaged.
19. When sun sets in a very red colour then there will be no rain and *thuribing* or rainbow stops rain.
20. They adjust time by observing shadow. During night they adjust time by noticing *Charhha Tara* (star) or *Harjuwari Tara* (star) or *Tin Tara* (star). Tin Tara rises in the eastern sky and with the approach of time it moves towards west.
21. When they see *jono chanu* (comet) they get afraid that there will be no rain and there will be famine and they will face hard time.
22. If they see that the colour of *sakhoa* leaves is red and there are several elevated portions just like boil are found on the leaves, it indicates that there will be pox in their village.
23. They locally call whirlwind as bandro bhut. If any body falls within it, they get afraid that the evil spirit will do harm to him.

They spit on it and do some magical performances to neutralise the evil effect.

24 Kohora or *dhund* or fog is according to them nothing but the water vapour, which is harmful for potato and lac cultivation.

25. Patthal or *pani sila*- the hailstone is harmful for mango and crops.

26. When sun rises slightly from south-eastern side then the days are small and cold days are coming but when the situation is just reverse that is the sun rises from north- east side then the days are long and hot.

27. If they see there is a circle-encircling the moon, it gives indications of rain. When the circle is found close to the moon, the rain will happen in places far from their village and when the circle is away from the moon, they believe that there will be rain in and around their village.

28. Eclipses are known as *garhan.*

29. In case of successful production of mango they know that there is no hailstone fallen on mango and the honey drops fall on the buds, and flowers of mango tree (which sticks on the mango bud and flower and hampers the growth of the flower into fruit and as a result these becomes dry and fall down), the honey is washed out.

30. According to them jackle, squirrel, chiti snake, hare, crow are considered as bad omen. During their journey if any of these is seen, then definitely there will be some disturbances.

31. An elephant, jara snake, dhaman snake etc are good omen.

32. If anybody stumbles, he postpones his journey.

Ethno-medicine: Traditional Knowledge in health and Hygiene:

The term ethno medicine generally gives emphasis on the study of belief and practices related to illness of an individual of a particular community. The tribal communities of the country are distributed in the different eco-settings. Till date most of them are dependent on nature, utilizing their environment, natural resources with the help of their traditional technology. Even to day they combat their ill health and other crisis situation with their indigenous methods of utilizing their natural resources. In the study of ethno medicine primarily it is important to see that what their conceptionis regarding disease and ill health- whether it is caused due to some physiological disorder or due to malevolent act of some outward agencies is to be mentioned. Next, who will ascertain it-a doctor or a medicine man or sorcerer of their tribeor any of the local communities. If he is a doctor then why they go to him leaving their own traditional one. If he is a medicine man or a sorcerer, then how he detects the disease. Is it through some ritual or magical performances or understood through symptoms or by holding pulse bit of the patient? When the medicine man or sorcerer detects the disease, than what the process of treatment is - only by application of medicine or along with that they perform some ritual or magical performances. When the disease detected is supposed to be caused only by the malevolent act of a spirit or if it is caused due to some deity's anger or if the deity is displeased, - then what process of treatment to cure the patient may be taken. When a medicine man or a sorcerer fails, then where they should go? In his success what is his remuneration? It should be ascertained what they think about death. It is known that the herbal medicines have important role in village situation, especially among the tribal. Now how they get the knowledge about the medicine, their process and application. If there is any social or religious obligation, restriction or taboo associated with collection, preparation and application. How the knowledge is transmitted from one to another generations.

The Asur habitats in the Netarhat plateau are sporadically distributed in various hilly terrain of this plateau and are completely devoid of any primary health centre. Therefore, situation compelled them to depend on the mercy of tribal medicine men who are primarily herbal practitioners. The empirical data also suggest that Asur tribal medicine man, named Raghunath Asur of Sakhuapani village not only treats medically the patients of the village but also he receives request from neighbouring villages for attending patients who are even the Oraon, Hill Korwa and the Nagesia tribe of this plateau. Now, primarily when he was asked that how he detects a disease, he answered that he keeps his keen observation on the patient and side-by-side takes the case history in relation to the disease from his/her parents and also from the patient to detect the actual disease and causes behind it. He also applies his magical power to detect whether any supernatural power has any act behind the disease. Raghunath told that not a single cause is responsible for a disease. He thinks in all the cases act of supernatural power is there. He cited some examples. In their village there are cases of falling from tree and getting fracture of body part. In such cases he is expert to cure his patients by fitting properly the broken part and plastering with herbal medicine in addition with oral medicines. But he argues that, a person generally falls due to the mischievous act of any of the malevolent spirit, which pushes and throws a person sitting on climbing a tree. Again in stomach pain or disorder, along with medicines needed to cure the disease, he identifies through magical performances, whether there is any other reason behind it. In several cases he comes to know through his magical power that the patient has taken the season's newly harvested item or fruit prior to the performance of the ceremony of offering of season's new food to the deities and ancestors which is an offence to them. As a result, for which they are displeased and felt insulted and caused that suffering to the person. So side-by-side along with medicines, he arranges for some rituals to satisfy the spirits and ancestors.

Traditionally among the Asur the post of medicine man is hereditary. Raghunath informed that he has inherited the post from his father who got it from his father. They believe that it is the god's gift to a person. His one of the forefathers acquired the power as a blessing from god and it is transmitted through generations up to him. But none of his sons are efficient to acquire the post. So it will be transmitted to efficient people who are keen to get the knowledge and it will be decided by their own jati panchayat. On the other hand the Asur are very keen to learn the magical performances. He told that they live in an uncanny atmosphere full with fear of some malevolent spirits. To overcome the fear it is very common to the Asurs to know several magical performances as protective measures. Generally the sons get the knowledge from father who very slowly transmits the knowledge to only that son who stays with him in the joint family. As soon as a son forms his own family separately, he gets no further knowledge. Due to this, there are several extended families found among the Asur community. They are very much afraid to talk about death. Death to them, as usual like others, is a very sorrowful event and the reason behind it as suspected by them is magical performance of a *dain* (witch), or of any malevolent spirit. When a sick person gets well, a ritual is performed as thanks giving to appease their deities and ancestors. The medicine man, sorcerer and the magical performer who is responsible to cure the patient is remunerated as per his demand and the patient's family's economic ability.

When Raghunath fails to cure a patient, then they consult other medicine men or shift the patient to nearby health centre at Netarhat which is faraway (i.e.35 Km) from the village.

Table: 5:2: Here, in the following lines the name of some of the herbal plants and its uses are given:

Sl No.	Name of the Disease	Symptom	Use of herbal plants
1	T.B.	Cough with blood	Lightly burn the leaf of *nagpheni* plant and then remove its upper layer with thorns and then consume it for a month.
2.	Gelatonai (Leprosy)	Prolonged wound with loosing of flesh	Root of *tinpatti* (Desmodium polycarpurn) with cocoanut oil, *sakar kanda*, root of *bhuiprash*, *math* kanda (nodes of bamboo shoot) and stool of *lambha* (hare) are mixed and applied in the affected place.
3	Pet dukhe	Stomachache.	The root of *kedar* plant is grinded and consumed.

4	Sarap kata	Snake bite	The root of *chirdhoa/chauthdhoa* and its leaf together are ground. The paste is applied in the affected part and then the sorcerer chants mantras to extract poison from the patient's body. They do not have belief in tying up the affected part to resist the poison to spread out through the patient's body.
5.	Boils	-	Collected anthills are ground softly and applied.
6.	Khojli (Eczema)	-	The seed of *bara sengal* flower (which is sweet in taste and favourite of children) is burnt into ashes and mix with karanj oil or cocoanut oil and heated in lamp and applied in the affected part.
7.	Gout/Gethia (Rheumatism)	Pain in joints	Tuber of *saru janam*, root of *tin patti* (Desmodium polycarpurn), root of *bandal aura*, sarkar kanda, root of *jabla siliyari*, potato, root of *bhaiparash*, root of *bhui kumbhi*, root of *dubri* or bark of *dubri* are altogether grounded and made paste with water and consumed as well as applied in the affected parts.
8	Bukhar/Jwar/ Jendra (Fever)	Temperature in body	The bark of *karam* (Adina cordifolia) tree is crushed and soaked in water. It is then boiled in water, added with some salt and then taken. Bark of *gethi* (Dioscorea bulbifera) tuber, which tastes bitter is crushed and taken with water.
9	To start mahinwari of a mother delivered a child recently	Pain in abdomen.	Gethi tubers are cut into pieces and then burnt into *chulha* (hearth) and added with *mahua* (Bassia latifolia) taken by new born's mother then menses is started.
10	Protection from snake	-	The root of *kaniwyat* is ground and sprinkle into their hut, if there is any snake it will leave the place because of its repelent smell.
11	Sardi Jukham (Cough and cold)	Running of nose and conjetion	The root of *tin Patti* plant (Desmodium Polycarpurn) is taken with water. **Kali marich** with salt are ground and consumed with water.

12	Phara Yatuna (Rough Skin)		Tomato (indigenous or deshi) is consumed.
13	Ghao (Toe eczema)		Harra (Terminalia Chebula) is heated and pasted. Then the paste is applied to the affected toe.
14	Anpachh (Indigestion)		Ashes of the fuel wood is mixed with water and consumed.
15	Lahiksen (Dysentery/ blood dysentery)		The root of *kedar* with wild grasses are ground and consumed with water.
16	Samang hasutana (Headache)		Root of *putri* (Croton rox-burghii) tree is rubbed and applied on the forehead. Garlic, mustard oil and *doob* grasses (Dog grass/creeping cynodon) are ground and the paste is applied.
17	Datahasua (Toothache)	Pains in gum and tooth	Bark of fruit of *putri* (Croton roxburghii) is ground and the paste is applied.
18.	Rangbaz/ Masipisi (Measles)	Several red allergy type rashes found all over body	Leaf of *chakkoar* tree (Hibiscus sabdariffa) is pasted and rubbed in the body.
19	Menstruation Problem with pain in stomach		Brak of *kumar amba* (the mango tree which is not yet flowering), bark of *piyar* (Buchanania latifolia) and *jovala kanda* tuber are mixed and grounded and then consumed.
20	Jwar (High Fever)	High body temperature	The root of *satawar* (Asparagus racemosus) and *putri* are mixed and added with water and consumed.
21	Malaria	Occurrence of high fever frequently.	The root of *parhi or Pathar kumrah* (Pueraria tuberosa) is ground with water and consumed.
22	Haddi tuta (Bone Fracture)		The tubers of *datram singhi* (Vitis tomentosa) and turmeric are mixed into paste and applied.
23	Jalan/ jalni (Burn)		The latex of *baghrandi* (Jatropha curcas) is mixed with salt and applied in the burning area.
24	Gethia dard (Gout pain)	Pain in the joints or joints pain	The bark and root of koreya (Holarrhena antidysenterica) are mixed into paste and applied in the affected part.

In all cases before application of herbal medicine they perform some rituals with chanting of mantras. It is also reported that before collection of the herbs from forest they usually perform following things –

a) Strictly avoid cohabitation with wife during night,
b) Leave the house before sunrise silently in empty stomach,
c) Prayer for *sing bonga,*
d) When they collect tubers, roots etc from forest, some portion are kept there for future rejuvenation.

They have also possesses knowledge of some diseases and their treatments of their animals. Some of those are given below:

Sl. No.	Name of the animal	Name of the disease	Symptoms	Treatment to cure
1.	Murga (Fowl/ Chicken)	Rangbaj (contagious disease)	Swelling of throat, keeps mouth open salivates, continuous swinging of head and white coloured loose motion, red coloured boil like swellings found on the body	Cauterisation by red-hot *hansua* (iron sickle) on the boils when the disease has just started. They burn incense in honour of diseased ancestors.
2.	Merom/Chhegri (Goat)	Rangbaj (contagious disease)	It lies down, several red coloured swellings like boils found on the body	Cauterisation by red-hot *hansua* (iron sickle) on the boils. Along with this they prepare medicine by the leaves and roots of a (variety of herb) known as *saramdiring* collected from jungle. They smash those in total by hands and mix with the fodder and let the sick one take it. It gets well; otherwise they bring it to nearby veterinary hospital at Bishunpur.)

3.	Suoa r (pig)	Gilti Rangbaj (contagious disease. If such a pig is consumed by men, then they may get loose motion or itches	Similar symptoms are noticed as found among the goat.	They collect the excreta of kundru (an animal of water probably turtle) from the river side Then this is mixed with *bhusa* (straw) It is a very effective medicine and only one dose is enough to control the disease and three doses are enough to cure the affected pig completely
4.	Gai (cow), Bail (bullock)	Gilti Rangbaj	All over the body it gets red boils. In this disease swelling of throat is found the cow or bull cannot breath properly and suffers from cough and cold, the colour of the tongue gets black, keeps mouth open, salivates, stops taking food.	Cauterisation with red-hot *hansua* (iron sickle) on the boils. With it as a medicine they prepare a mixture of Dhan(paddy), *bahera*,*bandarlatha* seeds and *chirchitta* plant. All these are mixed and ground together and let it be consumed with fodder.
5.	Do	Khurha	Ulcer or wound occurs on the boot of the animal.	They wash the ulcer with water of battery cell or boil Velva seed or bark in water and wash the place for several times, and the wound gets cured.
6.	Do	Chapka	Ulcer on tongue,	The bark and seeds of kohora plant are ground together and let it to consume it. Generally the cattle do not want to take it. So they keep it on a leaf along with some tamarind and salt.

7.	All types of cattle	Bouraha	There is a variety of grass, locally known as *matoasi ghash* and they call it as *bulbar ghash.* During grazing, sometimes those take this variety of grass with other grasses. Immediately such a cattle becomes mad.	Within 24 hours it should be given *kohora pani* (seeds of kohora plant mixed with water). Otherwise it dies
8.	Do	Dingtoat-adiyaye	Sometimes during grazing, there is a poison less snake named *sarudin* which suddenly bites. The exact spot gets swelling	.They prepare a band of straw and ignite it and cauterise the particular place with burning straw on the affected place.
9.	Do	Jwar	Fever	Cauterisation by a red-hot *hansua* (iron sickle).
10	Do	Ghao	Wound due to the attack or bite of any animal	Apply *dimak mitti* (mud of anthill) at the wound

From their natural habitats, which provide them an enormous range of indigenous medicinal plants, they utilize and conserve these for future use. Thus, the tribal medicine man in this area play a significant role in catering the health care needs of their locality at this Netarhat plateau. They provide plants centered culturally appropriate personalized health care that meets the needs and expectation of the patients in their vicinity. Encouragement should be given to tribal SHG (Self Help Group) for training, management and maintenance of medicinal herbal gardens, training should be imparted on processing, store, packaging and marketing and accordingly suitable amendments are required in Indian Patent Act.

Thus, the rich wealth of knowledge and associated practices regarding indigenous exploitation of natural resources by the tribal communities in our country should be properly documented in order to have potential industrial application leading to pharmacological developments that could help many people across the country. Therefore, we cannot afford to lose this natural resources and its associated indigenous knowledge

Transmission of Indigenous knowledge to next generation through process of socialization

Today their children are going to school to get formal education, which they think are not sufficient for them as they live in such an area where they always are scared with uncertainty and thus feel very insecured. To get confidence in mind they have several social customs and taboos. To cope up with the local ecological condition, from their very childhood they are enculturated and given training. Whenever they go for hunting and collection in forest, their children accompany them. In case of hunting their boys from 10 to 12 years of age accompany them. They drive the game close to the hunter by creating sound with *hurla*. They are taught to throw arrow on a particular object.Prior to that they practice to hit the aim by throwing of *gulel* (catapult). Children of both the sexes, especially the girls accompany them in collection of jungle products. They learn how to identify the places where the roots fruits and tubers can be found , what type of *putus* and *khukhries* are edible or poisonous, how to take out the tubers that grow beneath the soil, and also to preserve their food items for future use. They are taught to identify the path even in dense forest and where to go or not. In forest there are various evil spirits whom they should avoid and through several rituals and magical performances they keep those quiet. They are taught to identify if there is any animal on their way. They identify those by their half eaten fruits, their excreta and footprints. Each and every animal's footprint is different from other. They can identify when the animal pass through the path, by observing the freshness and temperature of the excreta. They are taught how to fell wood, what types of implements are necessary for it. They accompany their elders to identify the plants used as herbal medicine. Where there is a jungle of *putus* tree with blossom and where there are anthills, there are chances to meet a bear.

They have several riddles, myths, songs associated with their life and culture and through which one can understand their dependence on nature and also the conservation and preservation of forest in which their life is enmeshed.

Conclusion

In the emerging global knowledge economy a country's ability to build and mobilise knowledge capital is essential for sustainable development (World Bank, 1997). One of the components of any country's knowledge system is its indigenous/traditional knowledge bank. It encompasses the skills, experiences and insight of people applied to maintain or improve their livelihood. Many traditional knowledge systems are at risk of becoming extinct because of rapidly changing natural environment and fast pacing economic, political, and cultural changes on a global scale due to impact of globalisation, electronic media and so on even into the deep of the secluded rural area of the country.

Through on going process of globalisation the traditional cultural elements are rapidly vanishing. The cognisances of environment among the Asur in which the crust of cultural elements are embedded for their existence in such ecological niche is highly threatened. The sacred groves (*sarna*) among the Asur are rich in terms of biological wealth. There are number of *sarnas* in and around the studied village which not only provide various environmental, socio-cultural, religious and economic benefits to them but these also act for the preservation of natural local resources, climatic actions, ground water level etc.

Perception of time, season, and climate are only understood by means of natural phenomena which they have observed since their birth as well as learnt from their earlier generation. It is the only means for their survival in such ecological niche in order to cope up with their life in action with surrounding natural environment.

Forest provides a great cultural space in their livelihood. They pick up the elements from forest not only for their ailment but also for their livestock and for other economic and socio-religious occasions.

Use of Indigenous knowledge of Asur for Sustenance

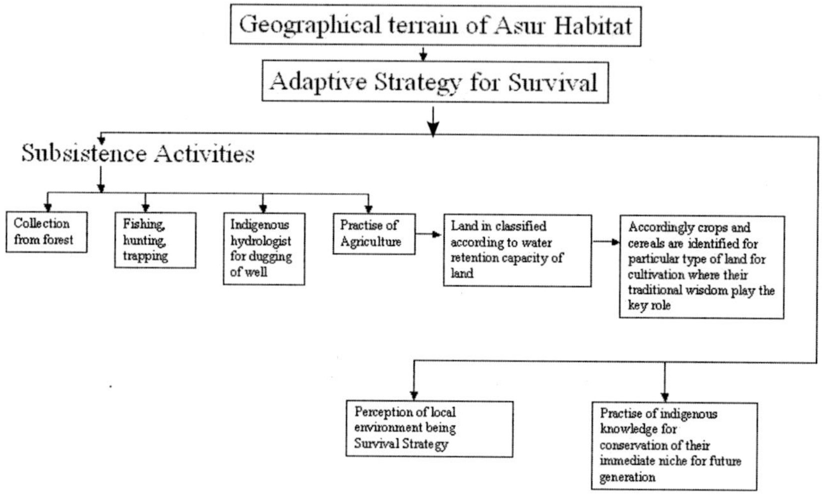

Thus, in common parlance the indigenous knowledge is the knowledge, which originates locally from people, their perception and day-to-day practical experiences in an environment. It finds expression through many cultural practices of the Asur, which are mentioned in the above chart as being a survival strategy. Asur—once famous for iron smelting work, now a PVTG group as well as indigenous people of the country constitute the rich repository of TK because of their nourishment and for being cherished under forest environment for generation.

Bibliography

Altman, Iruin and Martin M, Chemers. 1980. Culture and Environment; California: Brooks Cole Publishing Co.

Bates, Marston. 1953. 'Human Ecology', in Anthropology Today: an Encyclopedia Inventory (ed), A.L. Kroeber, Chicago: Chicago University Press.

Benneth, John, W. 1976. The Ecological Transition: Cultural Anthropology and Human Adaptation, New York: Pergamon Press, Inc.

Dasgupta, Samira. 1994. Birjia: Society and Culture (A Study in Cultural Ecological Perspective), Calcutta, Firma KLM Pvt. Ltd.

Leuva, K.K. 1963. Asur: a study of primitive iron smelters, New Delhi: Bharatiya Adimjati Sevak Sangh.

Prasad, Narmadeshwar. 1961. 'Asur', in Land and People of Tribal Bihar, Ranchi, Bihar Tribal Research Training Institute.

Misra, Kamal Kant. 2007. "Indigenous Environmental Knowledge Today: The Context and Relevance", in Traditional Knowledge in Contemporary Societies – Challenges and Opportunities, Edited by K.K. Misra, Bhopal and Delhi: IGRMS and Pratibha Prakashan.

Roy, S.C. 1926. "Asur Ancient and Modern", in Journal of the Bihar and Orissa Research Society, Vol. XII.

1. Collection of bans karil as food item during monsoon

2. Collection of bark for rope making

3. Asur –agricultural land.

4. Both the Authors with Asur Informants at Sakhuapani Village of Netarhat Plateau.

5. Maize Cultivation at Homestead land of Asur at Jovipat Village.

6. Mid-day Meal at Anganbari School at Sakhuapani Village

7. Group Interview at Sakhuapani- Asur Village

8. Mahulain Patta and Juru Patta for preparing rain coat and Chopi or hat.

9. Trap - Sim funda to catch jungle fowl.

10. Childhood duty among Asur

11. On the Way to Forest for Collection.

12. Asur Woman

13. Collection of Fire wood

14. On the Way to home after Day's collection from Forest.

INDEX

J

K

L

M